INTERVENTION
ON AMERICA

INTERVENTION ON AMERICA

A How-To Manual for Getting
America Into Recovery and Replacing
All Federally Elected Officials
in the Fall of 2012

Larry Fritzlan

© 2011 Larry Fritzlan

Published by

RWP Recovery Works Publishers

21 Tamal Vista Blvd., Ste. 226
Corte Madera, CA 94925

Cover and text design: *the*BookDesigners

ISBN: 978-0-9847573-0-5

First Printing, Nov. 2011
Printed in the U.S.A. on acid-free paper
10 9 8 7 6 5 4 3 2 1

I dedicate this book to my grandchildren, Loren and Elijah, and to all children, whom we must all serve. I also dedicate this book to Jackie, Erik, Camille, Jack, Kaitlyn, Erik, Killian, and Amanda. Each day I cheer as you courageously take your place as adults in an uncertain world.

ACKNOWLEDGEMENTS

This book is the product of so many good and loving people. I weep as I think of the role each has played for me. How could I have written this book if my father was not the crazy alcoholic? And how would I need to struggle and grow so if my mother had not set up such a challenging obstacle course? I love both of you and may your souls be at peace.

I would not be alive without the 12-Step programs and the countless individuals who are only a phone call away or only a mile away at a meeting. This huge, worldwide community is everywhere and has given me my sanity. Throughout this book I make references to AA and the 12-Step communities but I want to be clear that I do not speak for them. I am only speaking from my own experience.

Some, like Tom K., Jack C., and Todd J., have given me something that is immeasurable. You have seen the insanity of this disease up close and personal. You have seen the madness and did not flinch. Again and again, you pointed me toward the path that allowed me to recover my sanity.

My teachers and mentors. Michael Kahn, Jon Vander Zwaag, Stephanie Brown, Brant Cortright, Carolyn Foster, Judye Hess, Steven Bosky, Tim Cermak, Rick Lavine, and Jack Kornfeld. Your wisdom has inspired me and challenged me. This book and my work are indebted to your generosity.

Kristina Wandzilak, Bette Ann Weinstein, Vaughn Howland, George Patterson and my colleagues at the Network of Independent Interventionists. This honorable group is on the front lines of addiction every day and you are a great source of strength and guidance.

Leslie Keenan has held my hand and shepherded this project from my first written outburst to completion. Leslie, thank you. You are the Godmother of this book.

Julia McNeal, wizard with the pencil who created order to my writing. Thank you so much for your wisdom.

To Katy Butler, Nita Gage, and Carolyn Foster. You are the wise writers who have inspired me and modeled for me what successful writing looks like.

Shelley Frost has been my collaborator and creator of my digital face to the world. Thank you for your sense of humor and the sensitive handling of this mercurial client.

To my colleagues Bill Arigi, Jennifer Graham, Mary Beth McClure, Russell Hendlin, Stephanie Daigre, Paul Marra, and Richard Lipfield. On a daily basis we put our heads together in hope that we are making the right decisions in our work with our clients.

Stan Dale, the Human Awareness Institute, and the Potluckers. This amazing group of courageous individuals has taught me that high levels of love, intimacy, and sexuality are possible if we trust wise and undefended mentors and supportive communities. You have encouraged me to lean into my fear and discover what is possible.

My son David and his family, especially my grandchildren, Loren and Elijah. It is their future that has compelled me to push this book forward.

And my wife Avis Rumney, without whom this book would not have been written. Thank for your endless love and support. Your wise counsel, tireless editing and encouragement have made this book possible. Each day I marvel at what we have accomplished and daily wonder what our next adventure will be. I love you so.

CONTENTS

Confined in the dark, narrow cage of our own making which we take for the whole universe, very few of us can even begin to imagine another dimension of reality.

—SOGYAL RIMPOCHE

INTRODUCTION

I'm scared.

I wake up in the middle of the night like I'm in a nightmare. The world seems bleak and hopeless. My stomach is in a knot. I have an icy feeling in my gut. My mind is racing. I need to do something, but I don't know what to do.

It all seems so insane. I roll over. And over. And over.

"Why do I care? Just forget it! Go back to sleep. Don't worry about it. There have always been crazy times, and we got past them. Take a deep breath; it will all be fine, just go back to sleep. It will all be OK in the morning. Just a bad dream. Just a nightmare. Let it go."

But it keeps happening. It keeps waking me up. It won't go away. And now it happens in the daytime too.

What is "it?" What is the "it" that is so disturbing me? And why should *I* be disturbed? Nice job, nice family, nice friends, nice community. And yet I am so upset that I keep waking up with this pain, this hurt, this fear, this nightmare.

I can't let it go. I see things that just don't make sense. I see and hear things that cause my mind to recoil. A bit of news or a headline will cause me to lose my serenity and want to cry or break something. The car radio will send out a snippet of news, and I suddenly want to scream and I need to quickly turn it off. And I know that I am not alone. More and more I'm discovering that my friends are feeling the same things.

Sometimes I feel like I'm Rip Van Winkle, who went to sleep in a world that was innocent, simple, and hopeful, and woke up in a world that had gone insane. A world in which someone had figured out a way to wire everything to everything and then expose my senses to shocking news everywhere I went. Radio, TV, Computer, Facebook, Text Message, Internet, Cell Phone, Email, Twitter, iPad, and more were loudly blaring disturbing reality at me. It was easier when I was an addict. I numbed myself. I checked out. I went to sleep.

Now it hurts like someone took my skin off and left my nerves exposed. The electronic world is poking me and jabbing me and driving me slowly more and more insane.

What can I do? I must do something! But what? Where do I start?

I used to take our political system as a given. America's Democracy is supposed to be wonderful. Yes, we have always had graft and corruption and scandals. I read all about them in history classes. But now, something is different. Is it the new electronic world we live in? Now, I see it differently. Corruption is bad! It is not OK to be corrupt. We all know that. When I hear that President Obama has accepted cash from oil companies in order for Big Oil to drill, I see that as corruption. I know that this is wrong. Or I hear that Rick Perry, the governor of Texas, has enriched his supporters. I know that is wrong. This is corruption and everyone I know *knows this!* How can we simply look the other way when a politician is corrupt?

I get a knot in my stomach as I write this. This is really wrong! How can the media simply ignore this? How is it that the American citizenry is not marching in the streets?

I don't get it. *What am I missing?*

Our leaders are building the Keystone Pipeline, a pipeline to carry crude oil from the Athabasca Oil Sands in Alberta, Canada to refineries in Illinois, Oklahoma and the U.S. Gulf Coast. I have to think they are kidding. Haven't they heard the latest news is that the Artic Icecap is melting much faster than we thought? Perhaps it will be completely gone in less than 20 years and all of the polar bears will have drowned! Scientists are telling us this will happen! Noted academic and government scientists are raising their voices.

Why don't people get it? Or am I the crazy one?

Doesn't everyone understand the implications of these things? Yes, maybe the scientists are wrong, but what if they are right? What if the ice that reflects solar heat back into space goes away? What if our planet is like a car parked in the sun with its windows rolled up? What if we are just at the beginning of a runaway chain reaction that makes Earth like Venus? What if Earth's temperature rose to 500 degrees and everything died?

Maybe the scientists are wrong, but what if they are right?

Why aren't all of us freaking out?

Hello, is anyone home?

My friends are freaking out, but why isn't *everyone else freaking out?* Why is this not today's newspaper headlines:

"Earth Might Be Dying"?

Am I insane? Or is everyone else insane?

It is like we are all sitting around, and someone says, "I smell smoke," but no one responds. No one says anything, no one gets scared, no one is curious, and no one gets up to look. It is as if they forgot the saying, "Where there is smoke there is fire."

I see us doing that. Maybe it's nothing, but what if it is? What if we all have gone insane and are collectively committing suicide? Einstein predicted that we would do this, but I did not believe him when he implied that we were too stupid to live in harmony.

Is that why people are not speaking up? Because they're stupid? Or insane? Or are they all stoned?

The Keystone Pipeline is going to provide a lot of money to Big Business, but it will use up a lot of energy. Immense amounts of oil will be burned to dig up rocks in Canada and grind them all up. Immense amounts of natural gas will be burned to heat up the rocks. Immense amounts of carbon will be burned to move other carbon to places all over the country where we can burn yet more carbon.

Hello!

Aren't we going the wrong way? If we are destroying the ice-caps, shouldn't we stop burning carbon?

Have we all gone crazy?

But the news keeps coming at me. There are strident voices everywhere, and the new technology is giving them all a megaphone, and they all find some way to get to me. They keep finding a way to directly insert their probes into my brain. It is like I'm in a madhouse with insane people all screaming at once. I just want to pack up and move to "the country." But I can't. I just can't. I must do something.

Something to stop the voices.

I know that politicians are corrupt. I know they lie. We all make jokes about them doing this. But today they are so out of control that we can't ignore them. They are lying, cheating, and stealing from us.

And we continue to vote for them.

Did someone put LSD in the water?

Nearly *everyone agrees that things are not sane.* How can everyone at the gym, or standing in line at the grocery store, or wherever I go, not agree that there is blaring and obvious insanity all around us? How does it make sense that the media is telling us that America currently thinks that Rick Perry is the leading presidential candidate, when everyone I am close to sees he has traded cash for access to power? And it is the same with Obama! He signs off on drilling in exchange for cash. And the media enables this by reporting it as merely news, as if it is acceptable.

Over 80% of Americans currently distrust Washington. It is like the camera on the *Evening News* rounded a corner and caught Big Business and Big Union and the Fat Cats handing cash to elected officials. Boom! They got caught. They have been exposed.

And we all know this. We all know that all of our elected officials were bribed. Why are we not seriously pissed off at the fact that every single politician is corrupt? Am I the only one who is sickened by this?

I think of my grandchildren. I would die to protect their lives, and yet I am so embarrassed. How could I be part of what we have done to them? I am so ashamed.

In the lifetimes of my grandparents, my parents, and myself, we humans have done something startling. It is as if we are rats in a cage, and we started multiplying so fast that we have run out of room and are living in our own poop. It is all around us, and our cage is getting dirtier and dirtier. Our cage, this small blue ball moving through space, is getting hotter, dirtier, and scarier.

And yet our "leaders" tell us that they are going to fix it with this or that law or regulation. Over and over they tell us that, but the reality is that 90% of lions and tigers and whales and elephants are gone. How can a law or regulation change that? For millions of years Mother Nature was alive and well and, in the last one hundred years, we killed them!

I wake up with a start! Is this a dream, or is it actually true? Did we actually kill them?

Every day I see the damage done to children. One out of three children born today will get diabetes. How can we, as a species, neglect our children? No species survives if it does not take care of its children. How can a sane person, much less our "leaders" allow this to happen? Today's generation of children may not live as long as our generation, in spite of the advances in medicine! How did we create this? Did *I* create this?

Why can't I go back to sleep?

Look at the obese. They are multiplying like crazy, everywhere, while millions are starving. How is this happening? Am I hallucinating? Apparently not. There it is, on the cover of the *Wall Street Journal.* I can't get away from it.

Another jolt to my brain.

And our political system . . . . Has it always been like this? Is it FUBAR? (A military expression for Fucked Up Beyond All Repair.)

Why aren't the headlines *saying* it? Why can't the media tell the truth?

"America's Political System Failed!"

Seriously, it is maddening to take this all in. How does it make sense that we are not all yelling and screaming at the top of our lungs? The system is broken. It's rigged. It's corrupt. *Everyone knows this and no one is doing anything about it.* Our leaders are bald-faced lying to us, and we, like sheep, simply go along.

What am I missing?

It came to me that early morning, last April. I woke up with a start and I had an idea and started writing this book. I suddenly realized that *everything* made sense if I looked at the behavior of our politicians, of the business community, and of the voters of America through the lens of addiction. It was through this lens that the craziness and insanity I was experiencing suddenly *all* made sense.

Our political system *is* broken, we all know that. The politicians are in endless election cycles and need a lot of cash to keep their campaigns funded. They get the cash by selling special breaks to Big Business, Big Union, and the hyper-wealthy. We all know about this corrupt practice. The elected officials sell their honor, their ethics, their morality, and their souls for the cash. We know that, as well. This explains why they would harm America, the economy, the planet, and children -- to stay in power.

But what explains why the 536 federally elected officials, every one of them, would do this? Why would they be immoral? Why would they, to a person, be unethical?

As an addiction specialist, I believe that the brains of our leaders have been hijacked by an addictive process.

I believe that all 536 federally elected officials have the features of addiction -- their behavior resembles that of addicts. Their prefrontal cortex, the thinking, reasoning part of the brain, has been overpowered by their midbrain's need for more dopamine. Their compulsive drive for, among other things, power, greed, money, and gambling, explain why they would lie to us, steal from us, and put our children, our environment and our planet at risk. All addicts do it.

And the rest of us have slipped into denial. We want to believe we have sane leaders. We want to think they will do the right thing. We hear their words and promises and want to believe them. We can't believe that they are all mentally disordered because of what it would say about us, the folks who elected them. How could we elect leaders that were not very sane unless we were not very sane ourselves?

My job is to treat families who are living with addiction, and in this light, it suddenly all makes sense. Our elected officials meet many of the criteria for addition and are in denial. We are the enablers, those who prop up addicted systems, and we are also in denial.

When I saw it this way, it all made sense. And the solution also, quickly, made sense. When you have an addicted family system you need an Intervention. I'm an Interventionist. Perhaps America is ready.

PART ONE

1

ARE WE ALL ON THE TITANIC?

Our planet is in crisis. Our country is in crisis. We are on the Titanic and there is an iceberg looming ahead. Some of us see it, but we are not at the helm. And those who are at the helm don't see it – they are steering our country toward potential catastrophe. It's up to us who see what's going on to save the ship. We need to step up and take action while there might still be time.

There is hardly a person in America who is not heartbroken at our current plight. We are faced with serious problems. Here are a few:

- Global warming which threatens the entire planet. And we don't even have an energy policy in place.

- Environmental degradation. Wildlife, rivers, the Amazon Rainforest are being destroyed – our soil and air are rapidly becoming polluted.

- Massive corruption. Every single federally elected official has accepted cash from Big Business, Big Union, or the hyper-wealthy to rig the system in favor of the top 1%.

- A massive rip-off of the American people by Wall Street. This rip-off was caused by our federal officials who were given money by Wall Street to rig the system in their favor. And no one has gone to jail for this massive theft of money from Americans.

This is not acceptable. It is not OK.

Why is this so? Why are our political leaders so missing the obvious? They are like the captain of the Titanic. I believe that nearly everyone knows we have a problem, but no one's been able to coherently articulate it and then come up with a plan to address it.

These elected leaders promised us, just like an alcoholic promises to fix the mess he has created, that this time it would be different. And yet they continue to work out backroom deals, rigging the system to support their addictions to accumulating wealth, hoarding money, overspending, compulsive debting, compulsive gambling, and power.

And almost everyone wants change. This is one thing that both the right and the left can agree on. Almost everyone is looking for an answer.

Let's start with something we can all agree on.

We want children to be cared for. We want loving families. We want peace and tranquility in our lives. We want to live in balance with Mother Nature. We want our chosen leaders to guide us wisely. We want institutions that will protect us when things go wrong.

And almost all of us can agree with the Declaration of Independence:

"We hold these truths to be self-evident, that all men are created equal, that they are endowed by their Creator with certain inalienable Rights, that among these are Life, Liberty and the pursuit of Happiness."

No sane person would dispute this. We could poll all the current presidential candidates and they would all agree on this.

So, what happened?

Why are so many people angry and upset? Ask someone you meet on the street about our current politics and you will see powerful emotions come up. People feel anger, sadness, fear, hurt, outrage, disbelief, and bewilderment. Recent polls show that over 80% of Americans are unhappy with the way our current leaders are managing the country.

I believe we are at the "tipping point." It could go either way -- our country can survive and be stronger than ever, or it can fall.

Einstein said that human beings are capable of great things, but that we often choose to stay on a path of self-destruction.

There is no doubt that our country has many serious problems. Yet some would say, "Wait a minute. We live longer, homicide rates are down, fewer infants die, and we have more wealth." And it is true that the standards for many things have improved and clearly we are advancing in many areas. What concerns us is a different kind of problem. A new problem. We live in a very different world than we used to. A world that is going faster and faster. We are living at a time of development of a new paradigm, and it is chaotic. Most of us know the old, pre-technological reality is history. We can't go back to the days before Smartphones. The question is: will the new paradigm, the new world, be sane or insane?

(Sane = proceeding from a sound mind, rational; mentally sound; *especially:* able to anticipate and appraise the effect of one's actions; healthy in body. Insane = mentally disordered; exhibiting insanity.) (Merriam-Webster Dictionary)

For 99.99% of human history we have had to struggle to feed ourselves and to keep our children safe. But huge disruptive changes are occurring right now. We are in the midst of a technological revolution that is changing just about everything.

Many parts of our lives feel upside down. No longer do we all need to work hard just to feed ourselves and put a roof over our heads. We sit in cars for hours each day, and many of us have enough free time to watch an average of 5 hours of TV a day. *Nielsen's 'Three Screen Report' for the fourth quarter of 2010 says the average American now watches more than 151 hours of TV a month.* Or, we surf the Internet and "Facebook" for many hours a day. *The average kid spends 7.5 hours a day looking at electronic screens instead of outside playing, socializing with other kids, reading, and taking up hobbies.* (Kaiser Family Foundation) We are burning fossil fuel at ever-increasing rates. We have access to a vast array of legal and illegal mood-altering drugs and medicines. As a nation, we are rapidly becoming fat. The global economy has generated trillions of dollars that we can manipulate with a click of a mouse.

And we have the technology to offer better education to more children than ever before. We have medical advances that boggle the mind and provide more and more people with more opportunities for better health. We have communication technologies that soon will allow everyone to talk to everyone at any time. We can now Google all the wisdom of the ages as well as the ever-expanding knowledge of the moment. The wonders and practices of spirituality and transcendence are being disclosed for everyone to see. Brilliant minds talk to brilliant minds, and we have access to their conversations. We can all become Renaissance Men or Women. This amazing opportunity has never existed before. It is brand new!

But as things go faster and faster it feels like that wheels are about to come off. There are signs everywhere that we need to "get a grip" and change things. Strident political voices on the right and on the left are pointing out the flaws of the other side -- often with deadly accuracy. Parents are concerned and frightened about the world their children are growing up in. Teachers are concerned. Law enforcement is concerned. Environmental folks are concerned. So many things seem to be getting worse, not better.

What happened? Why is our formerly great nation now in so much trouble?

I would like to introduce the idea that our elected leaders' behaviors can best be described through the lens of addiction. Their behaviors, choices, and decisions that have led to the problems described above are the actions, I believe, of people exhibiting features of addiction. Clearly their thinking is disordered in ways that make no sense. I believe that, if we look closely, we will see that the actions of these 536 elected officials in fact do meet many criteria for the medical definition of addiction.

Here are the criteria for addiction (American Society for Addiction Medicine):

1. Loss of control. The addict does not have the power to stop.

2. Continuing despite adverse consequences. The addict continues even though bad things continue to happen.

3. Chronic. The behavior does not go away.

4. Craving. The addict has an urgent desire to "medicate," to get their "fix," with some behavior or substance.

The addict exhibits obsessive and compulsive behaviors that are driven by forces that appear to be beyond the addict's rational control.

The addict is so practiced at their behaviors that they cannot imagine doing anything different. They crave their substance, or desire to engage in their behavior, even if both the craving and the acquisition, or acting out of the behavior, have terrible consequences for themselves and others. The fact that their craving and acquiring have terrible consequences for their own children and for those around them somehow does not reach their consciousness. They have lost the ability to control their out-of-control behaviors: it does not stop, and it is getting worse. The addict has lost contact with reality and clearly is not sane.

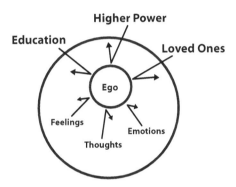

Figure 1: The Addict

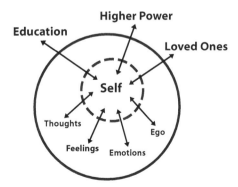

Figure 2: The Sane Person

Politicians' craving for power is obvious. For example, they subsidize production of high fructose corn syrup in order to get kickbacks from Big Food, and then use the money to support their election campaigns so they can remain in their position.

Our elected leaders and those who run Big Business are endlessly looking for a "fix." They are compelled to seek "more." They need "bigger and better." "Economic growth" is their religion. They exhibit *greed* in their continual quest for power, money, and material wealth. Their greed, their endless quest for more, has become an unquenchable monstrosity that literally is destroying our planet.

This is what Gandhi referred to when he wrote, "Earth provides enough to satisfy every man's need, but not every man's greed."

Our elected officials, leaders in Big Business, Big Food, Big Energy, Big Defense, Big Banks, Big Money, and Wall Street will do anything to "get more." Refer to the addiction criteria above, and it is easy to see the craving, the persistence despite adverse consequences, and the loss of control that they are exhibiting.

This is not news to perhaps 20% of Americans. Based on my experience as an interventionist, I believe that about one fifth of Americans, educated and not, rich and poor, have stood around and said, "These guys are nuts" and "Almost any sane person could do better."

This sane group of Americans has the power to actually put America into recovery. This group could show the rest of America how to be healthy adults. In the past, those seeking endless growth and power were annoying and boring and we avoided them. Today they are in charge. They have become very big, dangerous, and out of control. They have no compunction about killing their own children, and destroying the economy and the planet in their addictive desire to fill the empty hole, which is, as I will explain, in their own souls. Their greed is destroying our democracy.

Plenty of Americans are also addicted. They are addicted to drugs and alcohol, compulsive eating, compulsive working, cosmetic surgery, spending, exercise, nicotine, gambling, shopping, obsessively watching electronic screens, hoarding money, computer gaming -- however their greed manifests. When I add up all the folks in America suffering from these addictions, my guess is that more than half our population meets many or even most of the criteria for addiction. And like the alcoholic or drug addict, they are in denial of their loss of control and of their dependence on these substances and behaviors to get through the day. They don't even realize it.

Most of us know an active, practicing alcoholic who is in denial. These addicts are not sane. They usually die a sad and miserable death, unless an intervention occurs. They are out of control and it is hopeless to try to talk them out of their addiction. The only possibility is to pray for a miracle or to roll up our sleeves and do an intervention on them, *and on the enabling system that supports them.*

Please re-read that last sentence. If change is to occur, the focus needs to be on those unconscious folks who are unwittingly enabling the status quo, because the addict rarely will change without the enablers also changing.

Enabling is a dysfunctional approach that is intended to help, but that, in fact, allows the problem to get worse. With the best of intentions, an enabler will bail out the addict. The enabler will do for the addict what the addict needs do for himself or herself. Enablers allow the addict to continue their addictive behavior, unchallenged.

If over 50% of Americans have many of the features of addiction, I postulate that another 30% are codependently fused with their addicts. These 80% of Americans are actively or passively supporting the current captain and crew on the Titanic.

The reality is that we are that 80%! You and I, and every other American of voting age. We are the individuals who have been enabling this government to operate this way by choosing to re-elect these leaders. We, the citizens of America, voted these men and women into office. And we, the citizens of America, have not fired them!

I am responsible for this mess. And so are you. Left, right, and center. If change is to occur, we need to start with this truth. We can no longer stand around like drunks at 2 a.m. arguing with each other. We need to sober up. We need to start with the reality that it is we, ourselves, who created this unmanageable mess. Once we accept that reality, we can change. And then, we can elect ethical and moral adults to replace our current leaders in Washington.

It is vital to understand that you and I are supporting this addictive system. *We* are enabling our current mess. Here's how we did it, and do it:

1. We voted for a Democrat or a Republican (it doesn't matter which, they are both engaged in selling access to power).

2. We passively stood aside and did not vote.

3. We chose not to stand up against them (not marching, not throwing tea in the river, not writing a book, not blogging, etc.)

4. We fell for the old trap of trying to "work from within the system." (Something that *rarely ever* works in an addictive system).

It is next to hopeless for the members of an alcoholic family system to perform an intervention on themselves. And it is just as hopeless for those who are now in office, and those on the left or on the right, to fix America's current government. With an addicted family, we know that the addict is in denial of his addiction and is not sane. But the codependent-enablers are also in denial of how their very behavior actually supports and perpetuates the status quo. They simply cannot have an objective view of the system as a whole and of the complex and convoluted interrelationships of the individuals in the system. Everyone might think that he or she can change. The codependent-enablers endlessly try one thing after another with the hope that the addict will change -- but things only get worse. And the addict endlessly believes that he will get control of his addiction, but he never does. It is only when an interventionist steps in from outside the system and guides the family into a new paradigm that real change is possible.

It is the same with our current government. The left and the right, including those in office, are like the addicts and the enabling codependents who are endlessly trying to change the system. That will never work. Ever! We simply need to trust the process, follow the interventionist's suggestions, and move the system toward a new and unknown paradigm. (That is what this book is about.)

And, it turns out that even the sanest 20% of us are also in denial. We may grumble, but we have not yet put on our shoes and gone to the streets.

If you feel you're in that Sane 20%, as I do, it's time to wake up. We, you and I, need to come out of denial and see that we, the sanest among us, have actively or passively enabled the current mess and that we need to make a decision to actually do something to change the course of events, before it is too late.

Denial, as psychologists remind us, is a condition in which the mind makes things up that are not real. It is a defense mechanism that our ego uses to protect us from unpleasant feelings. A person in denial cannot tell the difference between reality and fantasy. We have all been amazed as someone who is obviously an alcoholic informs us that they "don't have a drinking problem." Clearly, they are not sane. Clearly they are "making things up."

In the 1960s, I read a report that said that one third of the world's population still believed the world was flat. In the time of Christopher Columbus, almost everyone believed that the world was flat and that if you sailed too far out to sea you would fall off the earth.

500 years elapsed between Christopher Columbus and that 1960s report. It seems that a billion people simply did not get the information. Their education was sorely lacking. Or maybe they lived in a community that believed in the odd proposition that we live on a one-sided flat earth.

There are a lot of myths in our lives. The myth of Santa Claus is a common one. One man, nine reindeer, in one night, sneaks into millions of homes and leaves gifts. No sane adult believes this is true.

In a recent study (http://www.geekosystem.com/which-is-bigger-the-earth-or-the-sun-okcupid/), the dating company *OK Cupid* polled over 600,000 American adults and asked them the question: "Which is larger, the earth or the sun?"

The bad news is that approximately 7% of the respondents actually believe that the earth is bigger than the sun, even though the sun is over a million times larger than the earth. Which means that approximately 15 million American adults are not quite in touch with at least that reality. And if we cannot get that right, I'm wondering what else we might be missing.

Americans believe many myths. "America is better than other countries; our citizens are superior and better educated." This is another myth. America ranks way down the list of the world's countries in mathematics, science, and reading. It is another example of how vulnerable we are to believing what we want to believe.

"Hydrocarbon Extraction" is one of the new myths we believe. According to this myth, we can extract more and more oil, gas, and coal from the earth to supply ever-increasing energy needs. The myth is that we can increase the rate of extraction indefinitely to create the "endless economic growth" our current political leaders and Big Business seek in their unquenchable craving for "more."

The Hydrocarbon Extraction myth began with the industrial revolution. We extracted carbon from the earth, ignited it to warm things up and make wheels go round. As time went on, we developed better tools and machines to reach deeper into the earth's crust. We got better and better at extracting carbon and found more and more ways to burn it. We moved into the desert and burned carbon to cool the air in our homes. Cars got bigger and bigger and burned more and more carbon. The pace of extraction accelerated, and the rate of carbon use increased. Then China, India, Brazil, and other countries began to outpace America with their voracious need to burn even more carbon.

> From NASA:
> "Human activities add a worldwide average of almost 1.4 metric tons of carbon per person per year to the atmosphere. Before industrialization, the concentration of carbon dioxide in the atmosphere was about 280 parts per million. By 1958, the concentration of carbon dioxide had increased to around 315 parts per million, and by 2007, it had risen to about 383 parts per million. These increases were due almost entirely to human activity." (http://www.nasa.gov/mission_pages/oco/news/oco-20090113.html)

People who are sane and paying attention are aware of the myth that we've been fed by those in power and influence. If the Hydrocarbon Extraction myth of infinite energy supply is not challenged, we will have dug up all the carbon, burned it all, killed Mother Nature, and created a planet too hot to sustain life, killing all of us.

This is not sane. This is insane.

> "Insanity: doing the same thing over and over again and expecting different results."
>
> —Albert Einstein

But our elected officials obviously believe that the carbon supply is infinite and burning it will not impact the planet, even though the evidence of global warming has been pouring in for years. Their denial and refusal to accept the truth is reflected in the absurd reality that oblivious officials and their Big Business enablers have utterly and completely failed to come up with *any* energy plan! "Full speed ahead and damn the torpedoes!" They are "continuing despite adverse consequences." They are behaving like addicts.

Not sane!

From the president on down they proclaim, "Drill baby drill!" Could any healthy person call these officials sane? They are not. From the mess they've created, and from my vantage point as an expert in addiction, it appears that we've elected a bunch of folks who went to Washington, became addicted to the Greed/Power Kool-Aid, and are insane. They became addicts.

We need to find a saner group to lead us. We need leaders who are not in denial. We need leaders who are wise, and who act like adults.

Looking at our current reality through the lens of addiction is, I believe, the best perspective to both understand and fix our current mess. Addiction treatment has been effectively restoring addicts and their families to sanity for decades. I believe the Sane 20% of us are capable of coming out of denial and initiating an intervention. I believe that we can put America into recovery and restore the country to sanity.

But first *we* must come out of denial, face reality, and be ready to act.

We are the ones who can change what's happening, and we must begin to visualize how we can bring this about. We simply need to visualize how we can do an Intervention on the whole broken American political system.

This book is about that Intervention.

I have intervened on hundreds of families dealing with addiction. The process is simple. Concerned family members call me and tell me about their addicted family. I meet with these concerned folks and gather information. We then see if there are other family members who are willing to join us. The question always is, "Are the enablers, those who support the addiction, willing to join the Intervention?" And the next question is, "Are the enablers themselves willing to consider changing?"

Then I gather everyone together, the addict and the enablers, and educate everyone about addiction, codependency, and recovery. I give each family member recommendations on how they can recover their sanity. Every addict and every codependent has the potential to recover and reclaim vibrant health, loving relationships, and a hopeful future. But it is vital to understand following point: the reality is that almost every addict is enabled by those around them. *Nearly all addicts will sober up if their enablers enter recovery and stop enabling. And addicts rarely change if their enablers are not willing to change!*

Most Americans are enablers. While many are very troubled and upset, the majority of Americans neither fully grasp the unfolding horror show nor have a clue about the radical steps necessary to bring about fundamental change. The majority of the electorate will grumble, but will re-elect Obama or one of the Republicans for President. They will re-elect most of the current senators and representatives, even though over 80% of the voting public distrusts Washington.

These frightened and confused Americans, the majority, are the ones we must talk to. They don't see that they are actually contributing to the problem. These citizens who are enabling this mess are like the family members in an alcoholic family system who are still buying booze for the alcoholic, while at the same time badgering him to stop drinking. They are like the ones who call in sick for the alcoholic when the alcoholic is too hungover to go to work. They are like the ones who let the addict lie around the house and get sicker. They are like the codependents who are going crazier and crazier trying to control everything and trying to make sense of the out-of-control reality.

We need to educate these enablers about their role in perpetuating our unfolding disaster. They are scared, hurt, and angry. We see them, the strident on the left and on the right. We see them on cable TV and on the radio and in blogs. They are making a lot of noise because they, too, are very frightened for America. They are like the frightened wife of an addict who is talking to anyone who will listen about the big mess she's in.

The sane and aware among us need to calmly but actively initiate this Intervention process. And we need to calmly invite the others to join us. And almost all of them will come, because they are fed up with the insanity too, and are hungry for leaders who are honorable. And they will eventually see the wisdom of what this means for them and for America. This has been my experience when intervening with addicted family systems -- in time, hopefully everyone gets on board and there's a positive outcome.

We Americans have inherited more wealth and abundance than mankind has ever known! And, like addicts, we have, in the blink of an eye, watched as our country has "hit bottom." We inherited a Rolls Royce and are in danger of driving it off a cliff in a drunken stupor.

Chief Seattle, the revered and honored Native American Suquamish Indian Chief, in 1854 reminded us that we need to protect the earth for the next seven generations. Of course we need to do that. Actually, we need to protect our planet for forever. But look at our oil use. The Artic icecap is melting, polar bears are drowning, and the fact that Obama and the Democrats and the Republicans want to keep on drilling makes every one of the Sane 20% weep.

Is there hope? Think about this.

Democrats and Republicans, like all of us, are amazed at what we Americans were able to do between December 7, 1941 and the end of World War II, Japan's formal surrender on September 2, 1945. We got focused, united around a purpose, built hundreds of thousands of ships, planes, tanks, trucks, and everything else that was needed to stop tyranny and create peace in Europe and Japan.

We rationed gas. We rationed food. Everyone pitched in. And in fewer than four years, we completed our mission. We created democracy and freedom where it had not existed.

We can do the same with renewable energy.

Today we have the technology to shut down the coal burning, mercury-spewing, carbon-emitting, planet-warming, electricity-generating coal industry. We could install wind generators and solar-powered generators and shut down these coal-burning plants. Industry, science, and technology have shown us that *we could have done this decades ago!*

If we think about what we did in World War II, we can see that this would be simple. We can see that we could do this in just a year or two -- if we had the vision, the unity, and the will. If we had another "Sputnik Moment."

Jeremy Rifkin, in his just-released book, *The Third Industrial Revolution,* clearly points out the amazing opportunity a new paradigm could offer us, if we put our minds to it. He writes that Americans, sadly, "continue to be in a state of denial, not wishing to acknowledge that the economic system that served us so well in the past is now on life support." But he offers us an obvious solution if we are sane enough to "get it." He seems to be saying that we have a simple choice. We can blindly continue down a path toward disaster, or wake up and embrace an amazing new paradigm.

Sadly, we have elected republicans who've been bought off by the coal producers, and we have elected democrats who've been bought off by the coal workers' union. These corrupt elected officials have been bribed to protect the status quo. This information is readily available. They don't deny accepting the cash. This dishonorable and corrupt behavior has been in the news for years. (It is like living with an alcoholic -- we are shocked at first, then we just get numb after awhile.) It is time for us to change this practice. Is it not obvious that what is happening is wrong and must be changed? There is a point when someone in an addicted family finally says, "I can't take it anymore," and calls an interventionist.

We could intervene with the economy: we could regulate Wall Street's greed. We could do the same with Big Food; food producers and our corrupt elected officials rig the system to push fat, sugar, and salt on our children! We could do the same with our drug problem. And our water problem. And our global warming problem. And our animal and plant extinction problem. And our homelessness problem.

In any of these situations, the Sane 20% could declare, "This has got to stop." They could call in an Interventionist, invite in others of the 80% who are still in denial, and let the Interventionist guide them in taking steps toward recovery. I discuss this process in Chapter 5 of Part One, and suggest some specific actions relevant to each of these areas in Part Three of this book.

In 1941 we had a problem. We unilaterally identified an enemy. We had leaders with a vision. And we had a population that supported these leaders. We all rolled up our sleeves, united, and went to work. We got that job done.

Today, we have a different enemy. Today the enemy is addiction and greed, coupled with denial. We need leaders with vision, and a population that supports these leaders, and we need to unite and go to work to create a solution to this problem.

In reality, there is not a person in America who woke up this morning and said, "Honey, let's vote for the same politicians as before, so they can screw our children (and their children, and all future generations) out of natural resources and ruin the planet! Who cares if our grandchildren live in horror on a dying planet? And who cares if they have to pay huge taxes because we ran up the nation's credit card to the breaking point and then handed the debt to them?"

No one says that. No one means that. And yet, that is what we have! *That is what you and I have created!*

Today, in back rooms in Washington, and State Senates and Houses and City Halls all over our country, special interest groups and government officials are "gaming the system" to feed their greed and addiction to gambling, spending, and power. And we continue to enable this.

We will all need to stop "playing victim" and blaming "them!" *We put them into office.* We need to take responsibility, grow up, and fix this.

I know life is complex, and the politicians endlessly remind us of this. But we know, in our gut, when something is wrong. Over 80% of Americans are in agreement that what our elected officials in Washington are doing is wrong. The left, the right, and the center agree on this. The "system" is broken. Our leaders have utterly failed to lead. They are like 4-year-olds, fighting over which one gets the ball. They are like urban gang members who are more interested in conforming to the party line than in thinking for themselves. They are like crack addicts, lying to get high one more time. They are like the alcoholic who masterfully tells us exactly what we want to hear.

As enablers, we really don't have any control over them. *What we have control over is ourselves and our actions.* We can stand up, vote, and replace all of them. We elected them to serve us and to do a job, but they have failed spectacularly. They must be fired and recalled. All 536. And firing and recalling will not be easy. They have manipulated the system to make sure that they don't have any competition. The current parties may appear to be in opposition to one another but, in reality, they work very carefully to make sure that no one will threaten their protected status.

ol •i •gar •chy   [ol-i-gahr-kee]
noun, plural -chies.
1. a form of government in which all power is vested in a few persons or in a dominant class or clique; government by the few.
2. a state or organization so ruled.
3. the persons or class so ruling.
(Merriam-Webster Dictionary)

Less than one percent of America, fewer than three million individuals, hold the reins of our government. Less than one percent -- these three million -- the elected officials, the ultra rich, Big Business, Big Union -- have the power to dictate the entire country's agenda. Less than one percent have manipulated the system in ways that benefit them but will cause the country to spiral into collapse. Those comprising the one percent are not like the honorable leaders we had during World War II. These leaders' self-serving behaviors are perverting democracy, bankrupting our economy, poisoning our children, and destroying the planet. This one percent, these three million, control the levers of power while the other 99% of us stand by and continue to enable this system.

We have a problem. We need to face the facts. We must stop enabling this.

America has become like one big alcoholic family system. We are all living with an alcoholic. He is that one percent. He is lying to us, he is stealing from us, and he is cheating on us. He has gotten in a fight with the neighbor again. He has stolen the credit cards again and won't stop spending. We can't sleep. We are in serious debt. We feel like we are going crazy. The children don't laugh much any more. We worry about the future. Things seem hopeless. The madness has been going on for a long time and, in spite of everything we have tried, it only seems to get worse.

Today, in 2011, we know a lot about addiction and recovery. We have many decades of experience with recovery, and we have seen how the recovery process has restored millions of addicts to sanity.

Interventions reverse the downward spiral toward insanity and death, and point the addictive system toward health, fun, and a return to an effective life. An effective intervention starts with the premise that *everyone* in the addictive family system plays a critical role in *keeping the system stuck in the way it is*. A successful family intervention occurs when everyone in the system changes. Otherwise, the madness almost always continues. If enablers refuse to change, the odds are slim that the addict will recover.

I propose an Intervention that will move America into a very different future, a different paradigm. But it will require that we, the Sane 20%, take action. We are 40 million voters, and we have the ability to swing any election. I believe we can follow clear direction and do what needs to be done.

Imagine this. Imagine these sane Americans -- these Concerned Others -- actually gathering in town centers across the country. Can you imagine forty million peaceful, loving women and men going to the streets for two hours every month and advocating for sanity? Can you imagine the impact? This has never happened before!

This is what happens in an Intervention: The Concerned Others contact the Interventionist and meet with him. The Interventionist guides each person in planning steps toward his or her recovery. The Concerned Others then talk with the other enablers in the family who are still in denial. They describe their meeting with the Interventionist and the recovery steps the Interventionist has recommended for each of them. They educate the enablers about addiction and recovery, and invite the enablers to join them in meeting with the Interventionist. The addict is also invited to participate, but with or without the addict, the other family members move forward to build healthier lives for themselves.

Intervention is a process that gradually wakes up those in denial and offers each family member a path toward recovery.

This would be the first step in the Intervention. But for the Intervention to be effective, we need the other family members, the other enablers, to join in recovery.

The goal over the next months would be to attract many of the other 79% who are confused and lost. The goal would be to lovingly invite them to join us. We would invite the 1% as well, the addicts, but whether or not they join us, we will proceed. The goal would be to educate the enablers (and the addicts) about the mess we are in and to educate them about what a better future would look like. As the enablers learn about addiction and understand its impact, hopefully they will begin to come out of denial and choose to join the Sane 20%. They, too, are desperately looking for leaders they can trust.

Once we have everyone gathered for the Intervention, I will make recommendations on what each of us needs to do to recover. Part Three of this book describes specific actions we can take. Each of us will need to change if we are going to change America. And if we change, we can replace our elected officials with sane and adult leaders.

All 536 of them. 1 President, 100 Senators and 435 Representatives.

Replaced.

In this book, I am inviting us to dream big. Who will replace these folks? Can we imagine electing men and women who are honorable and do not take money from special interests? Can we imagine electing people with vision who can come up with long-term solutions for what ails America?

Could our next President be you? Actually, it *will* be you. It will be the participants in the Intervention who will step up and lead America, one day at a time, to a saner future. We have no option if we care about our children, our country, and our planet.

I have seen the miracle of recovery unfolding around me for over three decades. I was once a suicidal, dangerous, insane addict who entered recovery in 1979. Today I'm different. I have seen what happens when one person initiates an Intervention, and a whole family goes from the death spiral of addiction to a life of hope and love and fun. This "recovery phenomenon" has been occurring all around us for numerous decades. I feel privileged to know of it, firsthand.

But for this Intervention on America to be successful, every one of us must step up. Just like in World War II, we all need to pitch in.

Being upset and complaining are the dubious luxury of a stable, sane, and safe world. That's not the world we live in. We are all on the Titanic and we need to re-write that story, or we're going down. The politicians at the helm of the ship don't see this – their eyes are focused on the dollar sign; they are driven by power and greed and the myth of endless growth. The politicians in power are steering our country toward potential catastrophe. They are blind to reality.

This book is not about Republican-bashing or Democrat-bashing, even though both parties are leading us off a cliff. These parties are both like clueless, spoiled brats who are blaming each other for not having their way. That is what addicts become.

After the Intervention, you and I need to imagine taking the reins. Each of us needs to visualize what is possible. And many of us will need to find the courage to lead. I don't want to run for office, but I believe we all have a duty to come out of our denial, stand up, and be ready to serve. Just like in World War II. We need to run for office, locally or at the state or federal level, and we need to work for the campaigns of those we support.

In Part Three of this book, I will propose what I believe is a sane and realistic paradigm for the Republican and Democratic parties. The current parties are not sane, neither of them, and we need to simply start over with a completely new cast of individuals.

We voters have been like the codependents in an addictive relationship. We have been hoping that "they" will change. We have begged them to be honest. We have pleaded with them. We have been listening to them for years as they've said, "this time will be different." "Really, this time I promise to regulate Wall Street." "I'm telling you the truth, this time I will come up with an education plan for all children." "Please, I swear I will stop spending money." "OK honey, I promise that this time we will not have any backroom deals, I will not see those lobbyists." "I swear, I will stop taking bribes from Big Business."

We have been the suckers. Ask the young people. They see that the current crop of leaders is so crazy that most of the youth have given up even caring. And *they* are America's future.

HOW TO USE THIS BOOK

Part One of this book is about how we got here. It's about educating folks to see the bigger picture. We have to *see* reality before we can accept it. And we have to accept it before we can do anything about it. Part One is about preparing us for the Intervention. It is necessary in any intervention process that we see the bigger picture, then we become willing to join in the Intervention.

Part Two of this book is about the medical and mental health practices of treating addiction. This part is really two stories interwoven. The first one is the story of my own recovery from addiction. The second story occurs in parallel with this story. It is the story of how America itself can also enter recovery and recover her ability to elect wise, honorable, spiritual, and sane leaders.

My own story is a miraculous one that millions of Americans could tell. It is the story of redemption. It is about how an addict's downward spiral toward insanity and death was interrupted, and about what happened that somehow turned it all around and restored him to sanity. Using the 12-Step recovery model, I tell my story about what it was like and what happened to bring about my recovery. At each step, I will explain how America and its citizens can use the same principles to recover our country's sanity.

Part Three of this book is about moving forward. If we are going to replace all 536 elected officials, we need to take action, and we need to have a plan. This is where a successful Intervention comes to fruition. This section describes specific actions we can take to create a better future.

The modern world holds a lot of promise. Subjugation, corruption, and repression are being exposed all over the world. The Internet allows access to all kinds of knowledge. The common woman or man or child has opportunities that have never existed before. Many of us now live lives that are rich and rewarding.

I believe that you and I are standing in the eye of a hurricane. We are in the midst of a paradigm shift. The old order is rapidly being recognized as unsustainable, unworkable, and potentially catastrophic. We literally are at the "end times" that some talk about. And at the same time, we are at the beginning of something very new and unknown. The future holds endless possibilities.

Mohamed Bouazizi, a fruit vendor in Tunisia set himself on fire to protest corruption. *That simple act collapsed a government in weeks!*

Facebook, one woman and one man recently brought down Hosni Mubarak, the dictator who ruled Egypt for decades. One man, one woman, and Facebook!

Wael Ghonim was arrested and tortured by the Egyptian secret police. Once free, he told his story on Facebook.

Asmaa Mahfouz, a 26-year-old Egyptian woman, was upset that

her peers were setting themselves on fire to protest the terrorism of Mubarak's insane government. She went on Facebook and announced that she, too, was willing to put her life at risk and *stand up* for sanity. She said, "People, I am going to Tahrir Square." Thousands followed her.

Frustrated and concerned Egyptians went to the streets, and within weeks Mubarak's government was brought down and Mubarak found himself in jail.

Julian Assange, Wikileaks, and the Internet have let all of us see more clearly the backroom dealing that we have always suspected.

We are at a tipping point.

We all must become Wael Ghonim and leverage the Internet to change the world.

We all must become Asmaa Mahfouz and use Facebook and Twitter to tell our friends that we are going to the streets.

We all must become Julian Assange and expose the corruption.

Sometimes I weep at this tragedy. I wonder if setting myself on fire might make a difference. The monks did it in Viet Nam. Self-immolation brought down the corrupt government of Algeria. I hope it doesn't happen here! But I feel like the canary in the coalmine as I imagine the horror of our species slipping away. What do I need to do? Sometimes I find that I need to numb myself from this insane possibility.

At other moments I am filled with joy. I wish the world could only know what I know about love and spirituality and sacred con-nection with others, and the wondrous joy of being in nature and the amazement of being a member of a very large community that is based on love, and acceptance, and making lives better. We all have the ability to see love and wonder everywhere! We all have the ability to dance and sing with everyone else in a loving and sane world. We all have the ability to prioritize children and nature above everything.

At those moments I am hopeful, and that is why I am writing this book. I visualize an amazing, beautiful, secure, loving, and peaceful world that is standing by to welcome every newborn child.

But to get there we need to first come out of denial. We need to realize that the change starts with me and with you. It needs to start with us.

Time and again I have seen the power of anger. A parent gets angry, takes a stand, a kid stops doing drugs. A spouse gets angry, hires an Interventionist, and a family becomes sane again. It's time to use our anger to help our country.

I'm hoping that this book will make everyone angry! We have enabled this, you and I. We have put our trust in people who are not well, not healthy. The have lied to us, and anger is an appropriate response. But then we need to take a deep breath and rationally look at our approach. We are wrong if we think we can change our leaders. Changing another person just isn't possible. Changing ourselves is the only effective solution.

The Serenity Prayer, written by Reinhold Niebuhr and used in recovering communities says it best:

"God, grant me the serenity to accept the things I cannot change. The courage to change the things I can. And the wisdom to know the difference."

People change because they choose to change.

It is essential that we understand this point very well. Many of us were hoping that our elected leaders would change (they keep saying they will!). But typically, addicts only change for the worse. There is only one thing we can change, and that is ourselves and our approach.

It is also futile to blame "them." "Blame" is a victim's game. We, the electorate, chose to be in relationship with our elected officials (and the special interest folks who run them). We, the electorate, voted for them, or passively supported the system by not voting. We, the American electorate, chose them. *And now we are freaking out at what we created.*

I believe we are hitting a bottom. This is good news!

Once we realize we are at a bottom, I'm hoping we can all see that we are powerless over Washington, and that our elected officials have made our lives and our planet unmanageable.

If things are going to be better, we need to have the courage to change the things we can, which is ourselves. We need to vote, we need to run for office, we need to march, we need to Twitter, and we need to link up on Facebook.

We need to dump the status quo into the crapper. If this Intervention is successful, it will disrupt a lot of entrenched interests. It will devastate folks who are on the take. It will scare those who are accustomed to buying special privileges. And it will terrify every politician, because all of them are about to lose their jobs.

We need a new game, a new approach, and a new philosophy. We need to think "outside the box."

WE NEED A NEW PARADIGM

This new paradigm, if it is to happen, will start with you and with me. 300 million people comprise the American public; two-thirds of them, adults. It is we who need to see that we all created this, and it is we who are responsible for changing it. *You and I are the government. They are 1%, and we are 99%.*

We need to run for President, for Senator, and for Representative.

But we also need to do what Gandhi and Martin Luther King and the young people in Egypt did. We need to stand up and go to the streets.

This book is also about the principles that I believe will safely support this disruptive change. I'm hoping that you, the Sane 20%, will also write a book, start a blog, and come up with your own ideas for supporting this Intervention and our Recovery. We need to encourage the smart and wise people we know to consider serving in Washington. The Internet age allows all of us access to all information. I believe the best people and the best ideas of this new paradigm will rise to the top.

And we do not know what this new paradigm is going to be. Until it happens, we humans are always struggling with a reality that is generally accepted by everyone. As a society and as a culture, we trundle on down the road completely unaware of a paradigm shift that is headed our way, and that will completely disrupt everything.

The western world has endured three blows that have forced humanity to grow up and accept that their worldview was, in fact, completely wrong:

At one point we believed that we were the privileged and that everything revolved around us. Earth was the center of the universe.

This cosmological view of the universe was accepted by all of the great thinkers of the time. That was until 1543 when a German published a book. No one saw it coming, and it disturbed and confused just about everyone who saw it. The Catholic Church banned this book for the next two centuries. The book was *On the Revolutions of the Celestial Spheres*. The author, Nicolaus Copernicus, pointed out the annoying fact that we were not the center of the universe, and that everything did not revolve around us. Keep this concept in mind. We will see that the concept of ego-centrism is a theme that is challenged by the next two paradigm shifts, and that is central to the Intervention that I propose for America.

The second blow to our exalted and unique status was the result of another book, this time by an Englishman. Charles Darwin's *On the Origin of Species* proposed an idea that was in direct conflict with religion and its followers. Darwin's evolution theories placed us humans as simply the latest version on an evolutionary branch of mammals called Apes. Yes we had bigger brains, but we were merely the product of millions of years of evolution.

And then, along came an Austrian named Sigmund Freud who further disrupted the worldview that we humans were conscious and actually had control of our lives. He said that each of us was a "labyrinth of impulses striving independently of one another toward action." (Freud, "A Difficulty in the Path of Psychoanalysis.") The psychologist Stephen Mitchell, in his book, *Can Love Last*, said "Our conscious experience is merely the tip of an immense iceberg of unconscious mental processes that really shape, unbeknownst to us, silently, impenetrably, and inexorably, our motives, our values, our actions."

These three paradigm shifts were gradual in their impact on civilization. Generations of people came and went as these ideas slowly shaped the culture and the education of the youth. Today, no one refutes Earth's place in the cosmos. Evolution, while still a challenge for some in the church, is accepted by science and by the majority of Americans. And many people understand that unconscious forces direct much of what we do.

The next paradigm shift, I believe, is unfolding today, all around us. Our ego-centrism is being challenged once again. Two forces are driving this shift. One force is the result of America's corrupted political system, combined with out-of-control and unsustainable growth. The other force is a technological revolution that, for the first time, is letting all of us see this terrifying reality in real time. Sensors all around us are telling us that we are hitting a bottom. I believe that we have two choices. One choice is to participate in the Intervention I am proposing. The other choice is to keep doing what we have been doing. Only the first choice will allow this great American democratic experiment to have a good outcome. Only the first choice will assure us that our children will have the opportunity to experience "life, liberty, and the pursuit of happiness."

From my perspective, I believe we can recover from this. The pieces are all in place. We simply need to come out of our collective denial and then take the next step in our growth.

All we have to do is change just about everything.

That is what an Intervention is about. I do them all the time. And they work.

Are *you* ready to be part of this Intervention and recover America's greatness?

Because if this Intervention works, and you folks all show up for it, we will have a new and wonderful problem. If we do not vote for any of the previous addicted and corrupt leaders, whom will we elect? Who will be our new, sane, adult, and ethical leaders?

The answer is that it will have to be you!

Let's get started.

2

ADDICTION IS A BIO-PSYCHO-SOCIAL-SPIRITUAL DISEASE

From my vantage point, our country's leaders' immoral actions, unethical behaviors, and bizarre thinking can best be described through the lens of addiction. Nearly all our elected officials meet some of the criteria for addiction, and the current mess our country is in can be well-explained from this perspective. America is like one, big, addicted family system. I believe that most Americans and all of our leaders have succumbed to a set of pathological beliefs and behaviors that have rendered us unable to see the larger picture. It is through the lens of addiction and recovery that we can visualize a path back to a healthy and sane future for America.

Addiction is a disease: it is the result of faulty brain circuitry; of brain wiring that is not healthy. If we understand addiction, and view our country's predicament as rooted in addiction, then we can understand that healing is possible. Effective treatment for addiction has been around for decades, and recovery is possible. *But if our country is to have a chance to recover its greatness, we, as individuals, need to accept the reality of how we have been enabling what is happening. We need to see that the current unfolding tragedy will certainly continue, unless we change our own behavior, because an enabled addict almost never goes into treatment.*

Let me say that another way. Addicts are out of control and will rarely seek treatment if someone is enabling them.

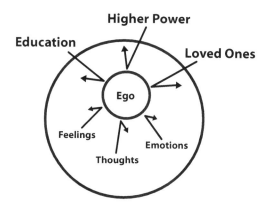

Figure 1: The Addict

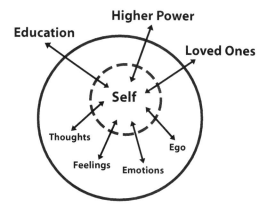

Figure 2: The Sane Person

Over 90% of addicts are in denial of their addiction -- they don't even know that they are addicts. And probably over 90% of the people in relationship with addicts, the enablers, are also in denial of how *they actually help the addiction to continue and progress.*

While we typically think of addiction as applying to drugs and alcohol, its scope is much larger. Many non-substance behaviors also will cause the brain to go insane and lose its ability to create a healthy, happy, and sane life. I will show you how these behaviors, our denial of them, and our social acceptance of them have led America to a crossroads that will decide our children's and our planet's future.

If we look at our current dilemma as if our country were one, big, addicted family system, we can see that all of our elected leaders, and the heads of Big Business and Big Union which collude with them, are insanely, unethically, and addictively behaving in ways that are driving the Titanic straight toward the iceberg. And we can see that many of us are quietly lost in our own addictions. And that a large number of us, by our actions -- or lack of action -- are enabling this system and are therefore responsible for sustaining this dysfunctional paradigm. If we are aware of addiction in a system (whether a family, a group, or the American political system) and we don't take action to counter the addiction, then we are enabling that system to stay the same, to stay sick. We then become just as responsible for perpetuating the status quo as those who actively act out their addictions.

Let me define addiction more fully, and tell you how I see our country is operating like an addicted system.

Addiction has baffled humans since the beginning of our history. For millennia, shamans and priests and witch doctors and . . . whoever, gave it their best shot, but sadly, most addicts went crazy and died early deaths. While a lot of folks tried a lot of things, no one had a reliable solution. Until 1935. Two drunks somehow found a "cure" that worked for a small part of the population. They founded Alcoholics Anonymous, and many millions of addicts since then have been able to find relief from their addiction through following the AA program.

AA, and its perceived reliance on God, turned off many people. But for those who were helped, it was a miracle that saved them and their families from tragic lives. It was a small group that was helped, but for this group, it was the way back to a normal life. Almost all of us know of someone who found a way out of addiction through AA.

In 1956, the American Medical Association, the physicians' own association, declared that addiction is a *medical disease* that requires specific treatment. In the 1960s, 70s and 80s, twin studies showed that there is, in fact, a biological component to addiction. Dr. Mark Shuckett's studies have demonstrated an hereditary component to alcoholism, and his research showed that the child of an alcoholic is 60% more likely to become an alcoholic than is the child of a non-alcoholic.

More recently, thinkers such as physician and author Dr. Gabor Mate (*In the Realm of Hungry Ghosts*) have offered a compelling argument that the cause of addiction for many of us is rooted in a "not good enough" early childhood. He, and many others, correctly state that all of us need to be loved, nurtured, and protected in those first months and years of our lives. This seems obvious. But without this intimate, calm, and constant attention from our early caregivers, the nervous system fails to develop normally. Individuals who have not received sufficient early nurturing are unusually vulnerable to stress. When these individuals mature, they lack the internal resources and security to "self soothe" when stressed. It is difficult for these individuals to regulate their emotions. Many of these individuals actually grow up with a deficit of dopamine, the chemical in our brain that makes us feel good, and will search for dozens of ways to artificially increase dopamine levels. It is as if these individuals don't have a skin to protect them from being irritable and restless. They will turn to substances (like alcohol, nicotine, heroin) and behaviors (like overeating, compulsive spending, compulsive sex, watching endless TV) to numb themselves and make their lives less painful.

In the years since the mid-1990s, with advances in neurobiology and PET scan technology, scientists are developing a clearer understanding of the brain pathways involved in addiction.

The science is conclusive: addiction is a brain disease.

- The addict's brain is biologically different from that of a non-addict.
- The addict's brain is psychologically impaired.
- The way the addict's brain socializes with others is typically dysfunctional.
- An addict's brain is often incapable of meaningful spiritual experiences.

Here, from the American Society of Addiction Medicine, is the "Definition of Addiction (Short Version)," emphasis mine:

> "Addiction is a *primary, chronic disease of brain reward, motivation, memory and related circuitry.* Dysfunction in these circuits leads to characteristic *biological, psychological, social and spiritual manifestations.* This is reflected in an individual *pathologically pursuing reward and/or relief* by substance use and other behaviors.
>
> Addiction is characterized by *inability to consistently abstain, impairment in behavioral control, craving, diminished recognition of significant problems with one's behaviors and interpersonal relationships,* and *a dysfunctional emotional response.* Like other chronic diseases, addiction often involves cycles of *relapse and remission.* Without treatment or engagement in recovery activities, addiction is *progressive* and can result in disability or premature death."

In short, the criteria for addiction include the following:

1. Craving. We have the urgent desire to "medicate" ourselves with some behavior or substance.

2. Loss of control. We do it even though we know it is not right.

3. Continuing despite adverse consequences. We do it even though bad things happen as a result.

4. Chronic. It persists, it recurs, and it is always present.

Or, as Eckhart Tolle says in characterizing addiction, "Quite simply this: you no longer feel that you have the power to stop. It seems stronger than you. It also gives you a false sense of pleasure, pleasure that invariably turns into pain." (*The Power of Now*)

Basically, what we need to understand from this is that the thinking, rational part of the addict's brain, the forebrain (prefrontal cortex or forebrain) has been hijacked by the midbrain (ventral tegmental area). The midbrain of the addict unconsciously directs the addict to act out their addiction. The rational, thinking forebrain might say "no," but in addicts, the midbrain overrides the thinking brain and *compels* the addict toward addictive behaviors. Non-addicts can "say no" to an urge to drink or binge or spend or masturbate or watch endless TV.

The thinking brain of non-addicts works fine when it comes to substances. The prefrontal cortex of these individuals can decide to have an alcohol-containing drink and to stop drinking at any time. But for the addict, the midbrain is in charge and overrides the thinking brain. The midbrain compels the alcoholic to continue to drink and drink and drink.

The addict has no control over this behavior. The midbrain's need to get high has usurped the thinking brain's capacity to reason. Then the thinking part of the brain compensates by "making things up" to justify the crazy behavior. The addict is no longer sane and will need treatment, or will get worse.

This, so far, speaks to the behavior of the addict. But the addict does not live in a vacuum. An addict is almost always part of a social system that allows him or her to continue engaging in these addictive behaviors.

The addict makes everyone near them crazy. The addict causes those close to the addict -- family, friends, employers, and larger social networks -- to develop their own bio-psycho-social-spiritual disorders (disorders that affect a person biologically, psychologically, socially and spiritually). These "co-addicts" or "codependents" are the enablers who prop up the addictive system that surrounds them. And these enablers can often be more disordered than the addict. These codependents often need help and treatment *even more* than the addict.

Without enablers, the codependents propping up the system, the addict's life will unravel and come crashing down. It usually takes that kind of crisis to cause an addict to seek treatment. We often say that the addict needs to "hit a bottom."

It is conjectured that the mortality rate for codependents, due to their disease, may be even higher than it is for addicts. The codependent's lack of sanity manifests in stress-related conditions, biological, and psychological disorders that can lead to death from cancer, obesity, stroke, their own addictions, heart disease, and even suicidal depression.

There is a force in all families to maintain the status quo, to keep things the same. This force, termed "homeostasis," is an unconscious drive in the family to "return to how things have always been." Families and organizations find safety in being able to predict how things are going to be.

Members of a family (or larger system) may say that they want the addict to stop his addictive behavior, but there can be a stronger force at work that can actually cause the family to undermine the addict's recovery, and can cause the addict to relapse in order to return the system to the familiar, predictable reality. This stronger force is the pull to maintain homeostasis. In some families, the addict fulfills the role of "the problem person." (Family therapists call the person the "I.P." or Identified Patient.) If the addict starts to get well, the family is thrown out of balance. To maintain homeostasis, the family needs the addict to relapse and get things back to "the way they were " so that the family members can focus again on the addict instead of facing their own roles in supporting the dysfunctional system.

I have known enablers to place a drink in front of an alcoholic the day he returned from an extended stay in a residential treatment program.

Lack of attention to the enablers is the single most significant reason for the high failure rate in addiction treatment. If members of the enabling system do not get treatment and stop enabling, there is a high probability that when the addict reunites with his or her enablers, the addict and the enablers will resume their addictive behavior.

Family members as well as the addict *must* enter treatment if sanity is to be achieved. *My point: We enablers must realize this and change ourselves if we are to effectively replace all 536 elected federal officials in the Fall of 2012.*

APPLYING THE DISEASE MODEL OF ADDICTION TO OUR COUNTRY

So, let's look at how the concept of addiction applies to our nation.

Since the 1950s, our country has changed radically. Technology has altered values of previous generations with respect to family, community, and mutual support for the common good. It has made it easy for us all to embrace modern ideals: the quest for material wealth, power, speed, more . . . bigger, better, faster. And it happened so fast, we couldn't see the implications of these profound changes.

I believe that a large segment of America's population is comprised of addicts and that much of our behavior meets the criteria for addiction:

- Craving.

- Loss of Control.

- Continuing Despite Adverse Consequences.

- Chronicity.

Here are some behaviors Americans exhibit that lead me to think many of us are addicts: We have lost sight of what is *enough*. Instead of simply satisfying our needs, we want more. The first criterion of addiction is *craving*. We yearn to do more or to acquire more in order to feel better. This desire for more has become a core part of the American psyche. We want more possessions, bigger houses, faster computers. And, because in this country we can, we set our sights still higher. Before the housing bubble burst, many of us were buying new appliances, remodeling our kitchens and adding extensions to our houses, because we had what seemed like limitless credit-card ceilings and home-equity lines of credit. We don't call it excess; we call it affluence or "economic growth." And we don't stop. We appear to have no brakes, no boundaries.

Our leaders, and Big Business, and many average citizens have *lost control*, the second aspect of addiction. We have lost the ability to stop and have a sane look at our lives. Do we really need a car with more horsepower and more gadgets? Do we really need another shade of lipstick? Do we really need a new flavor of ice cream or even to eat ice cream? Do we really need the latest multi-billion dollar jet fighter plane? Do we really need half the stuff our government spends money on?

Some of us say we're going to stop, but we don't. This has become an endless "New Year's Resolution" joke for us. If you are paying attention to the politicians, you will see this scenario repeated over and over again. They say that they will do something different, but it rarely happens. They have lied to us. They told us that Iraq had "weapons of mass destruction." President Obama said, "The health-care debate will be on C-Span." The first President Bush said, "Read my lips, no new taxes." And Watergate. It does not happen because they are addicts, and addicts, by definition, can't control their behavior. And we, the American electorate, enable their addictions.

Plus, our leaders make promises that they don't keep. Addicts do this all the time. Sometimes they're so focused on getting the next fix, they don't even remember what they've said they would do. Or they're trying to justify what they have or haven't done. Remember the housing-bubble crisis? Remember the hearings in Congress where the bankers got grilled? And then Congress formed the oversight committee to make regulations to protect the public. And guess what -- they went to the back rooms and took all the teeth out of the legislation. We can always depend on them *saying* that they will balance the budget, or get spending under control and fix the schools, or take better care of the veterans, or lower our taxes . . . . Addicts do not keep their promises. Lying is a way of life for the addict.

The third criterion of addiction is *continuing despite adverse consequences.* The wreckage of addiction surrounds us. We often say the addict is like a tornado, causing destruction wherever they are. All we have to do to verify this reality is to look around. We see a hotter planet, degraded soil, economic chaos, vanishing species, polluted water, increasing homelessness, and unhealthy, fat people.

The fourth criterion of addiction is that it is *chronic.* It is always present. *The disease will never go away.* The best we can do is to put it in remission through addiction treatment.

We enablers are also in denial of the process of addiction and its consequences. The enablers among us think that we can sustain our current approach and everything will be OK.

Except, we can't. We can't sustain this approach and we have known this reality for many, many years. We are in denial.

Denial (noun) de-ni-al
(1): refusal to admit the truth or reality (as of a statement or charge);
(2): assertion that an allegation is false
(Merriam-Webster Dictionary)

In other words, denial: making up convenient fantasies to avoid inconvenient truths.

It is as if we have put our heads in the sand and don't want to hear about animal extinction and global warming and ozone depletion and rising carbon dioxide levels and the endocrine disruptors in our drinking water and the death of the Amazon Rainforest and the vanishing Arctic and climate change, and the prospect of a third of all newborn children becoming diabetic, and mercury being rained down on our people by coal-burning plants, or the other myriad unfolding terrors.

Do we *really* think that we can keep doing what we are doing and it's all going to somehow be OK? Do we really think that someone is going to come along and magically solve this problem for us?

This is denial, and this is America's disease. We believe we are doing fine and we can keep doing what we are doing, and it's all going to work out.

If we were to come out of denial, if we could stand up and notice, where would we be? Smack in the middle of the mess we've made. No wonder we want to keep our heads in the sand and leave the mess for future generations to deal with! We landed on the planet in a time of more abundance than man had ever known and we are on track to leave our children with a horror beyond our imagination. In half a century we have totally screwed this up!

Us. You and me. We are the enablers in the addictive system.

But, like in any addictive system, at some point it all comes crashing down. We can no longer pretend that it will "all work out." Forces beyond our control are going to slam into us. The suddenness and disruption of the Arab Spring will come to us in ways we can't imagine if we don't grab the helm and plot a different course.

And the International Business Times, August 14, 2011, reported that the Intergovernmental Panel on Climate Change (IPCC) Fourth Assessment Report (released in 2007) forecasts that the Arctic will be ice-free in the summer by the year 2100. Recent reports by M.I.T. challenge that report and say the ice could disappear much, much sooner.

The Pixar movie, *WALL-E*, graphically showed us where we are headed if we don't wake up. In this award-winning Disney movie, we humans had to leave Earth because we had destroyed all life. Collectively, our addictive American family system had ravaged everything in our path.

And we enablers are making this *happen*, because we fail to stand up and take action to prevent it. It's not a movie, it's reality.

But we do have another option. We have the minds and the technology to create a very different outcome. If we are ready to change, to come out of denial and follow the wisdom of Gandhi and Martin Luther King and the young people in Egypt, we actually can pull off this Second American Revolution.

And, I believe, have a whole lot of fun doing it!

3

RECOVERY IS NOT ROCKET SCIENCE

Viewing the plight of our country, its citizens, and our politicians as an addictive system gives us hope. *There is hope because there is effective treatment for addiction and because full recovery is possible for anyone who seeks it. When Asmaa Mahfouz posted a video on YouTube and on Facebook asking Egyptians to stage a peaceful revolution in Tahrir Square, she declared,* "Hope disappears only when you say there is no hope."

We who are addicts and we who are the enabling codependents need to wake up and change -- only then can the addictive system be healed and a new, sane family and country be created.

If we look at our country in 2011, we could say that we are a nation with millions of addicts, governed and directed mostly by elected officials who are held hostage by greed, addictions, obsessions, or compulsions that have taken them away from their spiritual, moral, and ethical selves. It is these 536 elected officials who need to be replaced. We hope they will go to treatment and be available to help our country at some future time. But it is we who need to take responsibility for being the ones who elected them!

The term "recovery" is often misunderstood. It means simply recovering what our addiction took away. Or, as in my case, building a new, healthy self, because there probably never was one. One way to understand this is to imagine that a healthy 30-year-old man or woman slid into addiction for ten years. During those ten years, they would have been out of touch with reality and missing the normal developmental work that would have otherwise occurred. How long would it take to make up for this loss? My guess is that it would take diligent work over most of another ten years to regain *full health*.

Recovery is not just about the addict. An addict is part of a larger system that has damaged the other family members. The addict cannot sustain recovery and stay in the family system if the other family members don't also do the work to recover themselves. For recovery to succeed, either all of the individuals in the family need to recover or, sadly, the addict needs to accept that his family will never reach its full potential. For our country to recover, we need to visualize that we *all* enter recovery. Individually, we need to recover as addicts, and we need to recover as enablers, in order to be healthy ourselves. Then we can recover as a nation.

But recovery is not easy. It's not easy for anyone to change their brain's wiring if they are addicted to drugs or food or gambling or spending or accumulating wealth or compulsive sex or compulsive work or power. It's not easy for an addict's family. It's not going to be easy for a nation of people addicted to more, better, bigger, and faster. And change will not be easy for all the enablers who are addicted to, and support, these addicts. It's not going to be easy to stop falling for the charming campaign propaganda these addicts put on TV at election time. It's not going to be easy to change the whole interconnected system. In any family system, addiction seems to be fatally locked into place. The reality is that we do not have a choice not to change, unless we want to leave our grandkids with a history that ranks us as more heinous than the Third Reich. The destruction we are causing will be far greater than the havoc wreaked by that regime.

We simply do not have a choice.

For this Intervention to work, we will have to roll up our sleeves. Recovery is a lifetime process, and the good news is, in order to intervene on our country we have to begin the recovery process on ourselves.

Let me tell you about recovery from drug addiction, which I see as the model for our nation's recovery. I will talk about how recovery works for an individual, using my own process as an example. I'll address how I see this recovery process being applied to our nation.

Millions of people have recovered from addiction. In 2009,

Mark Willenbring, Director of the Treatment and Recovery Research Division of the National Institute on Alcohol Abuse and Alcoholism/National Institute of Health, estimated that there were over 20 million Americans in recovery from alcohol and other drugs. I could name dozens of famous actors, athletes, astronauts, business leaders, and more. I don't, because I am respecting the tradition of anonymity. Inside a judgmental world, we like to remain anonymous. In fact, anonymity creates an environment of safety that allows recovery to happen. I am telling you my story, because I know recovery works. I want my experience, strength and hope to offer hope for us in America's recovery.

For many people, recovery is very straightforward. Get help, get sober. I entered recovery in 1979. On November 14, 1979, after 25 years of addiction, I walked into a meeting and have been sober ever since. This is the case for countless other addicts. They get help in AA, and other 12-Step fellowships, and in addiction treatment programs, and they recover. Their families get help in Al-Anon, and in addiction or other mental health treatment, and they recover. Many of these people have fully recovered what they lost to addiction.

And while millions have walked this simple path, sadly, many millions never do recover from America's number-one mental health problem. It is estimated that most addicts fail to get treatment, live impaired lives, and often suffer early deaths.

The reality is that all members of addicted families are stressed. These families are often in crisis, and certainly not living up to their potential. The addict is dependent on a substance (or a behavior, in the case of gambling, compulsive sex, compulsive work, extreme exercise, gaming, overeating, overspending, hoarding, etc.). The enabling, codependent family members are typically *compulsively attached to their pathological relationship* with the addict. It is as if they are addicted to the addict and unable to change their destructive enabling behaviors.

"'The times they are a' changing," sang Bob Dylan. And boy are they. The treatment of addiction has finally reached a tipping point. We have known since the mid-1930s that addiction is a disease. Today we can benefit from the congruence of three forces in understanding addiction: neuroscience (especially brain scans), family dynamics (the work of Stephanie Brown, Ph.D., among others), and modern treatment approaches.

Today, we have the potential to understand addiction, to accept it as a brain disease, and to treat it accordingly. In the last chapter, I described the research showing that addiction is a brain disease. The addict's brain is biologically different from the brain of a non-addict. True, a lot of people, many doctors included, don't understand addiction. And 20 million Americans think the earth is bigger than the sun.

Basically, the addict's mind is not at home. Their rational, thinking, reasoning, logical, reflective brain has been kicked to the curb. This rational forebrain has been hijacked, pushed aside, and is no longer reliable. The addict, as neuroscience has shown, is not firing on all cylinders.

The second force that is tipping addiction treatment into the modern age is the understanding that addiction is a *family* disease. Psychologist Stephanie Brown has spearheaded the foundational work on family recovery in addiction treatment. Anyone familiar with addiction knows that the members of an addict's family are usually as crazy as the addict. And we know that, while the addict might recover, the other family members may or may not recover. As an Interventionist, I often find the codependents, the close family members, are crazier than the addict, and sometimes recommend that *they* are the ones that need intense, residential treatment.

Dr. Stephanie Brown's seminal research, first published in the 1980s and consolidated in her book, *The Alcoholic Family in Recovery* (1998), showed what those of us in recovery already know. If everyone in the family chose recovery, then the family got well. If the enabling members of the family didn't choose to pursue recovery, then the recovering addict moved on, left them in their dysfunctional lives, and got on with the business of having a life. Or, the addict went back to the family, reengaged with the crazy family system, relapsed, and the insanity resumed.

In my family, my father was the addict and my mother the codependent. He drank and she covered for him. This went on until I was 18 years old. Then my mother found Al-Anon. It took a very short period of time for her to "get it." She finally realized that she could not change her husband, no matter how much she pleaded, screamed, and begged. *But she could change herself.* With the support of Al-Anon, after nearly twenty years of living with an insane person, she recovered her capacity to think rationally.

After a brief period in recovery she said to my father, "I love you, I want to stay with you. But if you do not seek help for your drinking, I will get a divorce." For once she did not tell him what to do. She simply said what *she* would do if he continued his addiction. He refused to get help. She got a divorce and lived a serene and active life, filled with family, gardening, and friends. 15 years later, drunk, he killed himself at the age of 56.

A professional Intervention on our family decades ago might have resulted in a very different outcome. As it turned out, my three siblings and I grew up in that crazy house, left home as soon as possible, and have had little contact with each other since then. There simply was not enough goodness, love, and health for any of us to bond very deeply. To this day, my brother is an active addict who has been rejected by his friends, and my fear is that he will end his life like our father.

Professional Interventionists get this. They understand that the Intervention is initially going to be *on the system that supports the addict and not just on the addict.* They understand that the whole system is complicit in the addiction. All the family members are affected by the addiction, and each family member has the opportunity to create a more functional life for him or herself.

Unfortunately, among Interventionists, there are many amateurs who don't understand the systemic nature of this disease. They fail to see the role the family plays, and they collude with the family's belief that *the problem is just the addict.* The TV program, *Interventions,* has popularized this myth. These televised Interventions focus only on getting the addict into treatment, ignoring the fact that some family members may actively sabotage the addict's recovery in order to protect and maintain the familiar lifestyle, the status quo. The good news is that some of these Interventions work and the addict gets sober. But these Interventions leave the family out of the treatment process, and the relapse rate is much higher than when the family is included.

In my nearly 20 years of treating addiction from a family system's approach, I rarely see an addict get full recovery if the family members don't also choose recovery.

Clearly, I'm labeling the 536 elected Washington officials as addicts. For the sake of illustration, lets imagine that all 536 federally elected officials woke up today and said, "By golly. I'm an addict. I'm greedy and I'm addicted to power and money and accumulating wealth. I've been blind to what's going on in this country and to my part in it. I'm going to get help and get my head on straight. I'm going to go into treatment, and recover."

Most people might think that that was great. Wow, we got all those sleazy, corrupt, immoral and unethical folks out of office.

I wouldn't.

I wouldn't think it was great because *we* didn't change! We are the ones who elected them in the first place, and I believe that we would simply elect a similar bunch of addicted officials because that is what we are used to!

As individuals, these 536 would not be able to change and sustain recovery in the midst of the millions of people who would pull for the old way, for what was familiar and comfortable and didn't require anybody to do anything different. The force from us, the enablers, to maintain the homeostasis, or the status quo, in the system would undermine their recovery. Even if the President, the Senators, the members of the House of Representatives, and the leaders of Big Business and Big Union sought recovery, without the enablers also changing and moving toward recovery, recovery could not and would not be sustained. For the system to change, we all need to change.

An effective Intervention on all of us would lead to a process that would be able to shift our country into an entirely new way of being and create a different paradigm.

The third force that is tipping addiction treatment into the modern age is the recent increase in financial support for addiction treatment. This has powerful ramifications for our nation's recovery. For example, in California, voters approved a bond, Proposition 36, which provides money to divert drug-related criminals into treatment instead of sending them to jail.

So, what does "addiction treatment" look like? And what do we really mean by "recovery?"

In any Intervention, before we can look at what treatment is, it is important to understand the damage that the addiction has done. When we assess an addict, it is useful to look at the damage and the cost of addiction from a multi-dimensional perspective that incudes biological, psychological, social, and spiritual aspects.

The first of these, the biological damage, is the easiest to understand. Addicts ingest substances and engage in behaviors that mess up brain chemistry and brain wiring, and that harm body organs and body functioning. If we simply stop poisoning the brain and body, and stop other addictive behaviors, the brain, in time, will mostly return to health. How long the brain's return to health takes depends on the drug or addictive behavior history: which drug, which behavior, how much, how often, and for how long.

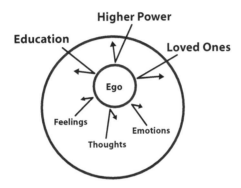

Figure 1: The Addict

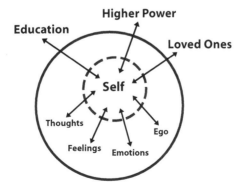

Figure 2: The Sane Person

The second kind of damage, psychological damage, is a little more complex. I will be talking about what constitutes mental health in the next chapter. Basically, the addict's single-minded focus on the next "fix" has cut him or herself off from a healthy view of reality. The midbrain is choosing addiction while the thinking, rational part of the brain is grappling with the impossible task of trying to make sense out of the midbrain's choices. The addict is out of control.

For example, one evening, my alcoholic brother announced to us that he was no longer going to drink. A few hours later, he was drinking. Someone asked him why he was drinking. His answer, "I changed my mind." Actually, he never even had the slightest chance to stop. All he could do was make up the story as he went along. All addicts do the same thing. We rationalize and justify and deny. We frantically make up stuff to give our ego the illusion of being in control, while everyone around us clearly sees the absence of sanity.

If we ask the bankers who took down our economy why they did it, they will come up with an answer, just like my brother did. The addict's ego always has an answer. And actually, addicts completely believe what they are saying at that moment, even though a day later they may have a completely different answer.

I was like that when I was caught in my addiction. I was out of control. I did my best to try to make sense out of my insane life. I could always come up with reasons to explain any action. And I *always* believed them!

Our lifetime of psychological development slows down or stops when we become addicted. This is particularly costly if the addiction started before the brain fully develops, at around age 25.

Life is a challenge. Every day, if we are living a healthy life, we are learning the next thing. We learn to walk. Then we're toilet trained. We cross the street alone. We learn to drive a car, take orders from a boss, develop relationships, raise children, etc. We learn literally millions and millions of tiny lessons, most so small and incremental that we don't even notice them. I like to think of the process like an endless escalator. The psychologist, Erik Erikson delineated eight stages of psychosocial development:

1 - Hope: Trust vs. Threat (Birth - 1 year)

2 - Will: Autonomy vs. Shame (2 - 4 years)

3 - Purpose: Initiative vs. Guilt (Preschool to 4)

4 - Competence: Industry vs. Inferiority (Childhood, 7-13)

5 - Fidelity: Identity vs. Role Confusion (Adolescents, 14 - 24)

6 - Love: Intimacy vs. Isolation (25 – 40)

7 - Care: Generativity vs. Stagnation (Middle Adulthood, 45 - 65)

8 - Wisdom: Ego Integrity vs. Despair (Seniors, 65+)

We need to master each stage before we can go onto the next stage. This is why addiction that starts in childhood is so very devastating. And addiction in a family is one of the most common causes of addiction in the next generation. Children need loving and sane parents. If there is any addiction in a family, there is a high possibility that the first five stages above will be disrupted, leaving the child vulnerable to anxiety or depression. An anxious or depressed child will quickly find a way to fix this by self-medicating with drugs or addictive behaviors. Having found an artificial solution to a disordered state, these children will become our future addicts and the next immense burden on our society.

The third kind of damage from addiction, social damage, is also immensely destructive to an individual, especially when addiction starts before age 25. When addictive behavior takes over, social development slows down or stops. I started drinking at age 14. When I got into recovery I realized how immature I was. Emotionally, I was still acting like a teenager even though I was in my forties. My development had been arrested when I started using substances to cope with life. If I wanted to grow up, I was going to need some help. It was as if I had not used my legs for 25 years. I could learn to live on my hands and knees, or I could ask for help and accept the guidance I needed to learn to stand up.

Our intimate relationships reflect our psychological and social development. We seek out people at a similar level of psychosocial development. Near the end of my addiction, most of the people I knew were also heavy drug users. My marriages to other addicts or codependents had all ended. I was alone.

And finally, the fourth kind of damage from addiction, spiritual damage, is reflected in an addict's almost complete absence of healthy spirituality. Addicts are busy trying to survive and get the next "fix." There is no spiritual connection. Faith, power, and salvation reside in the bottle, the pill, the next snack, or the unending quest for more money or power.

So let's return to the question: what does "addiction treatment" look like? If you Google "addiction treatment" you will find 18,200,000 listings offering thousands of approaches. But when you boil addiction treatment down, you will find that over 90% of addiction treatment basically looks the same as it has for many decades, because that is what we have figured out works.

Treatments for "process addictions," also known as behavioral addictions or non-substance-related addictions, use a protocol similar to treatment for substance addictions. They offer support to stop the addictive, obsessive, or compulsive behaviors. There are residential treatment programs, outpatient programs, and 12-Step meetings for these process or behavioral addictions.

I have treated families suffering from addiction for nearly 20 years. For chemically dependent individuals, treatment sometimes begins with a detox from the drugs. This may require help from a medical professional, if the addict has been using large quantities of alcohol or the benzodiazepine class of prescription drugs. Withdrawal from these substances can be problematic, even fatal. Once the addict is no longer under the influence, we teach the person tools to refrain from their addictive behavior, *just for today*. This could be as simple as going to a 12-Step meeting every day, as I did, and accepting the guidance of former addicts. Humans are social animals and we benefit from the support of others to whom we feel close and who are doing similar things.

If we are fortunate, in addition to the social support of a 12-Step program, we may be in an outpatient program that includes individual, family, and peer group counseling, as well as education and drug testing. Treatment may include moving into a sober living environment, a house where other sober men or women live.

Often we start treatment at a Residential Treatment Center (RTC). Residential treatment programs extend from 30 to 90 days. We always recommend that a residential stay be followed by "step down" to an Intensive Outpatient Program (IOP) and move into a sober living environment (SLE). The length of time in the IOP depends on what help the individual needs in order to stabilize enough to begin the next stage of recovery.

In my case, I drank and did drugs from age 14 to 39 -- twenty-five years. It has actually taken nearly 25 years of "treatment" (12-Step, psychotherapy, dealing with "life on life's terms) to heal and become what I might have been if I had not become an addict.

Nearly all long-standing and successful treatment programs are based on the 12-Step model, which provides a foundation for a lifetime of sustained recovery. Alternative programs exist that do not use the 12-Step approach, and they have helped many individuals abstain from their addiction. However, as we have seen, addiction is a chronic disorder. We have it for life, like diabetes, hypertension, and asthma. Most addicts and recovering enablers typically will need to stay close to their support network for life, if they wish to continue to grow and have flourishing lives and vibrant relationships. Though many alternative programs appeal to those looking for a softer, easier way, these programs often do not include anything akin to the free and readily available 12-Step backing that provides the extended support needed to address the chronic nature of addiction.

So, what are these twelve steps and what is so special about them? And how do they work? Once, when I was in early recovery and starting graduate school, I shyly confided to one of my professors that I was in recovery for addiction and that I was active in a local 12-Step meeting. His response surprised me, "Wow, that's wonderful. Do you know that the 12-Step programs are the fastest growing spiritual movement in the world?" I don't know about the world, but I do know about my local community. Marin County in California has 250,000 residents and over 300 AA meetings a week. And this number does not include numerous other 12-Step programs: Narcotics Anonymous, Al-Anon, Codependents Anonymous, Overeaters Anonymous, Food Addicts Anonymous, Smokers Anonymous, Nicotine Anonymous, Marijuana Anonymous, Heroin Anonymous, Clutterers Anonymous, Sex and Love Addicts Anonymous, Codependents of Sex and Love Addicts Anonymous, Pills Anonymous, Debtors Anonymous, Emotions Anonymous, Sexual Compulsives Anonymous, Online Gamers Anonymous, Survivors of Incest Anonymous, Shopaholics Anonymous, Gamblers Anonymous, Chronic Pain Anonymous, and many others. The 12-Step model is, in reality, a design for healthy living, and its rapid spread around the world gives testament to its value. And, many people who are suffering from psychiatric disorders or "problems with living" other than addictions can also benefit from the 12-Step approach.

Many churches make space available for 12-Step meetings. It is not unusual for there to be far more folks attending 12-Step meetings at a church than parishioners who go to weekly services!

THE TWELVE STEPS OF ALCOHOLICS ANONYMOUS

1. We admitted we were powerless over alcohol -- that our lives had become unmanageable.

2. Came to believe that a Power greater than ourselves could restore us to sanity.

3. Made a decision to turn our will and our lives over to the care of God, *as we understood Him.*

4. Made a searching and fearless moral inventory of ourselves.

5. Admitted to God, to ourselves, and to another human being the exact nature of our wrongs.

6. Were entirely ready to have God remove all these defects of character.

7. Humbly asked Him to remove our shortcomings.

8. Made a list of all persons we had harmed, and became willing to make amends to them all.

9. Made direct amends to such people wherever possible, except when to do so would injure them or others.

10. Continued to take personal inventory and when we were wrong promptly admitted it.

11. Sought through prayer and meditation to improve our conscious contact with God, *as we understood Him,* praying only for knowledge of His will for us and the power to carry that out.

12. Having had a spiritual awakening as the result of these Steps, we tried to carry this message to alcoholics, and to practice these principles in all our affairs.

Copyright A.A. World Services, Inc.

Let's look at the Twelve Steps from the perspective of a newly recovering addict: My brain isn't sane, I have been poisoning myself for some time, my relationships are a mess, and spirituality is not even on the radar screen.

When I first show up at a 12-Step meeting, I'm told not to engage in my addictive behaviors, one day at a time. I'm told to go to a 12-Step meeting every day for 90 days, to get a sponsor, and work the 12 Steps. At first it mostly does not make sense; things are in a whirl. My world seems upside down, but slowly things are dawning on me. Slowly, hope awakens. I feel a welcome relief as I learn that I'm not a bad person, I simply have a disease -- a very serious disease, but one that can be treated. If I follow the instructions, I can be reasonably certain my disease will go into remission.

One day at a time. Easy does it.

Slowly, as my brain clears, the first three steps start to make sense. They seem to boil down to this: "I'm very sick, something can help me get well, and I think I will follow the instructions on how to get well."

For America, it might be something like this: "America's political system is corrupt and out of control, a collective Intervention can restore America to sanity, and we are all willing to stand up and make that happen."

That's it.

Now for the longer version:

Step 1. "My craving midbrain drove me to act obsessively and compulsively. My actions were out of control, and my life was unmanageable and I was a mess." Admitting this takes a lot of courage -- to overcome our ego's denial and to accept this reality. But this step is critical. We first need to admit our problem. If we stay in denial, the rest of the Steps will not make any sense.

Step 2. "I began to see hope. I saw the sane folks around me that had been crazy. I began to believe I could become sane like them."

Step 3. "I began to open to the reality that if I wanted sanity I would need help, and therefore I made a decision to follow the suggestions of those who were recovering."

The actual Third Step suggests that we turn our will and our life over to God, as we understand God. Like many, I had a problem with organized religion. I had a wise sponsor who suggested that I set aside the "God thing" and turn my will and my life over to the group's collective wisdom and experience. That made sense. This group of addicts, after all, had helped me, a day at a time, to get a handle on my addiction. And to this day, over three decades later, I still attend a few regular meetings each week. My program saved my life, and I understand the chronic aspect of addiction: it does not go away; our only hope is that it goes into remission. I have seen too many people relapse, and some of them die, because they stop getting ongoing support. They forget that addiction is a chronic disease that needs ongoing attention like other chronic diseases.

Steps Four and Five are very similar to a comprehensive course of counseling or psychotherapy. We inventory the intimate details of our lives, often for the first time. In Step Four, we are finally able to see what the 12 Steps call our "defects of character." We look at the wrongs we have committed in our lives. We prepare for a new way of life that will be free of regrets and resentments. And then, in Step Five, we share this inventory of ourselves with another person. We were crazy and we did a lot of really selfish things that perhaps hurt a lot of people. Our shame and guilt are out in the open, and we can begin to take action to create a different and sane future for ourselves.

Typically, by the time we are working Steps Four and Five, our health is coming back, we have gotten over a bit of our defensiveness and arrogance, and we can actually accept the reality that we are flawed. It is often said that the active addict is an egomaniac with an inferiority complex. It's true. An active addict has a very defended and distorted ego and, at the same time, is carrying around a lot of shame that he or she has denied and repressed.

These are important Steps. A mind that is busy repressing and defending against conscious and unconscious thoughts is a mind that is too busy to make room for laughing, singing, dancing, and making love! The "I don't want to talk about it" mentality, sadly, means that the individual will miss out on a lot of love and life. If we work these Steps, perhaps along with getting professional counseling and developing a healthy lifestyle, we can develop psychosocial health.

As we do Steps Six and Seven, we understand that if we stick with the recovery process and develop a spiritual perspective, our defects of character and our shortcomings may lessen and perhaps, even be removed. We understand that our addiction-controlled past is not who we truly are. For the first time we can believe that we might be able to be really healthy!

In the process of inventorying our character defects in Step Four, we became aware of the individuals and institutions that we have harmed. Steps Eight and Nine give us the opportunity to address some of the damage we have caused in our relationships with others. And this is where the 12-Step process helps us heal these relationships. Steps Eight and Nine invite us to become healthy humans who are accountable and responsible. We finally are sane enough to look another person in the eye and take responsibility for our actions. We have the opportunity to make amends to them for our wrongs and also to make restitution for our actions. If we actually do this, we will no longer have to repress our guilt over these transgressions. We no longer have to look over our shoulder at those we have harmed. We can be free of the guilt that prevented us from being able to look others in the eyes and, for instance, tell them that we love them.

Step Ten keeps us accountable from day to day. Which is good, because it may take years before the addicts' and the codependents' brains are rewired in ways that are consistently functional. This Step reminds us to take daily inventory of our actions, and of ourselves. We note when we are wrong and make mistakes. And when we make mistakes, we make amends. We now are making a good start toward healing the social aspect of our disease.

The spiritual aspect of the Twelve Steps that we encounter again in Steps Eleven and Twelve is sometimes difficult to explain. Spirituality is "trans-egoic." It transcends our ego. And this concept is nearly impossible for someone, lost in addiction, to comprehend. For some, spirituality is a God consciousness. For others, it is an overwhelming sense of wonder, or an appreciation of the miracles of nature, or a connection with what is good in us and in our world. For still others, it includes our intuition and the experience of being able to embrace more than what we see and know in the physical world.

Being spiritual overwhelms our ability to fully describe it. I experience spirituality as love and a sense of immense "OK-ness" that I feel but do not have adequate words to explain.

Step Eleven invites us to connect with the spiritual, the world beyond the ego. By this point, hopefully, we have healed some of the damage that is biological (we have stopped poisoning our body or being obsessively driven by some behavior), psychological (we are no longer devoting a lot of energy to repressing our feelings and defending against unwanted realities), and social (we are beginning to have healthy relationships).

This Step reminds us to pray *only for the knowledge of God's will*. I don't get to pray for myself or for a rising stock market or for America or for rain or for anything else my ego can dream up. This Step invites us to relax and let go of living in fear or of feeling compelled to control the people and situations around us. Things will work out according to some divine plan. They always do.

The last step, Step Twelve, starts out with the phrase, "Having had a spiritual awakening." This is a bold promise. The reality is that almost everyone who diligently works the Steps reports that this actually happens -- that a spiritual part of us wakes up. We realize that something very special has happened to us. We realize that the unbelievable has occurred. We can look back and see that many people have, in small and large ways, guided us from insanity to sanity, from sickness to health, and more than that, to a place that is even better than we could ever have imagined that first day we entered recovery. I began to grasp that there was actually something more than just me! Something very fundamental had changed in that dark, wet container of electrical energy between my ears. I had somehow magically awakened to a reality that was very different and wonderful.

Neuroscientists often refer to the "plasticity" of the brain. This means that our brains are capable of radical change, usually to an extent that is unimaginable to the active addict. In reality, the addict *always underestimates* his ability to implement new behavior.

Step Twelve also invited me to "carry this message to those who still suffer." By this time I had become healthy enough to face the poor, broken addict, who is like I once was, and to be of service. I now could take a newcomer out to coffee and tell them about the "one day at a time" thing. What a remarkable thing. What a gift! I could give back what was so freely given to me.

It took me a year, a full twelve months, to work the 12 Steps. I went to a meeting almost every day, met with my sponsor weekly, and did not use addictive substances. I found that these Steps became principles that I could apply in "all my affairs," to every facet of my life. I also began to realize how impaired I had been. My development had been stunted starting at age 14. I had missed almost all the lessons after that. At the end of this first year of recovery, I realized that I was not much more grown up than a 15-year-old. I had finally awakened enough to see how asleep I had been. I didn't know it then, but I was to continue to "trudge the road of happy destiny." The last three decades of my recovery have been filled with so much wonder and love and joy that I could never begin to describe it all.

This is the beauty of the Twelve Steps and of recovery -- it is an opportunity to learn, from the ground up, how to be healthy. By stepping up, by taking action, recovery is possible. We who are recovering know how this works. And this is, I believe, the model for our nation's return to biological, psychological, social, and spiritual health. We step up, we take action, and the process unfolds. When we begin recovery, we don't know what the outcome will look like, we can't know, but we have faith that it will be better than how it was before. And we can't foresee what the future holds for our country's recovery, but we can believe that it will be a vast improvement from how things are now.

So let's look a little deeper at what a healthy America might look like.

4

ARE *ANY* OF US HEALTHY?

What is a healthy human? And how healthy can a human be?

The Internet, science, medicine, technology, modern drugs, sports, and social movements have pushed the envelope of human knowledge and capacity way beyond what our grandparents or even our parents could have imagined. "High-level wellness" today is not what Grandma knew.

I'm a former hippy (if anyone can outgrow that experience). Young people had a vision in the 1960s. Yes, there were "sex, drugs, and rock and roll." But it was more than that. We believed there were no limits to who or what we could become. We celebrated the brilliance and genius of every individual and every culture around the world. No longer was "being normal" a cultural expectation. If anything, to be called "normal" or "straight" was a put-down.

In 1997, Apple Computer aired a television ad called, "Think Different" that expressed this 1960s stance. The ad described the rebels, the rule-breakers, the visionaries, the ones who are crazy enough to think they just might change the world -- and who are the ones that do. The individuals in this ad showed us what is possible if we are allowed to fully develop. The list included Albert Einstein, Bob Dylan, Martin Luther King, Jr., Richard Branson, John Lennon, R. Buckminster Fuller, Thomas Edison, Muhammad Ali, Ted Turner, Maria Callas, Mahatma Gandhi, Amelia Earhart, Alfred Hitchcock, Martha Graham, Jim Henson (with Kermit the Frog), Frank Lloyd Wright, and Picasso.

The Sixties were a very turbulent time. Children were taking powerful psychedelic drugs. President Nixon was secretly bombing Cambodia. Brilliant minds from the east and the west were gathering at the Esalen Institute in Big Sur. Good and bad were swirling around us. A rising middle class was creating a shift in our awareness.

Humanistic psychology offered the perspective that mental health treatment could impact almost everyone. We began to understand the possibility that each of us had unlimited potential. Nelson Mandela, quoting Marianne Williamson, gave the following inaugural address when he was elected as the first black president of the formerly white government of South Africa:

> *"Our deepest fear is not that we are inadequate. Our deepest fear is that we are powerful beyond measure. It is our light, not our darkness, that most frightens us. We ask ourselves, who am I to be brilliant, gorgeous, talented, fabulous? Actually, who are you not to be? You are a child of God. Your playing small does not serve the world. There is nothing enlightened about shrinking so that other people won't feel insecure around you. We are all meant to shine, as children do. We were born to make manifest the glory of God that is within us. It's not just in some of us; it's in everyone. And as we let our own light shine, we unconsciously give other people permission to do the same. As we are liberated from our own fear, our presence automatically liberates others."*

There it is -- mental health. Every child has the potential to become an Einstein or a Maria Callas if given a chance. We have the wealth and technology to create a fantastic Eden for *each and every one of our children.*

But we haven't done this.

In fact, in many ways, things are worse now than in Grandma's time. Yes, science and technology are creating magic. But Americans, in their hearts and souls, can feel that something is missing. Instead of joyfully appreciating wise leaders for guiding us to a better future, we have a sad and dispirited population that is very frightened and frustrated. The fact that it seems like we are all on the Titanic heading for an iceberg is a narrative that we are collectively creating. Our crooked politicians and immoral business leaders are simply the most obvious symbols of a nation without wise and inspirational leaders. What we need is inspired, creative, and visionary innovators, like Steve Jobs, who truly Think Different.

We can create a new narrative. We can, like the Hippies in the Sixties, flip this. We can, just like they did in Egypt in 2011, replace a corrupt government. We can bring the positive aspects of all outstanding cultures into American life. We can be like Martin Luther King, Jr., and end legal discrimination. We can, like Gandhi, stand up and throw off the yokes of England. We, as a nation of visionaries, can take to the streets. We can do this! And we can have fun doing it!

We are brilliant and we are talented. We can all run for President and for Congress. Wouldn't that be fun? But first, like any addict, we need to become healthy ourselves.

What is health and what makes a person healthy? As a child growing up in an abusive, addicted family, I sure didn't know. I didn't have a clue what a functional relationship, marriage, or family looked like. Then I became an addict and was incapable of any meaningful personal development, until my late thirties. However, in the last three decades of my life, I've focused on doing the biological, psychological, social, and spiritual work needed to rewire my brain and move toward optimal health. If I can do this, anyone can do this.

Let's look at what health is, using the bio-psycho-social-spiritual perspective to explore what we know. In America, a healthy life is described by our Declaration of Independence -- that each of us is entitled to, "Life, liberty, and the pursuit of happiness." I believe this to be a basic description of a healthy life in society. Anything that precludes our bio-psycho-social-spiritual health will compromise our quest for these goals and prevent us from experiencing love, joy, and abundance during our lives. Any bio-psycho-social-spiritual barrier will prevent our having a full life. And, since we live in society, if we ourselves are impaired, we naturally will negatively impact the developmental potential of others.

Biologically, the American population is all over the map. On the streets of our cities we see the sick and the homeless; then we read about the 90-year-old woman who ran a marathon. We see rampant obesity and addiction. Yet nearly any sane person, given the information and resources we now possess, has the option of improving their health.

A biologically healthy and sane person would meet most of the following criteria:

- Free of physical or psychological addictions, or in effective treatment for them.

- Free of physical disease, or receiving effective treatment for the disease.

- Cardiovascularly fit, physically active, at least a half-hour of aerobic activity each day.

- Physically flexible.

- Strong, doing some sort of strength work regularly to keep bones and muscles strong.

- Body Mass Index, BMI, between 18.5 and 25 (http://en.wikipedia.org/wiki/Body_mass_index)

- Metabolically healthy (as shown by blood tests): cholesterol, triglycerides, red and white cell counts, etc. in a healthy range.

- Diet strong in plant-based foods (see the 2011 documentary, *Forks over Knives*).

Almost every one of us is capable of achieving a high degree of physical health. In fact, given the current level of medical knowledge and capability, it should be our cultural norm. I resent the fact that an unhealthy person pays the same health insurance premiums that I do.

I was unhealthy when I was in my addiction. Today, I am healthy by choice. We owe it to our children and to each other to be healthy. Some people were upset at President Obama's suggestion that we focus our nation's attention on obesity. They felt the government was intervening in our personal affairs. Actually, it would be best if we, ourselves, citizens of America, did the intervening. And, we need to get help to stop our enabling behaviors. I believe there is a cost to society when we enable addiction. The enablers' decision to continue to support addicts costs all of us.

Our psychological health is intertwined with our social health. Like many animals, humans evolved in social groups. We are social animals and need good social contacts to give us a well-rounded and healthy life. We need a society and culture that will provide us with healthy values, attitudes, and beliefs. This means growing up in healthy families and going to good quality schools. It means becoming "good enough" parents who raise "good enough" children. We need mentors to guide us, and we need to mentor others. Living in society as we do, we need to contribute to the common good. We need honest and trustworthy public servants in positions of power and influence, and we need these leaders to have the vision and wisdom to guide us to a better tomorrow.

Our psychological health is molded by our social world. Each one of us is born with genetically imprinted personality traits, but we grow up in a family. Our relationships with family members impact our early psychological growth. As we get older, we interact with other people -- friends, neighbors, teachers -- and these relationships influence our psychological development. We may develop a relationship with a partner. As we grow and mature, we develop more and more social ties within our community and the larger world.

There are a number of matrices for assessing our psychosocial health. One, the Global Assessment of Functioning (GAF), rates an individual's psychosocial capacities. It is a numeric scale (0 through 100), used by mental health clinicians and physicians to objectively rate the social, occupational, and psychological functioning of adults. This scale, presented below, is excerpted from the *Diagnostic and Statistical Manual for Mental Disorders* (DSM- IV TR, 2000, p. 34), a voluminous manual compiled by the American Medical Association:

91-100: Superior functioning in a wide range of activities, life's problems never seem to get out of hand, is sought out by others because of his or her many positive qualities. No symptoms.

81-90: Absent or minimal symptoms (e.g., mild anxiety before an exam), good functioning in all areas, interested and involved in a wide range of activities, socially effective, generally satisfied with life, no more than everyday problems or concerns (e.g., an occasional argument with family members).

71-80: If symptoms are present, they are transient and expectable reactions to psychosocial stressors (e.g., difficulty concentrating after family argument); no more than slight impairment in social occupational, or school functioning (e.g., temporarily falling behind in schoolwork).

61-70: Some mild symptoms (e.g., depressed mood and mild insomnia) OR some difficulty in social occupational, or school functioning (e.g., occasional truancy or theft within the household), but generally functioning pretty well, has some meaningful interpersonal relationships.

51-60: Moderate symptoms (e.g., flat affect and circumstantial speech, occasional panic attacks) OR moderate difficulty in social, occupational, or school functioning (e.g., few friends, conflicts with peers or co-workers).

41-50: Severe symptoms (e.g., suicidal ideation, severe obsessional rituals, frequent shoplifting) OR any serious impairment in social, occupational or school functioning (e.g., no friends, unable to keep a job).

31-40: Some impairment in reality testing or communication (e.g., speech is at times illogical, obscure, or irrelevant) OR major impairment in several areas, such as work or school, family relations, judgment, thinking, or mood (e.g., depressed man avoids friends, neglects family, and is unable to work; child frequently beats up younger children, is defiant at home, and is failing at school).

21-30: Behavior is considerably influenced by delusions or hallucinations OR serious impairment in communication or judgment (e.g., sometimes incoherent, acts grossly inappropriately, suicidal preoccupation) OR inability to function in almost all areas (e.g., stays in bed all day, no job, home, or friends).

11-20: Some danger of hurting self or others (e .g., suicidal attempts without clear expectation of death; frequently violent; manic excitement) OR occasionally fails to maintain minimal personal hygiene (e.g., smears feces) OR gross impairment in communication (e.g., largely incoherent or mute).

1-10: Persistent danger of severely hurting self or others (e.g., recurrent violence) OR persistent inability to maintain minimal personal hygiene OR serious suicidal act with clear expectation of death.

Prior to getting into recovery my score was in the 31- 40 range. I was not very sane. Today, after three decades of work on myself, I am in the 81-90 range, and continuing to work on the problems that keep me from functioning in the Superior range. Why would anyone who is sane not want to have better mental health? Isn't it our evolutionary imperative to struggle and improve? I believe that striving to be our best is hardwired in all of us – except for the addicts.

Another measure of psychological and social health is the assessment of "differentiation of self in relationship." This concept was developed by Murray Bowen, a medical doctor and one of the founders of family systems theory. Bowen describes a differentiated individual as someone in a close relationship who *can think rationally and clearly while at the same time experiencing strong emotions.*

A well-differentiated person rarely "loses it." They don't freak out, explode, rage, throw temper tantrums, or shut down while in close relationship with intimate others.

Many of us merge or fuse into codependent relationships with others when strong emotions get stirred up. We lose the ability to think rationally and logically and to hold onto our personal thought process at these times. Under stress we "lose it," we "freak out."

If we came from a healthy, differentiated family that in turn came from a healthy, differentiated family, then there is a good chance that we are healthy and differentiated also. If we came from an unhealthy family, then we have a problem. Sadly, we will probably have the same level of dysfunction in our life and our relationships as did our family of origin, unless we've consciously made the decision to work on changing ourselves. We may have been raised in a home where our father raised his voice and yelled at us. We may have been raised in a home where the parents fought in front of their kids. And we said, "I will not do that to my kids." But, if we are honest, if we look for the similarities and not the differences, we see that we are often doing the same things with our children that our parents did with us.

But we can change. We change when we have the motivation to change. Consider the following example:

Imagine that I will give you ten million dollars in cash if you can learn to play the violin well and speak passable Russian. You have two years to complete these tasks, and if you do, I will give you ten million dollars.

Many people would take on this challenge because the payoff is big, and almost everyone could accomplish the task. Almost everyone would study really hard to learn Russian and practice playing the violin for endless hours because of the reward. Our brains actually are capable of being rewired in an infinite variety of ways. It surprises me to see that many people fail to grasp the value of something worth much more than ten million dollars -- a happy, addiction-free life, full of loving relationships, joy, and serenity.

No amount of money can top that.

But addicts can't see past their addictions, even for money.

Another measure of psychological health is the capacity to identify and handle our feelings, and to be emotionally available to another person.

This is a hard one for many of us. Men, in general, have been programmed, brainwashed by our culture, to embody what I call the "John Wayne Syndrome" and to not "lose control." This repression of emotional aliveness leaves men emotionally handicapped.

Some in the media labeled Speaker of the House, John Boehner weak and incompetent because he showed vulnerability! If we ourselves are shut down emotionally, we will become anxious in the presence of someone who is emotionally available.

We all have feelings. When we are vital and alive, we experience a wide range of emotions. But those who fear "losing control" (by showing vulnerability, fear, sadness, tears, or even joy) actually *repress all emotions*. These sad folks become "talking heads" that don't have much fun and are pretty dull to be around. However, repressed emotions are usually going to be expressed somehow. These feelings will emerge indirectly if they are not expressed in healthy ways. Repressed anger can emerge as irritability or depression, or erupt in uncontrollable rage. Passive aggressive behavior is anger that leaks out indirectly.

In his book, *Emotional Intelligence*, Daniel Goleman, describes the concept of "Emotional Intelligence," which is our ability to understand and express a wide rage of emotions. With attention, we can raise our emotional IQ and become more alive, more present, and more expressive. As the wise saying goes, "Sing like no one is listening . . . dance like nobody's watching. " While there is no limit to our emotional expressiveness, many of us fall far short of full aliveness. How much would you pay to get back your emotional aliveness if, say, someone had kidnapped it and was holding it for ransom?

I like the phrase, "Intimacy = Into Me You See." People in psychologically and emotionally healthy relationships have the capacity for intimacy. These healthy men and women are capable of showing the soft, vulnerable feminine side as well as the logical, linear, goal-directed masculine side. They feel safe enough to fully express *all* their feelings and will typically choose to be with someone who will be able to hear their whole range of emotions. They can express anger freely (without rage), and they can show disappointment and easily cry in front of each other. Their emotions, like weather systems, come and go; some emotions are strong and some are mild. These healthy individuals are comfortable enough with who they are that they don't need to hide behind strong defenses.

Individuals who are emotionally healthy can develop emotionally healthy partnerships, and emotionally challenged individuals need help to become emotionally healthy. Intimate partners express their emotional selves in their physical and sexual connection. The psychologist David Schnarch gives couples an exercise to test and strengthen their emotional availability with each other: to "hug until relaxed." The goal is to fully hug your partner. Not shoulder to shoulder with some pats on the back like many of us do. No, Schnarch means full frontal contact from head to toe. He directs partners to hold each other this way and, at the same time, to bring their attention inside themselves and notice what they are feeling. Can they fully relax in the other's arms? Can they let go of self-consciousness or anxiety and maintain contact? Can they hug each other for as long as it takes to fully relax? The capacity to surrender and to relax into a loved one's arms is an expression of emotional intimacy. Sadly, many people are a long way from this level of intimacy and freedom.

Many of us are like turtles inside a hardened emotional shell. We are fearful of closeness and often hug each other in a quick, tense, perfunctory, backslapping, in a side-to-side way.

This exercise is geared to help partners develop emotional health. Many things get in the way of having the ability to hug until relaxed or to be undefended. We all use ego defenses to some extent. Some common defenses include:

- Rationalization: My behavior does not make sense but my ego will *make up a story* that can explain it. "I wasn't going to have a drink but everyone else was drinking."

- Denial: Just plain making things up! "What drinking problem? I'm not drinking." "What enabling, I'm just loving him."

- Projection: We see unwanted aspects of ourselves in others. For example, we feel angry but don't want to acknowledge the feeling, so we see our partner as the angry one. Homophobia is a classic example of projection. Most of us naturally have attractions for attractive people, regardless of gender. However, this feeling threatens a homophobic individual who believes that same-gender attraction is wrong, so they disown their attraction to a same-sex person and "project" this "badness" away from themselves and onto others who they then see as "bad."

We all have ego defenses, but the goal, the way to psychological and emotional health, is to lower our defenses enough to have more intimacy, love, and emotional aliveness.

The last aspect of health I'll discuss is spiritual health. Spirituality is the ability to see, feel, and experience a larger frame of reference. This is different from just *believing*, which is a rational thinking process and part of our ego. Spirituality may include religious aspects, but it is often more than what some religiously active people practice. People who are spiritual often do not talk about their spiritual practices. Lao Tzu in the classic Chinese text, *Tao Te Ching*, said, "Those who say, do not know. Those who know, do not say."

And the Buddha is reputed to have said, "If you see me, kill me." His point is that "Buddhahood" is a personal, inner, greater-than-ego experience. Spirituality is personal to each of us and is not an external thing that we focus on, belong to, or worship. It is difficult to talk about our spiritual experiences because spirituality transcends language. Many people are very spiritually healthy, and you would not know it unless you knew them well. They lead lives that are peaceful, loving, and responsible, and they experience a healthy balance of the bio-psycho-social-spiritual aspects of life.

The Beatles described the bliss of the man experiencing a peaceful existence in their song, "The Fool on the Hill." He seems like a fool because he is serene in the midst of everyone's frantic activity, but no one can comprehend his peacefulness.

Without a spiritual component to our lives, we are dependent on our ego for guidance. This can lead to a kind of spiritual sickness, which can manifest as egocentrism, extreme self-centeredness, or the Hungry Ghost syndrome, and addiction.

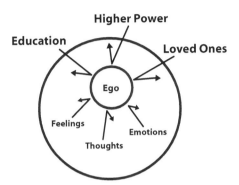

Figure 1: The Addict

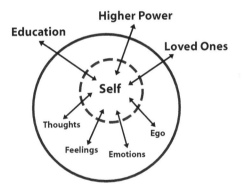

Figure 2: The Sane Person

Part Two of this book shows how the recovery process can help guide the addict, and anyone else who is ego-identified, into a more expansive sense of being. Carl Jung often talked about the development of Self as a normal process that occurs as we expand our view of ourselves to include a spiritual aspect. When we do this, we have transcended our ego. We still have an ego, but we realize that we are much more than just our ego.

Individuals suffering from addiction are nearly always spiritually bereft. These include the Wall Street perpetrators of the recent financial crash whose addictions to accumulating wealth, overspending, gambling, work and power relegated them to the realm of the Hungry Ghost. They were merely struggling egos frantically looking for relief by escaping reality through their addictions.

So we've looked at what constitutes health, and lack of health, in the spheres of biology, psychology, social relationships and spiritual life. We know that in addiction, these areas of functioning are compromised. And we know how "chemical addiction as a brain disease" works. Our midbrain *overrides, hijacks, and controls our addictive behavior.* Our reasoning, thinking, and rational forebrain is helpless. Without treatment, addicts will persist in their addictive practices. They will compulsively and obsessively go back to their addiction -- they crave it. Once started, they cannot stop -- they lose control. And bad things happen -- adverse consequences. And, it continues indefinitely -- it is chronic.

I want to expand the definition of "addiction" as it applies to the following individuals.

- •Individuals, like dictators, who kill their citizens. They are addicted to maintaining power (addiction to power, prestige, and control).

- •Individuals who walk away from their children and marriages in pursuit of money, power, or prestige (addiction to power, prestige, work, money, spending, accumulating).

- •Politicians who betray their values, their families, and their nation to gain power, influence, control, and money (addiction to power, prestige, control, work, money, spending, accumulating).

- •Lawyers who "game the system" and "create adversaries" for personal gain (addiction to money, power, work, accumulating, gambling).

- •Obese people (addiction to food).

- •Individuals who compulsively spend money (addiction to accumulating -- the more, better, bigger syndrome).

- •Individuals who debt compulsively (addiction to deprivation, accumulating, crisis, risk, gambling).

- •Individuals who look excessively at televisions or computers, or engage in excessive computer gaming (addiction to electronic screens, adrenalin).

- •Individuals who use pornography excessively or act out sexually (addiction to sex).

- •Individuals who are passive, ignore, try to control, or otherwise do not look at their part in supporting addiction. This could be supporting any politician, religious leader, or any individual they are in relationship with who engages in addictive or compulsive behaviors (addiction to enabling or codependence).

Those in the last category -- the enablers -- are the scaffolding that supports the addict's lifestyle. They, unknowingly, keep addictive systems alive.

Addicts in any of the above categories exhibit the same characteristics as drug addicts. They experience craving -- the unquenchable desire to pursue their goals even if it means betraying family and country; loss of control -- inability to stop doing what they are doing; continuing despite adverse consequences -- they harm themselves and others, and forsake love, family, and health to pursue their addictions; chronicity -- they may pause for a brief period, but they return to the behavior again and again.

A healthy individual is one who has an ego, *but who also* has a spiritual side, principles, a moral code, and a belief in the common good, which can mediate the ego's naturally selfish needs. Their prefrontal cortex and not their midbrain direct their choices. Those addicted to power and accumulation may use business or politics, or even religion to feed their ego's selfish needs, not to serve the public good. They are hungry ghosts. In the midst of opulence, they pursue more and more, hoping to feel better and trying to fill the empty hole in their souls with one more fix.

Hypocrisy is rampant among these individuals. They may go to church on Sunday, yet on Monday, they can justify working for a company that sells sugar to children or burning coal because "business is business." They may pray on TV, and then step behind the scenes and give special breaks to their campaign contributors. An individual with a spiritual orientation will *know* what is right, fair, ethical, and moral, and will act accordingly. An individual without a spiritual orientation will be unable to grasp the meaning of ethics and will defend or rationalize their position. These unhealthy individuals will stay hooked on TV, work, drugs, porn, food, sex, or risk.

Each of us has an ego. But if we are connected with a healthy community, espousing healthy morals and values, these influences can help temper our impulses, and we will be less likely to let our egos govern our behavior.

But right now, we are sorely lacking in healthy communities. The addicts in power aren't healthy; the enablers who support them aren't healthy. The Intervention I describe in the next chapter can shift the system. It can help enablers understand what's going on and help them wake up to the possibility of recovery and change. And if even some enablers begin to recover, the addictive system cannot sustain itself. The addicts almost always need their enablers to survive. (The politicians need their voters to survive.) The addictive system will almost always crash if the enablers choose recovery.

Perhaps the world has always had selfish and immoral leaders. Perhaps what is new is that the Internet has "turned the lights on." The Internet has allowed each of us to become like the Wikileaks founder, Julian Assange. We can become aware of the hypocrisy and awake to the lies because it is on the web for all to see. Suddenly, events can go viral and the whole world can learn about it. Recently, Osama Bin Laden was killed. In one day, billions of people heard about his death. This is a new development in our evolution, a part of the new paradigm, and it's exciting.

If we are healthy, we can see who is healthy and who is not. Sadly, looking at who's in charge in this country, it appears that we are not healthy, because the leaders we've chosen are not healthy. Hopefully this book will help guide those among us who are "firing on all cylinders" to "tell it like it is." When enough enablers begin to recover, then the addicts will have to change; or, if the addicts refuse to recover, we won't include them among the ranks of the healthy. We can't control anyone but ourselves. But we can choose to walk away from addicts, and we can choose sane leaders to guide us.

5

THE INTERVENTION

Our country is in crisis and operating like an addicted family. An intervention can halt the downward spiral of destruction in an addicted family -- and in our American family. Our country needs this kind of radical interruption and collapse to make room for recovery. Only by dismantling the current dysfunctional addictive system can we create space for the growth of a new and healthy America.

An Intervention is a process. A successful Intervention will result in the collapse of the dysfunctional, insane, addictive system and, over time, facilitate that system rebuilding itself in ways that lead to bio-psycho-social-spiritual wellness for all its members. *I am calling on the Sane 20% of American voters to wake up to the reality that they have the power to initiate an Intervention on America.*

An Intervention is a radical step. An Intervention is upsetting. A successful Intervention will cause members of the system to fundamentally change their ways of thinking and behaving. An Intervention is a critical act. It is a serious and acute undertaking on a grave situation. And I believe that this Sane 20% fully understands the severity of our current crisis. I believe that they are up to the challenging work needed to restore sanity to their family, in this case, the American Family. And I believe that if this core group of sober and rational people follows some basic instructions, they can initiate the process to actually put America into recovery, replace all 536 elected officials, and restore sanity to America.

I am a Professional Interventionist. I've been effectively leading Interventions on addictive systems for almost twenty years. I am
here, to be your Interventionist. I am writing to you, the Sane 20%,
the 40 million American voters. You simply need to follow my direction, and we can bring down the whole addicted American government. We can create the *American Revolution 2.0*. And we can replace
every elected official in the Fall of 2012.

So, let's get started.

Let me take you through the steps of an Intervention with the
family of an addict. Then we'll look at how this can work for our
country.

An Intervention starts when someone in an addicted family system calls me. Someone, some Concerned Other, understands that I
am an Interventionist.

The phone rings, I answer it and say, "Hello, this is Larry
Fritzlan." "Hello, my name is Sam and I have a problem."

The Intervention has just started.

The Intervention starts with this first phone call. Someone has
been suffering and has "had it." They have tolerated this problem
long enough and are ready for a change. They have heard about
Interventions and know that an Intervention is a pretty radical step but
are ready to consider it. They probably have been thinking about this
situation for a long time. At first, they were in denial of the problem. At
first, they were able to look the other way. But it got worse. And worse.
And finally something happened that pushed them over the edge. They
couldn't look the other way anymore. They had to do something.

I schedule a meeting with Sam, the Concerned Other. I want
to get the facts and understand the nature of the problem. I already
know the basics. A successful Intervention always starts with three
components: the Concerned Others, the Powerless Enablers, and at
least one Addict. This is fairly predictable. The system is stressed and
people are unhappy. Someone is addicted and others are enabling
this addictive system to continue the way it is.

But now someone has "broken the rule" about "not talking
about the addictive system." All addictive systems have this basic

understanding. Some members don't have a problem blaming the addict, but they are not interested in looking at their part in the problem. Their view is always some variation of this: "We all have a big problem here but we are going to pretend that we don't really have this problem, and if we do have a problem, we all agree it is all the addict's fault."

The addict has been going through life using substances and behaviors to increase dopamine in their midbrains. This works for them. Their "medicine" reduces their pain. And of course, they are in denial.

But someone is almost always enabling the addict. These enablers may harp on the addict. They may be angry with the addict. They may even see the problem as addiction. But they have not yet gotten to the stage where they realize that they, too, are addicted. They have not yet realized that they somehow are getting *their* midbrain-dopamine-surge by *trying to fix the addict*.

So Sam, our Concerned Other has broken the rule and is telling me a very predictable story. An addicted family system is spiraling down -- more and more out of control. Someone may die, and everyone is miserable.

But Sam is not going to take it anymore. He is ready to take this on. By this point he realizes that he really does not have a choice. What could be worse than what is going on now? If he does nothing, the addict could die. If he tells the truth, he will be shaking a hornet's nest. I educate him about how an Intervention works. I explain the basic facts. I explain that we can't change another person, only ourselves. I explain the enabling process, how the Powerless Enablers actually perpetuate the addiction by enabling and supporting it in myriad ways. Few Interventions will be successful if some of the Powerless Enablers refuse to participate in the Intervention. If these folks aren't willing to support the Intervention, then we have little hope of creating a situation in which the addict will choose treatment.

The next step, obviously, is to see if these Powerless Enablers are willing to join the Intervention team. Little is possible without them. The Addict and the Powerless Enablers are usually locked in a system. Typically, they have been engaged in a very predictable and badly choreographed dance that has been spiraling down for years. But they are also in pain and, like Sam, they just might be open to considering the possibility that something could be done about it.

There is every possibility that something can. An Intervention offers hope for change.

Sam is sent off to talk to the sanest of the Powerless Enablers. Can we get more people to join us? He assures me that there are a few others who will join, because he talked to them about calling me, and he knows that they are in agreement that something must be done.

Let's assume that this addictive family has 10 members -- spouses, parents, children, employer (the employer is usually a part of the addict's world, and therefore part of the family system -- and that Sam is able to get three more of them to agree to meet with me. We gather in my office or by conference call, and I listen to the predictable stories of an addicted system: lying, cheating, stealing, fear, attempts to get the addict to change, anger and exhaustion. This group of four is ready. We now have four Concerned Others. They are ready to "step up" and show up. They are willing to be part of the Intervention. They have a bunch of questions, but they have known something is wrong. They are naturally anxious about doing this thing called an "Intervention," but they are on board.

What about the Powerless Enablers? The other five members. They are in denial. They often have their own addictions (food, TV, drugs, shopping, etc.). They agree that there is a problem but can't see their part in it.

This is where good Interventionists have their work cut out for them. How can we get these Powerless Enablers to wake up? How can we get them to understand that they have an ongoing emotional investment in the addictive system? How can they trust someone fixing a problem they deny even exists?

Slowly and lovingly, we begin to invite these frightened Powerless Enablers into the process. We get them to describe how things have been. We get them to say out loud what has been going on. They get to hear other people say out loud what they have seen and heard. Slowly, reality begins to emerge.

Slowly, the Powerless Enablers come out of denial. Slowly, they begin to see that there is a brighter possibility. Slowly, they listen to the facts.

(Some don't; more on that in a moment.)

Now we have more people on our team. Hopefully everyone is now fully aware of the insanity of the family's addictive system. By now, everyone realizes that very dysfunctional behavior is occurring.

Remember what I said at the beginning of this chapter. An Intervention is a process. It begins with the first phone call and needs to be seen as an ongoing series of events that will reverse the family's downward spiral. It has often taken many years to get to this moment in the family's history, and a successful Intervention will take this into account and pace the recovery over an extended period. A comprehensive, systemic treatment program will be a least a year in length. But the recovery back to optimal health could take many years.

We do not hide any of this process from the Addict. There will no longer be secrets. After we have a solid team in place, the Addict is invited to join our meetings. I explain to him what I am doing. I tell him that I was contacted because "there was pain and unhappiness in the family." He, like all the other members, is treated respectfully and, of course, is free to leave at any time.

The process continues unfolding. I give members of the team, including the Addict, educational material. I ask them to attend some Al-Anon and AA meetings. And I keep meeting with them and facilitating the change.

Then we plan the "Intervention." The reality is that the "Intervention event" is simply the next of many steps. It certainly is not like the TV show, *Interventions*, which is held in low regard by professional Interventionists. This show is a "made to sell advertising" TV program that has little in common with sane mental health practices. It is a simplistic approach that sometimes has disastrous consequences for the participants. This "Surprise Model" is a relic of the past. This model was good news when it was first used in the 1960s. These Interventions were typically done by lay people, usually other recovering alcoholics. Some people got sober using this model, but many did not, and, regardless, it typically fails to treat the *system* that supported the addiction in the first place.

A modern, professional, Systemic Intervention event, properly conducted, does not resemble the scary scenes we've heard of or imagined. I typically schedule two, six-hour days to facilitate the Intervention event. It is important to remember that this time is simply the next opportunity to gather the whole family in one place, highlight the problems, educate them on their options, and, at the end of the second day, make recommendations for each of them.

I will recommend that everyone continue the recovery process. For any Addict or Enabler who is severely impaired, I will recommend a Residential Treatment Program to get them stabilized. I will always recommend a year-long Treatment Plan that includes a combination of professional, medical and mental health services, as well as the free and readily available 12-Step programs. It is in these 12-Step meetings that millions gather and lovingly support each other's recovery, one day at a time.

There is a theme, a central reality, which I recommend to everyone in the recovery process.

"Put the focus on yourself. Stand up for yourself. Make decisions about recovering your wellness. Take a look at your own addictions and codependent behaviors and address them. Support others who are doing the same. And also, respect others who choose not to change. You have no control over them. They are the captains of their lives, and you need to respect their choices. If they continue to turn down your support, this will probably mean that you will distance yourself from them because you are now choosing healthy people and healthy behaviors and are no longer willing to support or even be near any form of addiction."

Sadly, some family members may choose "to stay in the Problem and not seek the Solution." They may choose to stay in denial. Some may resist treatment. We have no control over these persons. What we offer is a path to "Life, Liberty, and the pursuit of Happiness," and they have a choice to take it or leave it.

The best strategy when Addicts or Enablers choose not to seek help is for those in recovery to move on and leave behind those who choose to stay in the disease.

The above is a description of how I do an Intervention, and it is a model of my proposal for an Intervention on America.

America needs an Interventionist to guide the country into recovery. What I propose is that the 20% of the American electorate who have the common sense to see what is really happening, hire me to facilitate an Intervention on America.

This Intervention will unfold in the same way as it does for an addicted family, only on a national level.

So, here goes:

You (the Sane 20% -- the 40 million voters) are the Concerned Others. You have picked up this book, and you want to know what the next step is. You know about the problems. You see addiction and enabling everywhere, and you see their catastrophic consequences. You see a corrupt government that has been bought off by Big Business, Big Union, and the hyper-wealthy. You see our elected officials, and the childish behavior that is out of hand. You see a President who is unable to lead. You see environmental damage. You understand. You are ready for the next step.

The next step is for you to start your own recovery process. Look at your own enabling behaviors, your own possible addictions, and begin your personal recovery. Next, with your help, we will invite the Powerless Enablers to participate in the process -- these are the other 160 million voters who do not yet see the extent of the problem. The goal is first to educate them about enabling and their role as enablers, and then to support them in engaging in their own recovery processes. Some will choose recovery, some won't. But with enough of a solid base -- perhaps thirty million additional voters -- we will have the foundation to go forward.

The next step is to invite into recovery the Addicts who run our nation. Wouldn't it be wonderful if they admitted to their addictions? Some will and some won't. Some will get into recovery and ultimately atone for their behavior. But that will take more time than we have to clean up our current mess.

The 12-Step recovery process, which I describe in Part Two, is a time-tested set of principles that merits serious consideration as a process for healthy living for every individual, every company, and every nation.

If America is to make it, if we are to have a sane and sustainable future, we need a better set of principles than the ones we are currently following. And we need to develop bio-psycho-social-spiritual health, as individuals and as a nation.

This Intervention on America is really quite straightforward. But it will be radically different from the "interventions" that seem to be going on all around us. Those on the right, the left, the Tea Partiers, MoveOn, the radio talk show hosts, the young, and the media -- everyone is trying to intervene. But they are trying to intervene from *within the addictive system. That will never work.* Every psychologist knows why. It won't work, because everyone in an addicted family system is part of the problem. They are in denial, see the "other side" as the problem, and fail to see their part in perpetuating the current paradigm. An addicted system needs an Interventionist from *outside* the system to point them toward a different paradigm, a very different place where sanity is possible.

I'm proposing that we, no matter what our political stance, seriously consider looking at the 12-Step model. Members of 12-Step recovery programs have, for over eighty years, quietly conducted themselves with integrity. This is even more remarkable when we consider that every single member in this group was probably quite insane at one point in their lives.

I believe these 12 Steps can be a means to recovery for our country, as well as to personal recovery. As you read Part Two, not only imagine yourself "working the steps," but imagine our country working the steps as well.

As we engage in recovery, we will become ready to take action. Part Three of this book, "Into Action," describes specific tasks we can take to move this country into recovery and into the second American Revolution. We can replace all our addicted elected officials with healthy adults. Once we are guided by healthy leaders, we can help America recover her wellness.

America has hit a bottom. It is time for each of us to reflect on this reality and step into recovery.

(And, you know who the Sam is that initiated the Intervention, don't you? He is none other than our beloved, old Uncle Sam. He wants YOU to stand up. Just like our forefathers did in the first American Revolution and in World War II.)

PART TWO

GETTING ON THE BUS, STEP ONE

Step One: *"We admitted we were powerless over alcohol – that our lives had become unmanageable."*

Getting on the bus, taking a trip, going anywhere, always starts with the first step. When we look back on all the stuff we have created and all of our accomplishments, we see that they all began with a single step toward a goal. That step was followed by many more steps, but none of those would have happened without the first step.

Recovering America's greatness will be like that. If we are to base this new paradigm on a return to sanity, we need to start somewhere. I'm proposing a model that has worked for millions of us. Actually, it has worked for some of the craziest people in America! This remarkably successful model has allowed insane, addicted individuals to recover sufficiently to: land on the moon, win several Academy Awards, and pitch a winning game in the World Series. It is the tried and true model of the 12 Steps.

Recovery is a process, not an event. It's like deciding on a career path. It is a lifestyle decision and it takes ongoing commitment if we are to make fundamental change. Whether as individuals or as a nation, recovery must start with Step One:

> We admitted we were powerless over alcohol -- that our lives had become unmanageable.

I would like to rephrase the wording of this Step slightly to be more inclusive and reflect the reality that the majority of Americans fit the criteria for addiction, as discussed in Part One.

> *We admitted we were powerless over (alcohol, drugs, gambling, food, power, spending, accumulating, work, other people, enabling, etc.) -- that our lives had become unmanageable.*

This Step is about acknowledging loss of control. This "loss of control" is a central issue for the addict and for the enablers. During the last years of my addiction, I woke with terrible hangovers and told myself every day that today would be different. Today I would not drink and do drugs. But I was an addict, and I would always drink and do drugs anyway. I could not stop.

From any perspective, a sane person has to admit that the American government is out of control. If we look at the 1%, the three million who hold the levers of power, we have to admit that they are not serving the other 99%.

(Sane = proceeding from a sound mind, rational; mentally sound; *especially:* able to anticipate and appraise the effect of one's actions; healthy in body. Insane = mentally disordered; exhibiting insanity. (Merriam-Webster Dictionary)

But let's start with us as individuals. Take a moment to try on for size the possibility that you have a problem that might loosely be called an addiction. Imagine, for a moment, that you are powerless over something. You might have a substance-use addiction (smoking, drugs, alcohol) or a people addiction (codependency, enabling, obsessive partner craving), or an obsessive-compulsive disorder, also called a "process addiction" (binge eating, shopping, out-of-control debting, hoarding, acting out sexually, gambling, cults, workaholism, uncontrolled rage, computer gaming).

Ask yourself the following questions about any of the above behaviors that you suspect you might have a problem with:

1. Have you ever lost time from work due to this behavior?
   YES __ NO __

2. Is this behavior making your home life unhappy?
YES __ NO __

3. Have you ever escaped into this behavior because you are shy with other people?
YES __ NO __

4. Has this behavior ever affected your reputation?
YES __ NO __

5. Have you ever felt remorse because of this behavior?
YES __ NO __

6. Have you ever gotten into financial difficulties as a result of this behavior? YES __ NO __

7. Has this behavior ever made you careless of your family's welfare? YES __ NO __

8. Has your ambition decreased since this behavior started?
YES __ NO __

9. Do you crave engaging in this behavior at a definite time?
YES __ NO __

10. Does this behavior cause you to have difficulty sleeping?
YES __ NO __

11. Has your efficiency decreased since starting this behavior?
YES __ NO __

12. Has this behavior ever jeopardized your job or business?
YES __ NO __

13. Have you ever engaged in this behavior to escape from worries or trouble?
YES __ NO __

14. Have you ever had a complete loss of memory as a result of this behavior?
YES __ NO __

15. Has your physician ever treated you for the consequences of this behavior?
YES __ NO __

16. Do you use this behavior to build up your self-confidence?
YES __ NO __

17. Have you ever been to a hospital or institution because of this behavior?
YES __ NO __

How did you do? Any "Yes" answers? If I were asked these questions thirty years ago, and not in denial, I would have answered "yes" to nearly all of them.

I believe that *many millions of Americans* meet the criteria for some sort of addictive behavior and answer "yes" to at least half of the questions above. And if we know that about ourselves, then we can actually *do something* to get help.

If you answered "No" to all of these, then you are among the very healthy. Or, you are in denial. No worries. Most of us are in denial about a lot of things. Sometimes I think that God put us here to see how many unconscious aspects of ourselves we can discover and then heal.

Step One basically has us honestly look at the complete picture. This is often not easy, but it is essential if we are to actually get well. There is no way around this fact. In the first part of this book, I gave an overview of the nature of the problem facing America.

Here are some examples of what our addicted elected officials are responsible for. We voted for them and this is what they did:

> We have a financial crisis, a housing crisis, an environmental crisis. The icecaps are shrinking, glaciers are melting, polar bears are drowning, coral reefs are dying, animals are *becoming extinct at a rate 1000 times greater than normal.* We are leaving our kids with a world that is a mess and a life expectancy shorter than our own.

These are some obvious examples of the insanity we are living with.

By voting for these politicians, we have enabled their addiction -- addiction to insane thinking that is destructive to our planet and to our population. It does not matter if we voted for the Democrat or Republican -- they are the same. We need to follow our own recovery program and cease being part of the problem. We need take an active role, a political role, in moving our country in a new direction and toward a solution.

For those of us who voted-in the current crop of leaders, Step One in recovery means acknowledging our powerlessness over our own addictive attachment to the addict. It appears that we have not been able to stop supporting crooked politicians and the status quo. We may not be able to control other people, but we can take responsibility for our own behavior.

A specific example of insanity and denial in our system is the Hydrocarbon Extraction Myth.

Let's see how this plays out, addictively speaking: Any sane person knows, and has known for years, that we have a big problem. We cannot endlessly increase our carbon burning. Anyone who has seen Al Gore's *An Inconvenient Truth* and is not upset is not, I believe, sane. We are melting the snow, the white "mirrors" that reflect sunlight back into space. This could set off irreversible global heating, and we could end up like Venus. (There is no life on Venus, it's too hot.) (Out-of-control negative consequences.)

The Federal Government, from President Obama on down, has known about this since the 1980s, but our elected officials still cry, "Drill, baby, drill!" (Denial.)

Today's *New York Times* has an editorial about this. The article reminds me of the endless nattering of drunks sitting on barstools at 2 a.m. It is also like the talk in a family with active addiction and codependency. The conversations are just re-hashes of arguments that have been going on for years.

The article contains the "Blah, blah, blah" of the establishment media that is just as addicted to the status quo as the rest of those in power. *The New York Times*, the leading left-leaning newspaper, is serious. They are seriously suggesting that we move the chairs in the dining room of the Titanic three inches closer to the wall! I'm sure *The Wall Street Journal* will reply in very serious language that, actually, the chairs need to be moved three inches in the opposite direction. They are clearly hopelessly addicted, in denial, and not sane. Does this seem unmanageable? And do you feel powerless to do anything? We created this! And we can change this.

The 12 Steps can offer all of us a new perspective, one that none of us has ever really imagined for or country. Try to imagine that on a certain date, we switched the side of the road we drive on and started driving on the left side. Imagine the confusion. Imagine the news stories. Imagine the buzz around the water cooler and the dinner table. This Intervention on America will be like that.

Paradigm shifts *can* happen that way. The Internet age has been a paradigm shift, but we hardly noticed it, because it developed over a few decades. The paradigm shift I am proposing will happen much faster.

We admitted that we were powerless, and that our lives were becoming unmanageable. There are many examples of unmanageability, personally and nationally.

A personal example: While I am free of alcohol and other drugs, I admit that I have simply switched to less dangerous substances and behaviors. Downing a pint of Haagan Dazs has gone from multiple times a week (thirty years ago) to once every few months. When the urge to "use" occurs -- to buy a pint of ice cream -- I am powerless. Another part of my brain takes over. It is as if my willpower has been hijacked and takes control of the steering wheel. I buy the pint of ice cream, come home, throw the lid in the trash, grab a spoon, and eat the whole thing. The next day I say the same thing that I said over and over again three decades ago, waking up after another night of using, "Oh no! Not again, I will not do this again!" I am very familiar with many addictions and have attended several 12-Step programs. I have used Al-Anon to differentiate myself from addicted family members. I have used Overeaters Anonymous to deal with food addiction (with the rare relapse!) and I have used Sex and Love Addicts Anonymous to learn how to have healthy intimate relationships.

I have created a team of friends, sponsors, doctors, therapists, and others that I can call on when my midbrain threatens to take control of my behaviors in ways that are not good for me.

Here are some examples of America's unmanageability. Good people go to Washington and get caught up in the disease of addiction. In order to get elected, they need money. To get money, they make deals with Big Business and Big Union to pass laws that are favorable to Big Business and Big Union. Big Business and Big Union kick down money to those who play along. That money buys media time for the politicians to sell themselves to us, the enablers, who are gullible and fail to see the charade. Or we see it, but are overwhelmed and feel helpless, and do nothing.

Here is another example. Big Oil props up the petrol dictators who buy our military-industrial complex guns and planes. They use these weapons to repress their people while we continue our addiction to their oil to run our Hummers and air-conditioned homes in the desert. We look away, in denial, because we are addicted to luxury. And the icecaps melt and the planet gets hotter.

Reactions to the above fall into two camps. Some of us feel sick. We have known this about our system for years and years, and it is just one more tragic bit of news confirming the nightmare we keep having. And we are the Concerned Others. Others of us, the Powerless Enablers, glaze over, deny it, and go eat something or sit in front of a TV for seven hours a day. It's "TMI," "Too Much Information" for our defended brains. We feel Powerless.

Here's another example, one that I know intimately. Today, in Marin County where I live, children in local high schools are selling OxyContin and other powerful narcotics to fellow students. They get these drugs from street dealers who get it from unethical and immoral doctors. Local doctors and the American Medical Society know about these immoral and unethical doctors who will write a prescription for powerful narcotics for anyone. The honorable doctors don't have the spine to actually confront the bad doctors because of the "code of silence" that prevents them from criticizing each other. It is exactly like the addicted family system. The American Medical Association fails to take action. Why? The pharmaceutical industry is protected by favorable laws passed by unethical politicians who need their "kickback" funds to run ads to "sell" us on why we should vote for them. And 15-year-olds die or get hooked for life on heroin-like drugs as a result.

This is for real. Does this feel unmanageable to you, and do you feel powerless to fix it?

The food industry is similarly rigged, corrupt, and deadly. Sugar is to food addicts what heroin is to heroin addicts. We know that it leads to obesity and diabetes. And now, research is showing that sugar is linked to cancer, heart disease, and strokes. The food industry is behaving just like the tobacco industry did before we pointed out the reality behind their scam. Big Food knows the negative consequences of ingesting sugar and high fructose corn syrup and still peddles the substance to children, through advertising. The food industry bribes politicians to keep the price of sugar and corn artificially low, through tariffs and subsidies. Our leaders keep these substances cheap so that Big Business can push their "drug" on the children, the poor, and the uneducated. These leaders are rigging the system, and even their own children are sickened! Their addictions have made them so crazy that they can't see clearly enough to care about their own children!

And while some of us are outraged, we are not taking action. The 20% who are sane and who see the travesty of the food industry haven't known what to do.

But wait. Aren't things getting better? "Cars are safer," "TV's are bigger and cheaper," "Infant deaths are decreasing," "We just got a new freeway," "A new bridge to nowhere," etc. The world is literally coming unglued and we listen to the politicians as if they are speaking the truth. Exactly the way family members in denial believe the lies of the active alcoholic.

It is true that some things are getting better. The Internet and instant media and the "inner Julian Assange" in each of us is waking up to reality and seeing the whole picture, seeing that the emperor actually has no clothes. Perhaps we are really getting to the point where we won't take it anymore and we will do what Egypt did -- what the Concerned Other does in the family system. Perhaps we really are at the point of saying this is insane, this is unmanageable, we are powerless, and we need help.

Recognizing the unmanageability in the above examples, we feel the pain that is part of what prepares us for an Intervention. Until something painful happens, we are prone to stay in denial.

Forty-three years ago, in 1968, I stood in front of thirty, second-grade black children. I was fresh out of college and working for the Chicago Public School System. I had just been assigned to substitute teach that day. I had no teaching experience, just a bachelor's degree in social sciences. I had not taken any education classes in college. I had never been mentored or done any kind of internship. It didn't matter, because this school was for black kids. Black kids in the inner cities had always gotten "teachers" like me.

I was scared. What does an untrained twenty-six-year-old man do with thirty, six-year-olds? I later found out that these children had had twenty different first grade teachers. Twenty! They had never had a real teacher! Of course they acted out, and I had no tools but the harsh, abusive voice that my alcoholic father had used to discipline me. So, in panic at my loss of control and lack of options, I yelled at them. That was all I knew to do to maintain order. I verbally abused and frightened these six-year-old children. Was I wrong? Of course. Was the system wrong? Of course.

I called in sick the next day. I have never forgiven myself for that, and this experience is a part of my past that helps fuel my commitment to change.

Republicans and Democrats put on their dog and pony shows with stories about "honor" and "loyalty" and "America" and the need to "make things better." These are like the grandiose rants of an alcoholic. And then it's business as usual. The politicians go behind curtains and make sweetheart deals to get the fixes that feed their addictions.

We are all aware of the 2008 Big Rip Off of Americans by Wall Street and their government enablers. Wall Street made billions, hundreds of millions went to our elected Big Government officials, and we got ripped off for our homes, our jobs, our retirements and our kids' college money. And no one went to jail! Why? Because Wall Street and our politicians are dependent on each other, just like a drug dealer is dependent on his customers, and the addict is dependent on his dealer.

But you got ripped off. And so did I. But we accepted this unacceptable behavior.

"OK, we will fix this," the politicians say. "This is a total tragedy and it will be fixed." All the politicians are "outraged" and they summon the big, bad, Wall Street Crooks to Washington. They put on a righteous, angry show for all the gullible voters to see on TV. "Don't worry, we will never let this happen again!" Just like the remorseful alcoholic who can't escape evidence of his destructive behavior and makes promises he can't keep.

If we have been paying attention we know they will never, ever, really change. They are addicts. Here is another example.

Elizabeth Warren, Harvard law professor, who seems ethical enough, was appointed Special Advisor to the Consumer Finance Protection Bureau. Her mandate was to come up with some laws that will actually prevent Wall Street from ripping us off again. So, she actually did come up with a plan that would set limits and might possibly restrict Wall Street and government officials' insatiable addiction to money and power.

She reported that things were going well. Her group had created a good set of laws that would prevent Wall Street from ripping us off again. She had watched and heard the politicians pledging to "fix the system" and expected to see the new laws quickly adopted. But, if you have been paying attention, you know what happened next.

The following is a transcript of Elizabeth Warren's interview with Jon Stewart on his TV program, The Daily Show, in April 2011. Ms. Warren then was Chairwoman of the Congressional Oversight Panel on the Toxic Assets Relief Program Program (TARP).

Ms. Warren: "We actually had the right tools to get that job done."

Jon Stewart: "And this is my favorite part of the fight. Tell us about round two."

Ms. Warren: "I thought the next part would be all about getting all the pieces of the agency put together. And it is, in part. And I'm having great fun doing that. But the fight isn't over. The fight moved from Main Street to the 'Dark Alleys.' And now the game is, 'now, let's see if we can stick a knife in the ribs of this Consumer Agency.' So, right now there are bills pending in Congress to delay the agency, to defund the agency, to defang, make it toothless so that the agency won't get anything done. And there are bills in both the House and the Senate to kill the agency outright before it is able to take even one step on behalf of middle class families."

There it is. The addicts (the politicians and Wall Street) made up a story about changing, but went right back to the garage where they had hidden their bottle of booze.

And a few months later, in July 2011, a committee of Republicans forced Elizabeth Warren off the Congressional Oversight Panel. Open Secrets, a non-profit organization, estimates that the Republicans on that committee who forced her out of the job had been paid over two million dollars by Big Banks!

And if there were even *one* non-addicted politician, they would yell and scream on the steps of the Senate about a colleague who was accepting kickbacks to throw the game!

If we don't change ourselves and vote them out of office, we will go back to sleep and vote the addict back into power, over and over again. Without recovery, we fall back into denial.

My mother put up with my addicted father for 18 years. Then she found Al-Anon and chose recovery. She realized that she had been enabling my father. She changed. She told him to get treatment or she would see a lawyer. She showed me how quick and effective an Intervention could be.

So, if we are paying attention, we see that Step One accurately describes our predicament in the midst of our country's current social and political landscape.

We admitted we were powerless over: alcohol, drugs, other people, gambling, food, power, money, accumulating, shoplifting, enabling, overworking, etc. -- that our lives had become unmanageable.

As an addiction specialist, I can say the following with some certainty:

- •10-15% of the population are addicted to chemicals other than nicotine
- •Nearly 30% of the population, age 12 and older, are addicted to nicotine
- •30% of the population are addicted to food
- •50 - 60% of the population are addicted to electronic screens: TV, computers, internet porn, gaming
- •Almost all politicians are addicted to money and power
- •Almost all leaders in Big Business and Big Union are addicted to money and power
- •100% of us who live with the any of the above people and who are not in active recovery from codependency are actively enabling the addiction. *If we voted, we are enabling what we currently have.*

The prevalence of all this addiction might be a good thing, because denial is becoming harder and harder to pull off. All we have to do is look around.

I'm hoping this book, and the Intervention, will send all of us into recovery. If we do this, we can recover America's greatness. I'm hoping that others will be like Julian Assange and "tell it like it is." I'm hoping that we all become like Asmaa Mahfouz in Egypt, post something on the Internet that counters an insane government, and says, "I'm going to the Square."

I'm hoping that we *have* hit a bottom. I'm hoping that we can truly admit that we are powerless, the situation is unmanageable, and we are ready for recovery. It is this kind of thinking that makes us available for the Intervention.

We all need to truly and soberly admit that America is really screwed up!

And then, we need to allow our world and ourselves to be restored to sanity.

And then, we can have a really amazing America.

First, we need to admit that we have lost control and things have become unmanageable. This must happen before the Intervention makes sense. We need to understand this point before we can visualize the steps needed to restore sanity to our lives. Are you ready to do that?

7

CAME TO BELIEVE THAT SANITY IS POSSIBLE, STEP TWO

Step Two: *"Came to believe that a Power greater than ourselves could restore us to sanity."*

What is the "Power greater than ourselves" that could make our world and each of us in it sane? Each of us, if impaired, can benefit from commitment to a comprehensive and proven path, a path that integrates the key elements of fully actualized humans. Those of us committed to this path can join together to create an optimal culture. The 12-Step path has been around for decades. It has been field-tested on some of the craziest of us, with great success. And it is the theoretical approach that medicine, science, and the government have adopted for treating America's number-one mental health problem.

This is the path that will help us heal ourselves as individuals and as a nation. This path, if followed, will give us hope and can motivate us to do what's necessary to create a healthy country. We have a problem, and luckily, we have a path to recover from our current crisis.

Let's look at Step Two of the 12 Steps.

> *"Came to believe that a Power greater than ourselves could restore us to sanity."*

Each of has "come to believe" in something. Some of us believe in baseball, or evangelic worship, or capitalism, or guns. All of us who are individually or socially or politically awake believe in what our founding fathers declared over two centuries ago, that we are entitled to "Life, Liberty, and the Pursuit of Happiness."

When I was nearing the end of my addicted days, about the only serious thing I could believe in were the chemicals and behaviors that would increase the dopamine in my midbrain. They were central to my life. If you had asked what I believed in, I might have told you that I believed in science or democracy or capitalism. But the reality was that I was a very shallow thinker. I was mostly unconscious, on autopilot. Survival was a day-to-day affair. Nearly all of my actions were geared primarily to "getting by," keeping the electricity on, paying my rent, and having enough money to keep my business going for another week. And, central to all of this was my all-consuming need to raise the dopamine levels in my brain.

Those last years of addiction were painful. The Golden Gate Bridge -- with its reputation as a place to commit suicide -- was only 10 minutes away. I remembered my father's death from carbon monoxide poisoning as he idled his car in a closed garage. I had a gun, and I was scared that I would suddenly go berserk and shoot myself. I was in hell.

Thank God, someone gave me the key to a new way of life. Someone gave me a directive: "See that key? See that hole in that door? OK, take the key, put it in the keyhole, turn it, then open the door and walk through."

That "key" came from a woman dressed in white, whom I met with when I attended a residential Stop Smoking program. She recognized my problem and gave me the solution. On my second day at the Stop Smoking program, I was told to go to their Residential Addiction Treatment Program for an assessment. I was clueless. I met with a nurse, a friendly woman in a white uniform. She asked me to fill out a questionnaire, the famous, "20 Questions of AA." She looked at my answers. Then she handed me some brochures about AA and addiction and said, "You need to consider the possibility that you have a problem. You might want to think about going to a meeting."

At the time, I was not well enough to "get it." It took nine more months of addiction madness before the information could seep through my diseased brain and arrive at a part of my consciousness that could grasp what she had said. Were it not for her words, I truly believe that I would not have lasted much longer.

That woman in white had accurately assessed my situation. She saw me as an addict. She saw what I could not yet see, because I was in denial and not sane. Finally, one gray November morning in 1979, I gave up and reached out for help.

I called the 12-Step Program number and went to a meeting. I was terribly confused and unsure of where I stood. I didn't trust anyone and didn't have a clue what the Program was about. I was invited out to coffee by a couple of guys after the meeting and they told me not to use addictive substances that day, to go to bed that night without using, and to get up the next day and meet them at another meeting.

I needed a life preserver, and I grabbed onto it. Still confused and dazed, I met them the next day at another meeting. Again, we had coffee and they suggested I not use addictive substances for that day. Looking back, I was holding onto the life preserver but still didn't know what was happening. On day four I suffered what I now believe was a psychotic break. I was hallucinating and felt like reality was leaving me. But I hung onto the life preserver. I kept not using, and I kept going to meetings.

In those next weeks my mind cleared a little. I was no longer sick every morning. I was not hungover. I was "coming to believe" that if I did not use chemicals I would get better. I was coming to believe that the "medicine" I had been taking was actually the cause of my suffering.

Let's look at the concept of "coming to believe." What is a "belief"? Where do beliefs come from? Are we brainwashed into them? Are we born with them? Can we change them? How do we know which beliefs are good and which ones are bad?

Parents and the surrounding society, if you will, indoctrinate babies. Russian babies are indoctrinated to speak Russian, Japanese babies, Japanese, and American babies, English. When we are children, our parents and teachers instill in us the beliefs of our society: lying and stealing are wrong; hurting others is bad; democracy and freedom of religion, for example, are good.

As a teen and young adult, watching my parents, I had come to believe that drugs and other addictive behaviors would make me OK. This, as it turned out, was erroneous. That thinking was not sane and ultimately drove me insane.

But recovery was showing me the insanity of my belief that chemicals were my friends. I was coming to understand the absurdity of spending 25 years chemically altering my brain. I was seeing that what I had believed in was dead wrong. My traumatic childhood had left me vulnerable to life's stresses, and I had taken drugs to numb my pain, anxiety, and depression. By this point in my sobriety I was beginning to see the fallacy in my thinking.

In the history of America, many of our beliefs have also changed. As strange as it seems, we used to believe that men or women with more melanin in their skin, a darker pigment, were different from -- and inferior to -- people with an ounce less of this chemical. We even made laws to sanction these beliefs. We could buy and sell people who had more melanin. We could beat them and rape them because they were "property." Today, we still believe that some people are "better" or "worse" because of their skin pigmentation. Racism still exists, and many Americans still devalue others based solely on the fact that they have more melanin in their skin.

Americans also "came to believe," for the first century-and-a-half of our country's history, that a person without a penis was not entitled to vote or participate in our democracy.

In the 1930s, the majority of Nazi Germany's population came to believe in the Third Reich. In some countries today, people believe that every little girl should have her clitoris removed. We used to believe that it was OK to put children to work in factories and mines. There was a time in America when the government approved of taking Native American children from their mothers and putting them in "re-education" facilities. Many people in our country believe it is OK to make mood-altering chemicals available to children and young adults whose brains are still developing. In some parts of the world, girls and young women are stolen and forced into prostitution or marriage. In other countries, there are people who believe it is OK to stone a woman to death if she has a sexual relationship that is not sanctioned by the men in her family.

Even though psychologists tell us that prolonged exposure to TV dramatically raises the rate of childhood psychiatric disorders, some parents still allow their children unsupervised access to TV. Some people believe it is OK to kill animals for sport; or that it is OK to destroy nature to create wealth.

Some beliefs are sane and some are not.

Where there is addiction, there is irrationality. And it turns out that most of us have aspects of addiction that affect our ability to have high-level wellness. This is the bad news. The good news is that once we know this, we can choose to get help. And the help, works.

Six months into my recovery, I was only as emotionally developed as perhaps a 17-year old. I still hung onto many pathological beliefs I'd inherited from my drug-addicted family of origin -- beliefs about parenting, relationships, and marriage, among many others. But one belief of mine had changed. I had come to believe that the dopamine-stimulating chemicals I'd been using for the past 25 years had harmed me and messed up my life. At this point I was still a long way from being able to think rationally. I was probably just buying into the jargon and brainwashing of this new group I had joined. But I was hanging out with this group for a reason -- they seemed to have found a way out of being depressed, suicidal, and hungover. And those who had been in recovery for many years were demonstrably living lives of incredible accomplishment. Slowly, the light was being turned on, but it was going to take a while. It can take many years to rewire a brain that has been addicted.

This is why professional addiction treatment providers recommend that addicts get long-term professional treatment -- at least a year. A 30- or 90-day "spin dry" in a residential treatment center is only the very, very beginning.

We can believe a lot of things, useful and not-so-useful. And, we can rewire our brains and believe in something else. We can do this as individuals, as a family, and as a culture. But it always starts with a single person making a decision to change him or herself. It must start with ourselves.

The second part of Step Two says *"that a Power greater than ourselves could restore us to sanity."*

What are "powers greater than ourselves?" If we suffer from extreme narcissism, we probably don't believe there are many powers greater than ourselves. But almost all of us do believe in something greater than our individual selves; exactly what that is, and what we call it varies. We may call it God, Mother Nature, Divine Will, Higher Power, or Higher Self. Or, it could be the Marines. They certainly are powerful. Actually, it is *anything* we decide is powerful. If we play victim, we assign power to others. If we are paranoid, we see powers generating conspiracies against us.

Sometimes power is threatening. Many people in America see the role of the Federal Government as both powerful and intrusive.

In reality, as a democratic society, we created powers greater than the individual to protect the rights of the individual. We created laws, and we give police the power to enforce the laws. If we are sick, we hope our doctor has the power to understand our broken parts. And if our house is on fire, the firemen are a power greater then ourselves, and we gladly turn our lives over to them.

Step Two is like that. The insane addict in early recovery is hanging onto a life preserver, wondering what is next and hoping for something better. The addict realizes he has been out of control and now hopes to be restored to sanity. He hopes to find a power greater than addiction.

In my first months of recovery, I understood little. I just knew things were not quite as bad as they'd been. Things were less scary. My migraines went away. I was beginning to imagine the possibility of hope, something I had not believed in for years.

Today, I have hope. I have hope because I am on the other side of my addiction. I have hope because I know this works.

I have hope for what this book and others like it can do. I have hope that people will wake up, like they did in Egypt. I have hope that people will take action.

And we don't have a choice. It is one thing for an addicted family to be stuck in their insanity for decades. But our larger family, the human family does not have a choice right now. And it already may be too late, because our planet and our civilization are at risk.

When I began working Step Two, my sponsor had me make a list of my then insane behaviors. Here are some of America's insane behaviors.

How we're treating the environment: Even if we stop burning all carbon tomorrow, we may have already crossed the line into runaway global warming. The temperature of the planet is quickly rising, the reflective snow is rapidly disappearing, and the permafrost is thawing. As reported in the journal *Nature*, if the permafrost melts, it will release vast amounts of carbon dioxide and methane, resulting in a wholesale destruction of our ecosystems and catastrophic extinction of life on the planet. If we shut down carbon burning tomorrow, we may still live in horror at the reality that, after millions of years, you and I and our elected officials have broken our planet and destroyed everything on it. The mockingbirds, the whales, the tigers, the elephants, the turtles, and your children's children -- it could all be gone soon unless radical change is initiated. Are we like a sailor trapped in a sinking submarine, waiting for the end to come?

How we are handling energy: Global warming has been in the news for decades. Wall Street and *The Wall Street Journal*, like all addicts, don't want to talk about it. Who can blame them? They are addicted to "economic growth" and are in denial. They will kick and scream like crazy at anything that might interfere with their fix. Their addiction and their insanity are solidly in place and highly predictable. They don't accept that the metaphor of the Titanic applies to us.

How we enable the rise in rates of obesity: The number of food addicts is increasing at an alarming rate. This rate is oddly similar to that of melting icecaps. These addicts are so dazed and depressed that we can't expect them to wake up and see beyond their next injection of fat and glucose and salt. We can predict that they will continue to fall for what our leaders, scads of cash from Big Food, and TV tell them to do. Their insanity is highly predictable.

Remember what happened when Michelle Obama proposed some sensible ideas to address the epidemic of childhood obesity in America? (The fact is that one third of babies born after the year 2000 will develop diabetes in their lifetime!) Big Business and Big Government and their lackeys went crazy at the fact that she had the gall to question their game! "Wait a minute, don't you dare mess with my drug! Back off! Who are you? Some sort of Commie or Socialist?" When you go to Washington, you need to understand that you never, ever expose the rigged game that everyone's playing. (That is the Rule in addicted systems -- "Do not ever talk about the addiction and the rigged game.")

The politicians are set as well. They have the best drug of all: a cocktail of power, money, and access to just about anything they desire. If they keep their act together, their "dog and pony show," they can keep getting elected forever. Do you think they would ever stand up and say, "Folks, this is all bullshit, it's all a game for us to con you and keep our addiction going"? Do you think they tip off their enablers? I sure wouldn't. I needed my bartenders and my drug dealers. An addict will protect his enablers at all costs, because without their enablers he will experience an immediate crisis.

We need to be careful around addicts. They will fight, tooth and nail, for their drug. It is impossible to change an addict. Please re-read that last sentence. This is key. We can't change addicts. We can't change the officials in charge of our government. We can't change the crooks on Wall Street into honest people. We can't change the people addicted to food or to screen images or to drugs. We can't change the enablers who will continue to prop up the whole rotten edifice called Modern America.

They won't change without an Intervention!
And an Intervention can change everything.

That's why the Sane 20% of Americans are the only ones who can make this Intervention happen. Those who see the problem can become willing to change. Step Two says that we came to believe that a power greater than ourselves could restore us to sanity. In my case the "power greater than myself" was the 12 Steps, the fellow-ship of men and women in the meetings, and a commitment to the ongoing recovery process. For America, the power greater than our-selves that will restore us to sanity is the Intervention, the 40 million voters going to the streets, the media attention this provokes, and the recovery process, all of which will result in 536 new elected officials voted into office November 6, 2012.

I've described how I conduct an Intervention on an addicted family. Someone in the addictive system is sane enough to call me and initiate the process. I gather the family together, including the addict. I listen to everyone's story and get the picture. I see the addict, and I see the addict's insanity. I see the enablers and I see the enablers' insanity. Without a sane person in the system, or at least an enabler who is willing to step up, I do not see how the family will make it.

Typically, the person who calls me is sane enough to see that there is a problem; I align with him or her. I use them to coax the enablers toward getting treatment for themselves. If they choose to get help, then we can create the fundamental change that can moti-vate the addict to choose treatment. If the enablers wake up, we can have some assurance that the family may recover.

An Intervention has four possible outcomes.

1. The enablers go into treatment and get sane. The addict goes into treatment and gets sane. The result is that the whole family recovers and gets sane.

2. The addict goes into treatment and gets sane. The enablers don't go into treatment and stay insane. The addict will eventually leave the insane enablers and join with sane people. (I did this.)

3. The addict won't go into treatment and stays insane. The enablers go into treatment and get sane. The enablers will eventually leave the insane addict and join with sane people. (My mother did this.)

4. No one goes into treatment and the whole family stays insane. Each individual family member must choose whether or not to enter recovery. Those who choose recovery make it, and those who don't will continue to live lives that are far from their potential.

As I re-read the last two sentences, I'm amazed at the fact that most addicts and enablers are afraid to invest a few hours a week to create happy, joyous, and sane lives. Sadly, it has been my experience that most members of an addicted family will choose insanity over sanity. That is how tragic this brain disease really is.

I also see four possible outcomes of an Intervention on America.

1. 20% of Americans read this book and are sane enough to call an Interventionist and to follow his instructions. This 20%, the Concerned Others, would then begin the formal Intervention that hopefully wakes up many of the other 79% who would join in and begin the recovery process. This majority would stop enabling the addicted 1%. This new majority would elect sane, adult Republicans and sane adult Democrats to lead the American family into long-term recovery. This would result in a stable and sane population and the possibility of saving the Earth. (We can't change other countries, but we can become a role model. And, Europe and China are far more advanced than America.)

2. 20% of Americans read this book and are sane enough to call an Interventionist and then follow his instructions. Unfortunately, the 79%, the Powerless Enablers, are so impaired that they don't

get it. They continue to be brainwashed by TV and lost in their own addictions, and they will again vote for one of the current addicted Democrats or Republicans. However, this 20%, this group of 40,000,000 sane Independents, Republicans, and Democrats, standing in the streets, would impact the outcome of elections and both parties would be forced toward the center. These people in the streets would inject sanity into the dialogue on energy policy, fiscal policy, corruption in government, etc. This would at least begin the public dialogue, but it might be too late to save our biosphere if fundamental change does not occur.

3. Some people read this book, and a movement slowly builds and, over time, more and more people understand the crisis and the solution, and some future America is able to accomplish #1, above. Sadly, millions of us will continue to weep at the insanity, as most Americans continue to support the degradation of Mother Nature and the mistreatment and killing of our own children. Our future will remain in dire jeopardy.

4. No one reads this book, and I weep at the insanity of *homo sapiens* and accept the fact that I gave it my best shot, using the tools I've been given, to help restore America to sanity.

Clearly I am proposing that we do this Intervention. I believe that we Americans can rise to the occasion, just as we did in the American Revolution, and in World War II, and when we ended slavery, and when we gave women the vote. I am proposing that the 12-Step recovery model, together with the principles of the American Revolution 2.0, is "the power that can restore us to sanity."

"Came to believe that a Power greater than ourselves could restore us to sanity."

If an Intervention is going to succeed on our insane government, it has to start with people willing to step outside the system leading the way. And it has to point toward a new paradigm, a new way, something we have not yet seen.

Some of us thought Obama would do it. Others thought Sarah Palin would do it. Or maybe Rush Limbaugh would guide us out of this mess. Or the Tea Party might get it done. Maybe MoveOn was the answer.

But they didn't. *They couldn't! They are in the system.*

This is vitally important to understand. Many of you are attached to the left or the right. Many of you are emotionally attached to the pathological belief that you can change someone else. Many of you on the far left or far right (it does not matter) identify with a group that is partisan and in opposition to the other side. You are emotionally attached to your position. Unfortunately, you are really like drunks arguing with each other. *"I* am right and *you* are wrong." You are trying to fix the problem from within the problem! You are like members of an addictive family, fighting with each other.

That fight has gone on for decades, and it is pretty obvious how it has been working for us. We need to move from the problem to the solution; we need to move from *putting the other party down* to sanely coming together and working this out. But this can't happen with our current leaders, inside the current system.

When I treat an addicted family, I actually suggest that during the first year, the family members not talk to each other about any emotionally charged issues unless they are in a therapist's office. Seriously. While they were in the addicted family, they were crazy and their relationships were crazy. The treatment recommends that each of them go off and get their own treatment and get well. After a year of treatment, they are much healthier and will have the possibility of healthy relationships. It is difficult for them to change if they stay close to each other after the Intervention, because they are still very attached to the way things have been.

It will be the same with the Intervention on America. We will need to remove all of our elected officials. Those folks only know how to play the old, corrupt game. We don't want them running the show, or even interacting with the new slate of officials. We will need a whole new crew to carry out the new paradigm.

"Came to believe that a Power greater than ourselves could restore us to sanity."

The "power" that is greater than ourselves is the collective America, the 40 million sane folks who see what needs to be done. And the means that can make this possible is our new, collaborative, democratic, and integrated "wired together" world.

This wired together world is what mobilized the oppressed and quickly organized Egyptians to bring down a corrupt dictatorship in weeks. This new technology is what rallied the oppressed Algerians to bring down Algeria's government in weeks, as well. It is the power of the Internet, of Facebook, email, texting, and Twitter. It is the capacity to instantaneously disseminate information that can exhort millions of people to take action.

The worldwide stirring of hope is another argument for an Intervention on America. It seems that the wired world has caused peoples around the globe to wake up, and then speak up, and finally stand up and act. Hope is what caused me to call a 12-Step Program in 1979 and start my recovery. Hope is the foundation of the mental health approach of the 12-Step Program. Hope is what Asmaa Mahfouz invoked in asking her comrades to join her at Tahrir Square. And hope is, hopefully, what may be stirring in you as you read this book.

The future is here. It has been looking us in the face for a while now. We've mostly missed it. We've been asleep, in denial, not thinking. But more and more people are seeing that a very different paradigm is beginning to turn the world upside down.

We are coming to believe. Wael Ghonim and Asmaa Mahfouz posted messages on Facebook, and the brutal dictatorship in Egypt fell. Our current officials in government and Big Business are terrified when they think of the power average people can bring to the table.

America is waking up to the fact that seemingly small events can lead to big changes. The next Facebook message could create fundamental change in our addicted government. Or perhaps this book will.

Any small group of people can initiate an Intervention. And with the power of the Internet, Facebook, texting, and Twitter, this new paradigm -- this idea of a world without corruption -- can travel around the world in milliseconds. We have the means to suddenly spread this idea, worldwide. As I write, the news is full of the rising tide of people around the world taking to the streets and calling for sanity.

The pieces are all in place. The facts are in.

"A power greater than ourselves!" "Could restore us to sanity!"

Bingo! That power to restore us to sanity is all of us coming together! The means are the little devices in your hands, the modern cell phone which can be the means to unite people to peacefully join this Intervention.

But we have to get to the tipping point. The 40 million of us who are awake need to write the books, post on Facebook, Tweet, run for President, talk to others, go to the streets. We have to be brave. We see that our children are at risk and the planet is failing, and we are becoming more depressed. We need to wake up and stand up. We need to "not take it any more." We need to get into recovery ourselves. We need to help others into recovery. We need to listen to the Interventionist. We need to trust the recovery process to initiate a restoration of sanity.

Betty Ford inspired millions to enter treatment for alcoholism. There are hundreds of thousands of 12-Step meetings around the country. They work! They do! Food addicts, drug addicts, sex addicts, codependent addicts, TV addicts, love addicts, gambling addicts -- addicts who get treatment can recover. And can wake up and get healthy. So can we. And then we can protect our children, our democracy, and the planet.

Healthy role models for recovery surround us and recovering addicts are among all of us. Marin County, in northern California with a population of 250,000, has nearly 400 weekly 12-Step support groups for recovering addicts and enablers. Some meetings have two or three hundred attendees.

These people are all recovering from addiction. They are being restored to sanity. One day at a time.

Renowned anthropologist Margaret Mead said: "Never underestimate the power of a small group of committed people to change the world. In fact, it is the only thing that ever has."

So, write a book. Start a website. This is *my* shot. Can I change the world? Can I save it? Can you? Individually, no. But together, we can. We can form that small group of committed people who can change the world.

Only one third of Americans supported the American Revolution, but it succeeded! The Sane 20% of us can bring about a successful American Revolution 2.0.

We can't predict the future. We do know that we have badly damaged Mother Earth. We don't know if she can be saved. But if a hundred years from now we look back and see that the Earth was saved, it will be because a small group of people began the Intervention that got the job done. We don't have a choice. We really need to believe that together we can restore America to sanity.

8

MADE A DECISION TO CHANGE, STEP THREE

Step Three: *"Made a decision to turn our will and our lives over to the care of God as we understood Him."*

My ego, my small self, always believed I was OK and in charge of my life. I think that our ego, by nature, lives under the illusion of "being in control."

But despite my denial, I was an addict and I was *out* of control. I would get up in the morning and swear, "I will not do it again. I *will* stay clean and sober today." We know how that ends. The addict's prefrontal cortex does not govern their behavior. Their midbrain, which they have zero power over, is what directs their addictive behaviors.

I'm sure that when Barack Obama returned to his motel room after visiting some small town in southern Illinois, he would dream wonderful thoughts of standing up for principles and "telling it like it is." But then he went to Washington and sadly realized that he had to "work things out" with Big Business, Big Unions, and the hyper-wealthy who fund his re-election campaigns. He found that he had to go along with the corrupt, self-serving, money and power addicts.

And Rush Limbaugh, back in his early days in Sacramento, when things were quiet and he had time to reflect, was also able to see the larger picture. But things changed when he was invited to play with the Big Boys and Big Business. Soon he, too, was swept along by the allure of running with the Big Dogs on the right.

If we are lucky, we find something meaningful to believe in, something that we surrender to, some power greater than ourselves. The question is, are we choosing a "power" that supports our self-centered wants -- our small, protected self, our ego defenses -- or are we choosing a "power" that challenges us to differentiate, seek improved mental health and more intimacy in our loving relationships, be more effective at working things out with others, develop a deeper spiritual connection, and be more in harmony with Mother Nature?

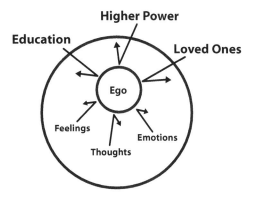

Figure 1: The Addict

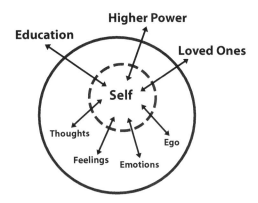

Figure 2: The Sane Person

In 1959, when I was a senior in high school, Episcopal priest, Reverend Meyers, inspired me. I listened with great interest when he said he was going to the south to join the Civil Rights Movement. I almost went with him. That was the first time in my life that I consciously considered "turning my will and my life over" to something important, some higher cause, some Great Idea, something beyond my immediate needs, something beyond my ego.

Five years later, I "came to believe in 'another power' greater than myself." The Viet Nam war was heating up, and I planned on joining the Marines. I recall my excitement and pride at the thought of belonging to a movement, of "turning my will and my life over" to the United States Marines! Millions know the pride of surrendering to the Marines or some other large group. It feels good. We are moved by this inner "something" that makes us feel more alive.

Instead, a few years later, I joined the anti-war movement. In the summer of 1968 my wife, my sister, and I were living in Chicago. We were among the peaceful demonstrators when the police went berserk and beat and tear-gassed the crowds.

Then there was the Peace and Love movement of the Sixties. I turned my will and my life over again, and moved to the Haight Ashbury district of San Francisco to immerse myself in the Summer of Love movement. I became a hippy.

Think for a moment. Have you turned your will and your life over to something bigger than yourself? If you have, you know that followers of a cause exhibit unique characteristics, act certain ways, and sometimes even adopt distinct language and dress.

Being a hippy was like that. I turned my will and my life over to a language, ("cool," "groovy," "far out"). We had our Higher Powers: Timothy Leary, Bob Dylan, The Grateful Dead, Indian gurus. We had our standard costumes -- outrageous, fun, anti-establishment garb.

Fifteen years later, I again became ready to turn my will and my life over to something greater than myself: to a process that would take me out of my addictions and ultimately restore me to sanity. I joined a 12-Step Program.

As a part of the recovery process, 12-Step programs suggest that members get a "sponsor" and "work the steps." A sponsor is like a mentor, someone with a little more experience than the newcomer. I chose a sponsor almost immediately, and by the time I started working Step Three, perhaps after three months of sobriety, a small part of my brain was coming back on line.

Frankly, I don't think my brain had been working very well up to this point. Yes, I could survive, keep the utilities from being shut off, and drive well enough to keep my driver's license, that sort of stuff. However, in order to actually *think effectively*, we need to have a lot of ducks in a row. We need to be free of drugs, have proper nutrition, and get enough exercise to pump blood to our brains and get oxygen to our neurons. And, we need to have a modicum of mental health, to not be burdened by a lot of psychological defenses and other neurotic behaviors. Unfortunately, except for being "free of drugs," I was barely meeting the other criteria. It would take years of work to get all the cylinders firing together, to get the biological, psychological, social, and spiritual aspects of myself up to anything like optimal performance.

I had "worked" Steps One and Two with my sponsor but, looking back, I don't know how conscious I was. I knew that when I used drugs, my life went insane. That was the essence of Step One -- admitting that I was addicted, out of control, powerless, and accepting that my life had become unmanageable. I bought the Step Two thing about being restored to sanity because, in fact, I wanted that, and it seemed to be happening.

But I will never forget the day I started to work on Step Three. I had a yellow legal pad and I was doing what my sponsor suggested. "Write about the Step," he said. It was then that my mind focused on the actual words in Step Three.

> *"Made a decision to turn our will and our lives over to the care of God as we understood Him."*

I got scared. I think I wrote something like: "How can I turn my life over to something else? What will happen to 'me'?" I had not yet begun to move beyond the "ego identification stage." I guess I was afraid that if I gave myself to God then "I" would no longer exist. Losing my "self" did not seem like a good idea. But at least I was considering the possibility of relating to the world from something beyond just my ego.

That was my first problem. The second problem was the thought of giving up my "self" to some random "God."

My grandparents on my father's side had been fundamentalist

Christian missionaries in India for 25 years, and were a bit over the top with "the religion thing." I was eight when my mother was stricken with polio and my younger brothers and I were sent to live with our grandparents. In many ways, my grandparents were kind and loving people. They lived on very modest retirement savings and supplemented their income by raising and selling chickens and rabbits. But they were fanatics when it came to teaching me, age eight, and my two younger brothers, ages five and six, to "fear God." When my brothers and I arrived at my grandparents' house, we weren't even allowed into their home until we got down on our knees at the front door and "admitted we were sinners!"

(How can a five-year -old even know what a sinner is?)

For some goofy reason, my grandparents wanted us to be really fearful of God. They told us that God might judge us as bad and kill us in our sleep by dropping "fire and brimstone" on us, if we strayed from some rigid party line that I was not yet privy to. It worked. I became afraid of this God-person. From that time, up until when I started to drink myself to sleep, I was really scared as I lay alone in my bed!

However, their teachings also provided a solution. They taught me a prayer that just might protect me if I did sin:

"Now I lay me down to sleep. I pray the Lord my soul to keep. If I die before I wake, I pray the Lord my soul to take."

Thanks! Scare the crap out of me, tell me that I might die while I'm asleep, and then give me a ditty that "might" work if I say it just right and don't think bad thoughts!

It was only when I started to drink and use drugs regularly, in my teens, that I was able to numb myself and generate enough ego defenses to rationalize away the "God thing." I became agnostic.

Then, twenty years later, I was faced with the "God thing" again. With great trepidation, I told my sponsor my story about the God that would kill children in their sleep. He must have heard this before, because he laughed! He laughed and told me to consider another possibility. Could I turn my will and my life over to G.O.D.?

G.O.D.?

"Good Orderly Direction," he said. "Or Group Of Drunks. Or Group Of Drug Addicts." "Could you turn your will and life over

to a 12-Step Program, groups which offer good, orderly direction?"
My brain was a little slow but I was able to grasp his idea.

Sure, maybe I could do that, I thought. I was still stuck with
needing to defend my ego. My ego was like a rat in a deep hole. It
was hard to imagine trusting anything or anybody. But I went along.
After all, this happy band of recovering addicts sure knew how to
stay sober and I wanted that. Besides, he told me this parable that
made it a little easier. It went like this:

"Two frogs are sitting on a lily pad. One decides to jump off.
How many frogs are left?"

I had a college degree and I let him know I was a quick study: the
answer was obvious and there was only one frog left on the lily pad.
He smiled that self-righteous smile that wily old 12-Step sponsors
smile when dealing with a mentally retarded, newly sober addict.
"Wrong," he said. "It only 'decided' to jump off. It didn't jump. Both
frogs are still on the lily pad."

Oh. That actually gave me even more of an out. I only needed
to make a "decision" to turn my will and my life over to the Good
Orderly Direction. I could "take it back" and continue to let my
ego run things. But pretty quickly I figured out that I was better off
going along with the program, because the life I had been living was
a mess. So I had the opportunity to "make a decision" and change. I
had an opportunity to turn my will and my life over to a process that
was offering me daily examples of formerly crazy people, many driving new cars and telling stories of how much their lives had changed
as a result of staying sober and working these Steps.

History is full of examples of people "turning our will and our lives"
over to something – a cause, an association. A group of individuals with
impoverished egos who needed to find a "problem outside of themselves" formed the Klu Klux Klan. These men turned "their will and
their lives over" to the group norms (racism, hate, bigotry, murder) and
wore absurd costumes. Another example is the frightened people who
"turned their will and their lives" over to Hitler and the Third Reich.

This surrender to a power greater than ourselves can go both
ways. It can be in service of developing a holistic Self, a healthy
integration of all of our aspects, and support our ongoing growth.
Or it can be in service of our ego, our fear, keep us small, stifle our
development, and keep us scared and separate from one another,
like the KKK or the Nazi party of the 1930s.

Organized religion offers examples of both possibilities. Mother Theresa, a devout Catholic, dedicated her life to helping those who were poor, sick, orphaned, and dying. At the opposite extreme are the fringe groups who obscenely preach hate and separation under the name of God. This latter group can even justify killing another human under the umbrella of their beliefs. I believe that there would be more peace in the world if everyone simply walked away from any religion that supports the ego. All great religions and perennial philosophies of the world advocate for peace and love.

One requirement for becoming a licensed psychotherapist is doing internships to gain experience. In 1993, I was an intern in San Quentin, California's notorious prison. I worked in a program there called Prisons to Success. I counseled prison inmates and then coordinated with churches in their home communities to help facilitate inmates' return to life after prison. The program was ahead of its time and, sadly, the prison authorities were unable to keep it going. While my participation was short-lived, I saw that organized religion could offer an amazing service to ex-convicts who needed help reintegrating into society.

If we look around and are honest about those who identify with their ego, we can understand the problem. As a society, we have elected and are governed by people who identify with ego and are addicted to beliefs and behaviors that support their self-serving lives, but impoverish us. They fit the larger definition of addiction, a condition that precludes their having any kind of functioning, spiritual Self.

As a society, we may be better than Nazi Germany, but leaders addicted to power and money are still governing us. Race relations in America are much better than when the KKK's influence was widespread, but still the majority of our population fails to own up to its internal bias and unconscious racism. I have found, by working Step Three, the undoing of those addictions and fears generated by the ego is not only possible, *it simply happens*.

What does Step Three look like for those of us who are codependents, those of us who are enabling the addicts? In Step One, we saw how crazy things really are. In Step Two, we realized that we needed to believe in something that could restore us to sanity, and get us out of the hopeless morass we had created in our country by continuing to re-elect leaders who were corrupt. We began to understand that we had to curtail our self-righteousness and let go of the idea that we could change another person. We realized we had to have faith that there was a solution, but that we needed to look beyond ourselves for that solution.

In Step Three, we become willing to rely on some power or process that is bigger than we are, and that will lead to more sanity than before. We muster our courage and put our trust in this "greater power." We become willing to let go of what we know – and what we know doesn't work – and allow room for a better future. We agree to follow the guidance of this "power greater" than our ego, rather than to stubbornly insist that our way is the right way.

This is a brilliant process and just needs to be replicated on the national level. How can I call it a brilliant process? The reality is that we recovering people have been keeping this approach nearly secret from you for 80 years. What is the second word in most 12-Step Programs? Anonymous. We are all around you, millions of us. We have been quietly doing our thing. This has been a grand social experiment that began in 1935. This experiment took the craziest of us and somehow turned us into some of the sanest! It really works.

But how can we apply Step Three to a whole country? What is the "power greater than ourselves" that a country could turn its will and its life over to?

That is what this book is about. This "power greater than ourselves" that will restore America to sanity is a process, an Intervention that leads to a new paradigm, something that we have not seen before and has not yet been fully defined. We could say that we are going to turn our country's will and life over to love, or spirituality, or a union with Nature. But in reality I believe that what we are going to turn our will and our lives over to is very simple. We, the sane 40 million, already have the answer. *We are already sane and we are simply going to use our collective common sense.* We are going to turn our will and our lives over to our common cause, our belief that there are sane and wise people who can collaboratively initiate an ongoing process that will transform America.

What a concept!

In my early recovery I would often ask my sponsor, my doctor, or my therapist the following questions: "What will my future look like? How will recovery change me? What will happen next? How does recovery work?" I was told to "trust the process" and follow the simple suggestions. The 12-Step communities are solidly in place and will easily provide the model of this new paradigm for us. But we need to do the footwork.

We can go back to the Declaration of Independence for guidance. Our forefathers had a vision, and much of what we seek today mirrors the principles and ideals put forth in 1776: a government that represents the people, and laws that support the common good.

But that is not what we currently have. Our corrupt leaders today represent the wishes of those who give them money. They clearly do not represent us.

(It is easy to visualize us on the Titanic and to see that we have a big, big problem when we look at the facts. The satellite images and the GPS are telling us that we are headed straight toward an iceberg. We can wake up, grab the helm, and take action, or we can stand around and ignore the disaster just over the horizon.)

Can we believe in a power greater than ourselves that can restore us to sanity? Can we make a decision to turn our will and our lives over to this "power greater than ourselves?" Can we get behind the idea of this Intervention on America? Can we imagine this idea going viral and actually happening? This is what is possible when an idea crystalizes a group of people who are ready to receive it.

Can we come to believe in a greater power that can lead to a replacement of the current carbon-burning, greedy, money and power addicted political system? Will we actually "step up" and take action?

Asmaa Mahfouz suggested to the Egyptians, "Instead of setting ourselves on fire, let's do something positive. Meet me at Tahrir Square." Wouldn't it be fun to do that here? We did it in the Sixties and we can do it again. The young people I work with idolize that movement and would readily show up. Wouldn't it be fun to be the crowds of joyful yet purposeful individuals assembling and making the statement that, "We are standing up and creating what we want America to be."

I believe it is a no-brainer. Millions of people live in harmony with Mother Nature and use zero or very little carbon. They live "off the grid," relying on solar, wind or hydropower to supply their energy needs. Millions of people live in communities where the welfare of children and family is foremost. There are communities where parents limit children's exposure to TV, feed their families diets rich in plant-based foods, and have active spiritual lives. Millions of people avail themselves of spiritual practices that support our evolution. The 12-Step community is one example. Millions of people live lives of high-level wellness. These folks actively attend to their bio-psycho-social-spiritual needs.

We who are recovering know how this works. We know how to stand up and take action, to make a leap of faith into a new paradigm. America has good enough institutions: our Constitution, democracy, rule of law, the two-party system, etc. But addicts have hijacked what these things really stand for. We need to remove the addicts from the system. We need to replace the addicted, fear-based system with an entirely new paradigm that is based on cooperation, collaboration and consensus.

With this book, I humbly propose an Intervention that we can all support. It is insanity to keep doing what we've been doing and expect anything to be different. If we can believe that this idea, this Intervention on American, is a worthy idea, then we can make a decision. We can become like the two frogs on the lily pad. Then we need to consider what happens after we make the decision.

Do we continue to sit on the lily pad or do we jump? Can we move beyond thinking to action?

9

COMING OUT OF DENIAL, STEP FOUR

Step Four: *"Made a searching and fearless moral inventory of ourselves."*

Before we can change anything in the world, we need to take a good look at ourselves. Before we can expect to usher in a world of sanity and functional relationships, we need to make sure that we, ourselves, are sane.

The sane, educated, spiritual, and functional Americans need to examine themselves and solidify their own health and recovery in order to bring the rest of country along into this Intervention. We need to be a healthy population before we can be a healthy country. Step Four asks us to do exactly that.

"Made a searching and fearless moral inventory of ourselves."

We have to get honest with ourselves and with our country. We need to get past the denial inherent in our own "stuff " and take a realistic look at America's "stuff."

For the individual addict, this means compiling as complete and specific a list as possible of the harm we've done: actions we regret, or feel ashamed or guilty about, resentments we've harbored, ways we've wronged or hurt others, and ways we've harmed ourselves. We need to inventory these things as well as our positive aspects.

At first, I was naïve about this Step. I did not fully grasp what it was asking of me. I had no problem telling you where I was born or what a jerk my father was, that kind of stuff. But my sponsor pointed out that "fearless and searching " meant that I needed to look deeper. At that point I had been to enough meetings to know that I and nearly everyone else was, as the Big Book (*Alcoholics Anonymous*, generally simply called the Big Book) says, "a liar, cheat, and a thief." This is a pretty amazing fact. What is it about addiction that causes us to lie, cheat, and steal from others? Why is this a universal fact, and how might this apply to our leaders and their corrupt behaviors?

"Self centered to the extreme" is another description often used in 12-Step work. I believe that the mind of an addict is impoverished. The addict's mind is frantically trying to make sense of a world that is out of control. When we are addicted, we are missing some big part of ourselves. We will see, as we work the Steps, that we are able, unlike Humpty Dumpty, to actually put ourselves back together again! From my years of work with addiction, I believe our insanity results from the fact that addicts are only working with part of their brain. The analogy I like to use is that of driving a car. Imagine that you are driving, and every now and then someone grabs the wheel and swerves around a corner or suddenly shifts lanes in the middle of traffic. You would be so absorbed in trying to regain control that you would not be able to do much else. This is what an addict's rational, prefrontal cortex is busy doing while another part of the brain actually makes the decisions.

This doesn't leave much room for serenity, fun, loving relationships, and productive behavior. This is a brain in a constant state of urgency and crisis.

So I began the humbling work of looking at yucky parts of myself. I did steal from various businesses, mostly petty stuff, but it was still hard to go back over my whole life, identify these actions, and write them down. I had lied to a lot of people. I went down the list of family members, friends, lovers, and ex-wives. I saw that I had been a tornado in their lives. I was told to take my time, and bring each of these instances into my awareness, and then write it down. The harder stuff was things I had done as a child or a teen. I did not have good supervision, and I was able to act out in ways that were very shameful and hard to acknowledge. But the suggestion was that I be fearless and thorough.

Ouch. I really don't want to think about *that!* I'd rather just "forget all about it." In reality we don't forget, we just push these things into the basements of our minds. This Step's goal is to bring it all up into the light of day, and then let it go.

More and more things came to mind for me. It was as if I had had a whole life that I was hiding from. How could I be real if I was hiding away from me?

Step Four also asks us to look at our resentments toward others. It is not surprising that addicts are angry with others. We typically have behaved so badly that it makes sense that our ego would twist reality around and make the other person wrong! It's a neat trick, but won't fly if we want to grow up and get healthy. A resentment is actually a gift, if we are honest and willing to see our part in the relationship or event.

Because I had waited until I was in my late thirties to get sober, I had quite a list of "stuff." And not all of it was bad. We need to list our good stuff as well. I had been an accomplished photojournalist and owned a retail shop in the North Beach area of San Francisco that I was quite proud of. But this list of good stuff was much shorter than the other list.

The 4th Step is also vital for enablers. It is the first action step in the 12-Step process. If we are addicted to trying to change someone, if we are codependents, we need to acknowledge the harm we have done to others as well as ourselves. How has our egocentric need to change another person actually harmed them? Has our enabling prevented them from facing their own lives? One woman asked me to intervene on her 64-year-old son . . . who was still living at home!

As citizens of America we need to acknowledge the harm we have done to others, our country, our environment, and ourselves, whether by our actions or by inaction. We need to look at *all* the ways we have contributed to our country's current state of affairs. How have *we* gone along with the lies of Big Business, Big Government, and Big Oil? What is our part in the financial debacle in our nation? How much gas and oil do we consume? How big is our carbon footprint? How do we support the fast-food industry that we may castigate?

We can all agree that we need honorable, ethical, and moral leaders instead of power-hungry politicians who are taking advantage of us. How often have you heard this? "*They* took advantage of us!" But we can't simply blame them. We need to take responsibility for voting for them. We voted them into office, or stuck our heads in the sand and looked the other way while they acted in immoral or unethical ways.

What does "taking an inventory," mean for the politician taking bribes, the CEO of Big Chemical dumping poison into the environment, or a Wall Street banker evicting the little guy to get yet more money? That's none of our business – it's theirs! It's not up to us to list their wrongdoings or to get them to admit the error of their ways. If they choose, they can do their own 4th-Step inventory. It's obvious how their actions have harmed our country and our environment and we can decide not to vote for them, or to recall them, or to protest their actions. *We* are a Democracy. We citizens *are* the country. The elected officials are but our "trusted servants." It is *we* who are responsible for their behavior and the current mess. We are the enablers. Which is really great news! Because we can choose to *stop* enabling and stop voting for those who accept bribes from unions and businesses.

It is as if we sent our addicted parent to run the family shoe store and then got mad at them for screwing it up. It is not useful to spend our energy getting mad at the corrupt elected officials. *We sent them to Washington.* We simply need to do this Intervention and send a new crop of principled officials to Washington.

12-Step programs acknowledge that we cannot "take another person's inventory." It's up to each individual to decide whether they are willing to look at the impact of their behavior and see if they want to change and develop an authentic, healthy self.

If our leaders in government, and Big Business and Big Union, don't want to take responsibility, that's their business. We still need to take responsibility for our part -- we voted for them, or bought their products, or turned a blind eye to their actions.

Why do a 4th Step? We do it because we want to heal and recover from a life based on ego. Every path to high-level wellness includes a process of acknowledging the mistakes we have made.

So let's start. Let's start with what's good about America. We have a lot to be grateful for. Our nation has endured for over 200 years. We have established law and order. We support freedom of the individual. Our economy has flourished for decades. Our universities attract students from all over the world. Our culture supports medicine, science, education, sports, and the arts.

Apple, Facebook, fiber optics, the Internet, and Google are homegrown and have created the foundation of the whole world's next paradigm shift.

In the Fourth Step of the 12-Step recovery process, we take a wide-eyed and honest appraisal of ourselves. We look at all of our behaviors.

I think it's useful to consider the paradigm shift to a democratic republic that occurred in the 1770s. Can you imagine what would have happened if the paradigm shift of the American Revolution had not taken place? I believe we are on the cusp of the next one. "Democracy" was just a being given lip-service back "in the day." Only the property owners could vote in Great Britain, and the monarch ruled with little direct input from his countrymen. Little did King George III envision the split in the British Empire and the fate of British reign in America. The long-standing dominance of the monarchy was challenged by our founding fathers and they replaced it with a new, sovereign, nation based on democracy.

Our founding fathers repudiated the laws of England and wrote a Declaration of Independence that emancipated us from colonial rule. They declared the right of the people to abolish government when that government became destructive, and listed the ways King George had violated their rights. They affirmed Life, Liberty and the Pursuit of Happiness as inalienable human rights. The citizens fought a war to defend these rights, and then established a democratic government with a Presidency, a Senate and House of Representatives, and a Supreme Court.

However, today we can look around and see the failings of our democratic institutions. We need to take a fearless and searching inventory of what we've created. Over time, every established institution needs this. Young people have fresh eyes and they see the messy hypocrisy that is clearly present in our current government.

In the Declaration of Independence, our forefathers listed the transgressions of King George and the injustices that they sought freedom from. Then they declared the principles which were to serve as the foundation of their future democratic republic. We are at a similar juncture today. We see the past. We see the mess we have allowed to evolve under our watch. And we are poised to move forward, to support and embrace a shift.

Let's continue with our "searching and fearless moral inventory" of America.

The list of transgressions by our government leaders, Big Business, Big Union and the hyper-wealthy is long. Some of these, like global warming, I've already described. Let me give you a couple of other examples, keeping in mind that it is these kinds of practices that a paradigm shift would eliminate.

We all agree that we must protect children at all costs. Every society values children. Even the folks in prison understand that the worst among them are the child abusers. In the 1960s, a group from Big Business stood in front of Congress and swore that tobacco use was not linked to lung cancer or other diseases. They all knew it was a lie. But they were addicted to what tobacco sales provided for them.

Again, in 1994, ignoring decades of research, CEO's of seven major tobacco companies testified in a congressional subcommittee on health and the environment that tobacco is not addictive! An equally immoral group of congresspersons, knowing that tobacco will kill almost half its users, looked the other way while the tobacco industry's "drug dealers" used creative advertising to push this deadly drug on children! It was finally an outraged public, and overwhelming medical research, that embarrassed politicians to take action. Otherwise Joe Camel would still be on the back cover of children's magazines! President Reagan's "War on Drugs" did not include tobacco, and by now you know why. Nearly all of them were getting kickbacks from the tobacco companies!

And we have watched in horror as this band of corrupt officials marches on.

And these same politicians, who colluded in backroom deals that made nicotine available to children, realized that they were creating nicotine addicts who would pay big bucks for their "fix." Everyone knows that an addict will not let money get in the way of his or her "fix." So they taxed tobacco. A lot. And kept raising the tax. A rational person might hope that nicotine tax revenues would be used to promote reduction in tobacco use and fund education about consequences of tobacco use and drug treatment for nicotine addicts. And that is what the politicians promised. Of course this did not happen. It seems that a little money went toward research on the effects of tobacco use, but most of the funds quickly got diverted to other programs. And the promised TV ads warning against the harmful effects of smoking soon went away. Children are still smoking and many will be crippled and die because of their addiction.

Most of our elected leaders have children. You would think that they would do what they could do to see that their own children would grow up in a drug-free world. Clearly, their addiction to money and power were more important than the safety of their own children. That is why a "fearless " inventory can be so effective for an addict, or an enabler.

Even today, we subject children to secondhand smoke that sentences hundreds of thousands of them to chronic diseases like asthma and other cardiopulmonary disorders.

Pediatricians and child psychologists have for years been telling "leaders" in Congress that TV is negatively impacting the development of children. TV is like a drug for children. The electronic images excite a part of the brain that short-circuits healthy brain pathways and stunts normal development. Excessive TV retards children's bio-psycho-social-spiritual development. We have known this for decades. Congress knows this but won't dare speak about it to parents because it would upset the folks who fund their re-election. They cannot say anything about this "child neglect" practice, or they will lose their money 'fix' from Big Media and Big Food and others who sell their products on TV. They don't speak and warn millions of innocent parents who use their TVs as babysitters that TV is addictive. Using TV this way puts children at a disadvantage. (These parents wonder why their kids are later diagnosed with Attention Deficit Disorder and are put on powerful stimulants to counteract the effects of this neglect.)

Go to the zoo. Go to the monkey cage. Watch the young monkeys. They are doing what young monkeys have done for millions of years. Now imagine that we gave each of them a TV and they spent their days watching TV instead of running, jumping, swinging, interacting with the older monkeys, getting in fights, making up, forming cliques, taking naps, dreaming, watching bugs, looking at the sky. They would become habituated to the TV, and we'd have zoos full of spaced out, retarded, emotionally immature, socially awkward, neurotic monkeys who would be prone to mental disorders, and addictions. A whole industry of psychologists, therapists, consultants, and special programs would then be required to take care of these screwed up monkeys.

We need wise leaders that we trust to guide us, to lead us, to educate us. *Instead we have addicted leaders who look the other way and rip us off. We need much less government, but much smarter government.* I want our wise and trusted servants to come to us and help us be better parents and better citizens. I want my elected leaders to say something like this, "Hey, science and mental health professionals are telling us that children are better off playing outside and interacting with other humans than sitting around and watching flickering images on a TV or computer or iPod and should be supervised to see that they aren't exposed to excessive amounts."

A good example of a wise leader's message came from Michelle Obama. She suggested that eating more plant-based food would help reverse the obesity epidemic. The obesity problem remains because many politicians get kickbacks from Big Food and Big Unions. The politicians became outraged and criticized Michelle for this reasonable and intelligent move. One out of three children is headed toward debilitating diabetes, and the elected officials will never criticize Big Food because they want their kickbacks. (Michelle gets my vote for giving us the rare, sane message out of Washington.)

I am fortunate to live and work and socialize with a number of educated parents. None of them use TVs as babysitters for their childcare. None. Many of these professionals are not even hooked up to cable. They might have a TV so the whole family can watch movies together. That "endless drone sound," present in some homes, is evidence of a new type of addiction that I call "Electronic Screen Addiction" (E.S.A.). It is a form of often compulsive behavior that effectively disrupts our bio-psycho-social-spiritual development. Parents who put their children at a disadvantage in this way need to be educated about the harmful effects of overexposure to electronic screens.

It is easy to assess families suffering from E.S.A. No matter what time of day you enter their homes, the television is on. These folks seem unable to be present; the TV comes between them so that intimate, authentic communication is impaired. Children in these homes are at high risk of never appreciating nature and not developing healthy emotional intelligence. Emotional intelligence is what allows us to interact with others and to participate in close, fun, and intimate relationships.

Another example of the upsetting state of affairs is the "Democratic-Lawyer Complex." This pattern is active in the back rooms of political offices around the country. Many doctors pay over $100,000 a year in malpractice insurance just for the right to practice medicine and avoid lawsuits. The Democrats acquiesce to the lawyers' demands, the lawyers donate money to the politicians that supports the campaign financing, the Republicans complain, but not too much, because they know they will get their chance to get kickbacks from those who fund *their elections.*

Big Union is another such situation. Democrats receive up to 75% of their kickbacks and bribes from large unions. You can confirm this by visiting http://www.opensecrets.org/. How can someone serve us, when they are beholden to special interests?

These politicians may have been honorable people before they went to Washington. Let's stand back at look at one example I have already mentioned -- spreading toxic chemicals into the air while mining coal. Today, in Pennsylvania, union workers are waking up and going to work removing the tops of mountains in order to dig up coal. This causes a deadly spewing of mercury into the air. The politicians might like to stop this and heal the planet, but they are beholden to the bribes they receive from the coal workers' union. Perhaps the coal worker and the politician see the problem, but have no way of addressing it. They are stuck in a system that is broken.

What about our collective "isms"? Racism, sexism, ageism, and other ways we pigeonhole, marginalize, discriminate, or otherwise diminish someone else because they are not like "my people." We need to include this in our inventory of ourselves.

In 1990, I stood on Mount Tamalpias, in Northern California, at an event led by the poet Robert Bly. I was standing with a hundred other, mostly white, men. We had been discussing how we'd distanced ourselves from men of color and what we could do about it. I recall stepping into the middle of the circle to speak. I admitted I was a racist and said I was a racist, because I lived in a racist society.

I still live in a racist society. I was probably five or six years old when I heard my father say, "You have to watch out for Negroes. They will cut you with a knife!" My father was simply reflecting the racist world he lived in.

In the chapter, "Are Any of Us Healthy?" I talked about projection. If we are doing a fearless and searching moral inventory of ourselves, we need to look at this process. If we don't have a healthy ego or a realistic and balanced self-image, we are prone to "project" our shadow, the unwanted aspects of ourselves, onto someone else. It could be Blacks (or Spics, or Miks, or Fags, or Bitches, or Bastards, or Slopes, or Chinks, or Gays, or whomever). They become the target for the unconscious parts of ourselves that we don't want or don't like. "I don't want to acknowledge some 'bad' part of me, so I will see it 'out there in *them*' and then hate that particular group of people."

We all have rapscallion parts of ourselves. Freud is reputed to have said, "A murder a day in our minds keeps the psychiatrist away." He was suggesting that any one of us could conjure up just about anything in our minds. On three occasions I have attended 10-day, silent mediation retreats. For ten days we sat and meditated and walked and ate in total silence. I was warned ahead of time that as my mind settled down and became still I would become aware of how it endlessly is generating all kinds of material. It was humbling to experience this. I saw that in my mind I was capable of murderous thoughts and images, as well as of fantastic, loving thoughts and images. My inner Hitler, emerged and I imagined harming others. And I experienced my inner Christ who saw infinite love everywhere. The Seven Deadly Sins were alive and well. I later discovered that this is quite common, that everyone's ego is regularly generating these thoughts and images. We see them, if we slow down enough to become aware of them. The problem is that most of our minds are like hamsters on a wheel, endlessly seeking relief and never allowing ourselves to find long periods of silence to reveal these aspects of ourselves. The 4th Step asks us to stop the wheel, and take this inventory.

These psychological defenses are not a big deal, as long as we are psychologically healthy and know it is only our mind, "running away with me," as the song goes. They become a problem when we defend against them and let them leak out in other ways, in rageful and passive-aggressive behaviors.

This can become deadly, particularly when individuals in a group collectively fail to realize it. They get confused and project their own "evil" onto others and then go kill them! Many thoughtful psychologists have speculated that President Bush was unconsciously working out unfinished business with his father via the war on Iraq. Blacks have tragically had to endure for years mentally ill white people who chose to project their "shadow" onto them in the insane belief that by killing people with more melanin in their skin they were getting rid of "badness." The problem is that the "badness" actually resides inside the racists' or warmongers' minds. This, similarly, is what happened to the Jews in WWII. Al Qaida, today, is killing innocents whom they see as "evil."

I believe that 100% of Americans over 40 will find their internal racism if they are truly honest with themselves. I am aware of my own racism, regardless of how openhearted I also may be. I was active in the Civil Rights movement in the 1960s. A group of us were jailed in 1963; we were protesting housing laws that discriminated against blacks in East Lansing, Michigan. I taught in black schools. I have dated black women. And yet today, when I see a black person, a part of me contracts. At these moments I remember that my father and my society programmed me to imagine "them" as different because of their skin color.

As I was working Step Four, I began to understand that I was a good kid and that my parents did the best they could. But they were the product of a different age. I was spanked, and later beaten, by my alcoholic father and codependent mother. When I began drinking, I too did terrible things. I did many things that were very wrong. I hurt and abused others; I had buried a lot of shame and guilt, deep in my unconscious. As I followed the directions of my sponsor and worked Step Four, I began to acknowledge painful truths that I had kept from myself, as well as from any other person. As citizens who want a better America, we need to do the same thing.

If we are to recover our birthright and become healthy, we will need to "fess up." We will need to get real and "spill the beans." We will have to find the courage to be honest with ourselves and to bring to light our deepest, darkest secrets. It is essential that our inventory of our secrets, of the actions we regret, of our shame and guilt, be fearless and thorough.

The "I don't want to think about it or talk about it" mentality condemns us to a sad and impoverished life. And a lonely life. Holding on to our secrets condemns us to separation from our more joyful selves, and from connection to the rest of humanity. We all screw up! We do. We all make mistakes. We would not be human if we didn't. It is in the *acknowledgment* of our humanness and our ability to *acknowledge to others* our faults (Step Five), that we enter the family of man. It is only when we are able to be fully honest that we can be trusted by others.

I believe that this inability to be honest goes to the core of our political process. Our leaders are not being honest. They are also "liars, cheats, and thieves." Would it be great if they admitted this? Imagine what a politician taking a 4th Step might sound like:

"OK, it's true. You elected me but I have been lying to you. I've lied to you about taking kickbacks from the lobbyists, special interests, and Big Business and Big Union. Yes, they give me millions of dollars in cash. Yes, they put together slick publicity on TV that promotes me. And yes, I use expensive marketing people to create TV ads that are meant to scare you so you won't see the real, rigged game we are all playing.

"And yes, I am beholden to these folks. I hate it, but when I came to Washington I realized that everyone here does it. It is the culture. It is a culture of lies, deceit, money laundering, pandering, bribing, and other corrupt stuff. And I may trash the other party, but the reality is that they are the same as our party. We suck up to the money and then rig the system so that they, and we, make more money."

Not only do the near majority of our elected 536 lie, but also it's probable that they themselves are so embedded in the mess that they don't even know it!

Here is an example. In April of 2011 Senator Jon Kyl, speaking to the Senate, said, "Planned Parenthood spends 90% of their time performing abortions." Various news media checked the statistic, and found the number is really 3%. A sane person would say, "Oops, sorry, I made a mistake. Let me correct the facts." So, how did Senator Kyl respond to his lie? His spokesman offered the following:

"His remark was not intended to be a factual statement but rather to illustrate that Planned Parenthood, an organization that receives millions of taxpayer dollars, does subsidize abortions."

But wait, he lied. Where is the admission of the wrong? Where is the correction and where is the apology?

He lied and didn't even know he lied! He said it like it was perfectly fine to make up facts! And everyone accepted it. No outrage from his colleagues. No mention of the stain on the reputation of the other senators that one of their own lied and did not apologize. No demand for a correction from the leaders of his party. Or even from the Democrats. And where was the media?

It was left to the comedian, Jon Stewart to be the rare media person who pointed this out this shocking incongruency. This is an example of how the mainstream media colludes with the addictive political system. If asked about this, the Washington media might say something like the following.

> *"Oh, they all do it, they all lie. It's how Washington works. All of us media folks have to play along if we are to have access to them. If we point out the truth, we will be excluded from the halls of power. So the reality is that we can't tell the truth either. We, and our news outlets are lying to the American public as well."*

I wish they would say that. If we are to move forward, we must be honest with ourselves and with each other. This is the essence of Steps Four and Five.

We read in the book, *Alcoholics Anonymous*, that addicts are "liars, cheats, and thieves." And that is my point. Our leaders, the media, and the moneyed few are addicts. They are liars, cheats and thieves, and we need to initiate an Intervention. We can replace all 536 in the fall of 2012.

America has many realities that need to be publically acknowledged. We need to erect monuments to these errors. Our "searching and fearless moral inventory" needs to include how we enslaved blacks, terrorized Native Americans, and denied women their rights. We, as a nation, have yet to own up to our immoral behaviors.

By acknowledging and listing our mistakes, we begin to unburden ourselves from a past that renders us too mired in guilt and shame to move forward. We begin to see more clearly where we have been and where we are now.

Once we have done this fearless and searching inventory of ourselves, we are now ready to move on to the next step, Step Five.

10

TELLING THE TRUTH, STEP FIVE

Step Five: *"Admitted to God, to ourselves, and to another human being the exact nature of our wrongs."*

I believe that being able to experience love and spirituality requires us to dissolve the boundaries that separate us from one another. Love and spirituality: neither can fully exist if we are spending our psychic energy defending something. Imagine hanging from a rope and being afraid to let go because you will fall into the unknown. This is what it is like when we hold onto secrets. We fear terrible things may happen if we let go and reveal what we've kept hidden. Step Five shows us that the rope we are hanging from has us dangling only one inch from the ground! When we let go and reveal our secrets we actually feel much *better. The ego's fear of losing control is incredible!*

> *"Admitted to God, to ourselves, and to another human being the exact nature of our wrongs."*

This Step is brilliant. When Bill Wilson and the other early founders of AA wrote Step Five, they were asking the addict to knock down the barriers separating him from others, and to develop the capacity for intimacy and rationality. This Step invites us to find the courage to fully join the human race. There is something profound about the process of looking another human in the eye, being vulnerable, and saying out loud the things we have repressed, resisted, or denied, because we have been afraid.

Imagine that you have a basement in your home and that you have been storing stuff in it. Whenever something is in the way, you put it in the basement. If you don't want it, it goes to the basement. If it makes you uncomfortable, it goes to the basement. Imagine that you have been doing this for your whole life.

It is now overflowing with decades of piled up junk. It has become moldy and dusty and filled with spider webs, and it reeks of decay. Now imagine that you decide to clean it all out, remodel it, and beautifully decorate it. Working the Fifth Step is exactly like this. Cleaning that basement will take a while, but you are determined to see it through and improve your home. You know you will need some help as you start the process, and you know that if you keep working on it, a day at a time, you will eventually get the job done.

You get to work. You get a dumpster for the trash and a place for the stuff you will give away or sell. Slowly, more and more space is exposed. It's hard work. It's dirty work. How did things get so messed up? How did this disaster go unnoticed? You find things that you had long ago forgotten about. Some of them may be hard to look at, but now and then you find something special. At last, the basement is empty and thoroughly cleaned out. The long-closed windows are opened and the breeze wafts in. Sunlight brightens the once-dark space.

Remodeling begins. Basic structures are fortified with up-to-date codes. Enhancements are considered. Next, the interior decorator makes design choices, and it looks wonderful. Finally, you can let the basement be part of your life. It can be a valuable extension of your home. No longer do you have that nagging thought, "Something needs to be done, something is wrong!"

Working the Fifth Step is admitting to another person what is in our "basement."

In the process of disclosing our secrets and our shameful actions out loud, to another person, we move that particular bit of distorted reality from the dustbin of our unconsciousness into the light, where we can own that it is part of who we are. It is an aspect of ourselves that we come to accept. We no longer need to ignore repressed memories.

The addict's ego generates defenses to hide from himself the sad reality of his condition, while the recovering addict acknowledges the insanity that characterized his life prior to choosing recovery.

When I was using drugs and insane, I announced repeatedly, "I'm fine, I don't have a drug problem." My ego was defensively saying, "I'm not insane." By the time I got to this Step, I was no longer in denial and easily acknowledged my addiction and loss of control. I could say, without defensiveness, "When I was in my addiction I was clearly not sane, no question about it."

If we have done a fearless and searching moral inventory in Step Four, we will have a lot of information to communicate to the person we ask to hear our list in Step Five.

Legend has it that in the early days of 12-Step Programs, recovering addicts would grab someone off the street and take them into a coffee shop and tell their history to this stranger. But the practice in my part of the country is to sit with a sponsor and admit "*the exact nature of our wrongs.*" For my Fifth Step, my sponsor, invited me to his modest home. It was a warm spring evening in 1980. He provided a six-pack of Coke and a can of Planters salted peanuts. I arrived with my yellow pad and butterflies in my stomach. He started off the meeting telling me a few raunchy Fifth Step jokes. I'm sure it was to set the mood and make it easier for me to talk about the things I'd done that I'd never revealed to anyone before.

Most of what I admitted to my sponsor was probably not a surprise to this man who had been in recovery for three years. There is a constellation of behaviors common to most addicts. The details may vary, but the behaviors are those of a person whose rational, moral, thinking brain has been hijacked by his impulsive midbrain. According to the Big Book of Alcoholics Anonymous, all addicts are, as I have mentioned numerous times, "liars, cheats, and thieves."

I was no exception. I had used all my defenses to justify, rationalize, and deny my behaviors. True to the Big Book's characterization of an addict, I was a thief. I once worked as a bartender at Michigan State University's local hangout. The huge, Coral Gables Restaurant had two bars and as many as six bartenders on duty at a time. I imagined that most of us drank on the job; I know I did. And I stole. Each night I would shove a twenty-dollar bill into my beer-splattered sneakers. And I shoplifted. I was putting myself through college; I was often hungry and stole my dinner. And, I justified my lack of morals to myself. Although I was a little startled once when I woke up after a drunken party and realized that I had stolen someone's shoes.

During high school I worked at the A&P supermarket in the Detroit area. On my shifts, I often tossed six-packs of beer into the garbage. I'd come back later with my friends to retrieve them. My relationships were characterized by selfishness, deception, and lies. I always had a story that justified my behavior, and I often blamed another person for my problems.

When I was doing my 5th Step, it wasn't difficult for me to reveal most of these facts to my sponsor. In some ways I suppose I was a little proud of my skills at thievery. After all, hadn't I been through a period when Nixon and others had lied and started a war; and when Watergate had demonstrated how corrupt our highest leaders were? Our highest leader had lied to the American people, including me. It was not too much of a stretch for me to rationalize my behavior.

Can you now see why we have such a crisis of morals in this country? Our leaders are exactly the "liars, thieves, and cheats" that I had been. Our children watch our politicians and Wall Street financiers lie and steal. How do we explain that to them? No wonder so many young people have difficulty knowing what is right, when our most important "leaders" are actually publically lying to us!

So what about admitting our part in contributing to this crisis? We have elected leaders who lack morals, then we grumble to each other when these politicians act immorally. We voted these politicians into office, but few of us protested when they acted badly, told lies, or didn't act in the best interests of their constituency. We just sat around and complained. Or perhaps we played the "Blame Game:" We identified with one party, got together with like-minded people, and agreed that the "other side" was the problem.

If we are to have a brain that works, and the freedom to feel and express our emotions, we will benefit significantly from admitting the exact nature of our wrongs to someone we trust. Many people simply "don't want to talk about it." In his book, *I Don't Want to Talk about It: Overcoming the Secret Legacy of Male Depression*, psychotherapist Terrence Real explored the father-to-son legacy of rage, depression, workaholism, and distancing relationships that millions of men suffer from, by stuffing feelings they don't feel entitled to express. It is sad for me, as a psychotherapist, to know about these poor folks who are deprived of having a full life. I am so grateful for the person who pointed out my addiction. And, I am *so very grateful* for becoming an addict! I would not be where I am without that condition and the recovery process that resulted in the restoration of my sanity. Often, without a bottom, or a crisis to overcome, change is not possible. A case could be made that America will look back and be grateful for the financial meltdown, unemployment, global warming crisis, and inept Congress because these events offered us the "bottom" from which to do a "restart."

Earlier, I referred to a speech by New Jersey's Governor, Chris Christie, in which he said that past governors had lied to their audiences. Wouldn't it be wonderful if more of our leaders actually did "fess up" and apologize for deceiving us? Unfortunately, addicts are actually usually unaware of their addictions. We will be much happier if we never forget that last sentence. Addicts lie -- but they don't know they are doing it! We all know they are lying, and yet we choose to ignore it, because we don't know that we have any options. If we want sanity, I believe our only hope is a complete paradigm shift because the addict almost never changes without us changing first. And that's as true of the addicts in Congress or on Wall Street as it is for the addict or codependent in our own families.

National change will happen only when each of us wakes up to our own addictions, or wakes up to how we enable addictions. And then, only when we do the work to recover. Most of us are racist, for example, and need to acknowledge that fact. We do not need to know immediately what we will *do* about it. That will come later on in the Steps. For now, we are simply acknowledging our personal and cultural wrongs.

Here is a partial list of the *"exact nature of our wrongs"* that we Americans need to admit. I'm sure you can add to this list.

We have talked about the practice of judging God's children by the color of their skin. Americans have much wrongdoing to admit on this topic. Slavery, the owning of another person, was wrong. Our history is full of the wrongs we did to those men and women. We kidnapped them from their home countries, and forced them into slavery. We beat them, raped them, and ultimately, lynched them.

In this country, people over a certain age have been raised in a homophobic culture and are homophobic. The 5th Step gives us the opportunity to simply acknowledge the insanity of discriminating against a person because of their sexual interests and orientations.

One of the most shameful things that we Americans need to

admit is the unconscionable ways that we treated Native Americans. We murdered, raped, and stole from these indigenous peoples. We took children from their mothers and put them in "re-education facilities" in order to make them more like us. Genocide? Ten million Native Americans lived here before Christopher Columbus "found" these lands, and the white man has reduced that population to 2.4 million. The Northwest Ordinance of 1787 forbade these people from speaking their own languages and, starting in 1930, 70,000 Native American women were involuntarily sterilized, often without their even knowing it.

Then there's sexism. At times in human history, there have been matriarchal societies. By and large, those cultures were more peaceful than patriarchies. Women are naturally more peaceful than men. America started out as a patriarchal society. Women were not allowed to vote, were not given fair wages, and were treated as second-class citizens in many ways. Today, women still hold relatively few positions of power in business or government. Men and women in America have been programmed to support, enable, and sustain this unfair patriarchy.

And there is the myth of democracy, which is held not as a myth, but as a highly regarded system of beliefs, in much of America. In Asia, many believe in the myth of socialism or communism or whatever China today is calling its political ideology. Those who believe these myths are often willing to go to war over them. At the moment, the democracy myth appears to be the most "fair," but anyone who reads the papers or follows the news knows that many aspects of applied democracy are not sane. Gerrymandering is one example. Those addicted to money and power (the politicians) manipulate the geographic boundaries of election districts to favor certain partisan groups; this thwarts fair elections, explains why so few vote, and guarantees that the same folks return to Washington and elsewhere, over and over. The two parties work together to do this. We enablers, for the most part, simply accept this situation, even though we all know it undermines democracy. Throughout the history of America, addiction to power has systematically deprived women, blacks, and the poorly educated of the right to vote. This is still going on, and certainly has not been in service of democracy.

Capitalism is a financial myth that hides numerous wrongs. It is a myth that is held sacrosanct by those who benefit from it and by those who enable it. Our recent financial meltdown is a current example of something that has gone on throughout the history of America. Capitalism is wonderful in many ways, but it is flawed. I am lucky to own a home, but, like many of us, I lost a lot of equity in my home in the recent financial meltdown. My money went to Wall Street, and then to Wall Street's enablers, the politicians who receive kickbacks so they will protect the capitalists who gamed the system.

"Admitted to God, to ourselves, and to another human being the exact nature of our wrongs."

All of us, that is, all of us except the members of our oligarchy, need to acknowledge that we have enabled "this." And by "this" I mean all of the above, in addition to the current, critical, state of affairs. Currently we are all supporting a corrupt, immoral, and unethical political system that is ripping us off, poisoning our waters and lands, making children sick, and putting our planet at risk. If we are to work Step Five and admit our faults, we will all have to acknowledge our part in propping up this oligarchy. Only an addict, lost in addiction, could fail to see the problem.

The above is a partial list of America's wrongs. But the real point of enumerating them, is for all of us to begin to see our vulnerability to a corrupt culture that is operating only as a mere shadow of its potential.

It is essential to follow through on this Step's directive "to own up to our flaws" so that we can move forward. It is through working this Step that we can begin to look objectively at our character, and the character defects that define us and our country. And, as we take responsibility for our behavior, we can clearly see the goal of this Intervention.

Only then can we do the work needed to begin the healing process, both individually and as a nation.

11

REWIRING OUR BRAINS, STEP SIX

Step Six: *"Were entirely ready to have God remove all these defects of character."*

Step Six asks us to become "entirely ready" to have our "character defects" removed. I don't know anyone who woke up one day, and was grateful for his or her character defects and wanted to hold onto them. I believe that most of us, upon recognizing our character defects, would like them removed. How that happens is another question. Working the Steps is a transformational process. As we slowly transition from an ego-identification to a Self-identification, our egocentric approach and our character defects become less and less a part of who we truly are.

> *"Were entirely ready to have God remove all these defects of character."*

This Step is about becoming *willing* to let go of our old delusional beliefs. This is not simply about doing the cognitive work to change how we think, although we certainly need to examine our beliefs, but it is also about the process of preparing our brains for developing an Authentic Self.

Many of us have had momentary spiritual experiences that have allowed us to transcend our egos and our hardwired ego identification. It is in these transcendent times, these spiritual experiences, that we can see the folly of our personalities and the egocentric approaches of our lives. For a moment we can see that a life based on ego is a mere shadow of what is actually possible. In these spiritual moments we see the infinite in all of its wonder. We are able to "look down" on our "stuff" and see our ego and its defensive, and hardwired stance. These moments are typically short-lived and very rare for the ego-identified addict. We addicts are usually ignorant of our dysfunctional and limiting beliefs. As Freud once said, "Most people live lives of quiet desperation." The addict and the ego-identified do not comprehend the tragedy of their failure to understand what could be possible.

Take someone who is strongly racist for example. They would not suddenly have this insight, "Wow, I'm ready to have my racism removed." No. Racism, like any strong belief, is part of a carefully constructed cognitive *and* emotional structure. Changing a long-standing and foundational belief requires a comprehensive and lengthy process, such as this 12-Step process. Or long term, spiritually-based, in-depth therapy. But neither of these approaches will work if the individual is not first willing to change. *We must want to change before any change will occur.* The racist is strongly and unconsciously motivated to *defend and perpetuate* their cognitive stance -- deep down, they don't want to change. An individual's racism is typically a reflection of their childhood programming, surrounding culture, and their personal belief system. The racist and the addict's "system software," and its attendant brain wiring, have been extensively constructed over a lifetime. The racist, like the addict, is highly motivated to *not change*, regardless of what information they may encounter that contradicts their belief system. In fact, additional information which challenges their hardwired beliefs will make them even more defensive and less able to change. In other words, the wiring of their neuronal networks enslaves them and it would take years of hard work to rewire their brains, even if they were highly motivated to change, which few racists or addicts are, unless something extraordinary occurs.

Addicts and racists are only a few of us humans who are delusional and who hold onto beliefs that are not sane. The following is a list of delusional beliefs that are held by some elected officials, and some of the candidates who propose to lead America:

• Climate change is a hoax

• Evolution is a hoax

- Saddam Hussein was involved in the 9/11 attacks
- Barack Obama was not born in the United States

And these beliefs also have large numbers of followers:

- The Apollo moon landing was a hoax
- 9/11 was an inside job by the Bush administration
- The Holocaust did not happen
- AIDS is not caused by HIV
- Vaccines cause autism

It turns out that those who believe the ideas above, if challenged, will use "fight or flight" reflexes -- just like addicts. The above folks, and addicts, just plain cannot take in contradictory information. Information that contradicts their position will make them *feel bad*. They don't want to feel bad, so they typically will go on the defensive and possibly even attack – or they will flee into their "medicine," their addictive behavior or substance.

It is delusional to try to talk a racist out of his/her position. It is delusional to try to talk an addict out of his/her position. And it is delusional to try to talk a codependent out of his/her enabling position. The codependent's delusional belief that he or she can change an addict, sadly keeps millions of addicted families stuck in their dysfunction. I believe the addiction treatment industry fails miserably by treating just the addict instead of the whole, addicted system. But when industry treats just one person, I believe they often *treat the wrong person!* Of course the addict is sick and needs treatment, but in many cases we need to attend to the enablers first. If these codependent enablers don't change, then the addict will return from treatment to the same sick system and, usually, relapse. Often, the enablers are often much more impaired than the addict.

Their egos simply cannot allow them to take Step One. *They cannot admit that they are powerless over the addiction and that their lives have become unmanageable.*

Or, as H.L. Mencken said: *"The most common of all follies is to believe passionately in the palpably not true. It is the chief occupation of mankind."*

I believe that our character is a hardwired result of our genetics, in combination with influences from the world we live in. Where did we learn to speak English? We didn't each invent it. We were not born already knowing it. We were programmed and wired by our culture to believe, think, and speak the way we do. It is only through the hard work of getting our bio-psycho-social-spiritual house in order that we can untether ourselves from our egos and from the external cultural messages, and that we can begin to differentiate and construct a Self, and actually begin to think for ourselves.

As we work this Step we will need to look back over the first five Steps. When we stand back and look at the previous work we have done, we will be able to see the larger picture. And, from that vantage point, we will become ready to have these defects of character removed.

How does America do Step Six? I believe the facts are clear. We have committed genocide against Native Americans, we have enslaved Africans, we have pushed women to a lower-class status, and we have soiled our land and dirtied our waters and air. These and others behaviors are America's "wrongs." Nearly all of these behaviors and actions originate from ego. We have committed wrongs because of our defects of character: our fear of others who look or are different from us, our need to dominate and control, our desire to feel important, our fear of being seen as inadequate. These are some of the character defects that we Americans have, and we all need to acknowledge these character defects before they can be removed.

But, as I have said, in order to change we first must want to change. Addicts, our politicians, and the far left and far right do not want to change. *Their position is hardwired and we are delusional if we do not get the implications of this reality.* Fundamental change in America's political culture will occur only when the sane among us are willing to stand up for sanity. I believe that we humans, we Americans, have finally differentiated enough, have finally grown up enough, to have a sizeable group large enough to initiate this paradigm shift. This group, working cooperatively toward positive change, is capable of collectively removing our country's character defects.

Through our work in Step Six, both individually and as participants in the group which is cooperating to initiate positive change, we have become entirely ready to have our defects removed. This prepares us to take the next Step toward recovery, Step Seven.

12

LETTING THEM GO, STEP SEVEN

Step 7: *"Humbly asked Him to remove our shortcomings."*

As a result of working the previous Steps we have acknowledged our shortcomings, and now we are asking "Him" to remove them. Most people acknowledge that there are powers greater than ourselves: Mother Nature, Higher Power, God, Allah, The Force, etc. This Step is inviting us to find some "higher wisdom," something beyond our ego, to support the process of our development.

It has been my experience that working the Steps and practicing these principles for over three decades has moved my awareness into more of an alignment with my "higher self," what the psychologist Carl Jung called "Self." (See Diagram, following page)

Recovering addicts do this all the time. (And if these crazy people can do it, almost anyone can do it!) If we are willing to be curious, we will find a whole world of information, and large communities, supporting this process. But willingness is essential. No one will ever move from a defensive, egocentric approach unless they are willing. My life is testament to this process. For the last thirty years I have slowly been realigning a Self that had previously been formed around a broken and frightened ego. I have used the 12-Step programs, psychotherapy, workshops, retreats, vision quests, mentors, guides, and associating with like-minded folks to facilitate this process.

But it appears that most people have not made this kind of transition. All we have to do is look at our world to see that egocentrism

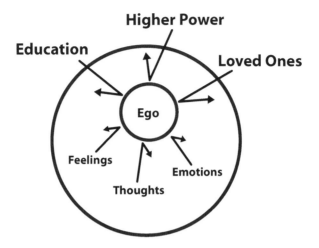

Figure 1: The Addict

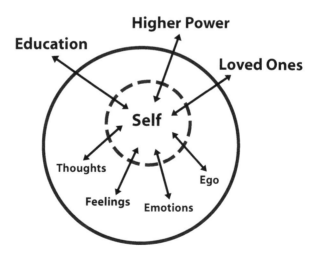

Figure 2: The Sane Person

is still the central organizing principle. The world is a true reflection of you and me, the "collective us." We Americans have indulged in unjust wars, racism, greed, deception, environmental degradation, genocide, and lies. The behavior of our oligarchy, our elected officials, special interests, and their enablers clearly are self-serving and ego-identified.

In Step Seven we ask to have our shortcomings removed, because we see clearly how they have hindered us. We can see how they can undermine the new values and lifestyle we wish to adopt.

In this Step, we solidify a fundamental change in attitude. We renew our commitment to the process of recovery as we move from being driven by survival-based and self-focused fear. We adopt a broader view of humanity and of a world in which we can embrace ourselves, others, and powers greater than our small, egoic selves. We fortify our acceptance of ourselves as growing, changing, and evolving persons. We do this by humbly turning to a power greater than ourselves. We have little to lose. We can always return to our "it's all about me" stance. But we can see that a lot of really crazy people have somehow done something that makes them smile and laugh a lot and talk about how this process has made them feel better. At some point we need to simply trust this process to improve our mental health and our relationships.

We are beginning to feel the momentum of this "letting go" process. We see that we did not die when we told our sponsor (or therapist) our shameful stuff. An excitement often occurs as we come to understand that change actually feels really *good*.

We are coming out of our defended stance and opening to an amazing world full of love and fun!

We now are aware of what it really takes to change. We have done enough personal work to realize that the addicts in our lives are not going to change. We accept this often-painful reality. They will not change unless they choose to "give up" and "do the work." And *we* can never get someone to give up their defensive position. That is a choice only they can make. *(And they will be much more likely to do this if we stop enabling.)*

The madness of the belief that we can change someone never fails to amaze me. We so want our addict to "just do the right thing," and we can spend our lifetime getting sicker and sicker as we hold onto this pathogenic desire.

We cannot change anyone other than ourselves.

The "letting go" that we do in this Step means that we accept that we are generally powerless over the outcome of our efforts, and that we are going to *trust* that things will get better. But in order to change, we must be willing to do our own footwork. Firmly grasping this perspective requires active work on our part. We need to make different choices, practice new behaviors and change how we think. We will need to continue to do the internal and external work. That is often hard, because of the addictive culture that surrounds us and urges us to stay the same. It will take commitment and follow-through, one day at a time, to continue on the path of recovery.

The authors of this Step do not expect us to rewire our brains *simply by asking.*

But we do need to start by asking. And this is the start. We can rewire our brains, just like we can rewire our homes. But it is not easy since our brain's wiring is millions of times more complex. But it is doable. Remember the exercise where you get ten million dollars if you can rewire your brains sufficiently to play the violin and speak Russian? Almost all able-bodied adults can do this. When we look around at the American population, we see that very few of us grasp the power of the brain to learn and change. Some say that we use only three percent of our brains. We all can have our character defects removed if we choose, but it takes serious daily commitment to the path of recovery for this to happen.

This is one of the miracles of addiction and recovery: If we get it, if we recognize our situation and get into recovery, we have the opportunity to launch ourselves on a path where we can actually do this "rewiring job." We cannot just "think it" and have it become true. We have to walk a different walk. I believe this quest for a Self, this rewiring job, requires a lot of muscle, and time. We need muscles to enroll ourselves in a treatment program. We need muscles to talk to counselors. We need to use muscles to walk into meetings where we gather with people in recovery. We need to use muscles to read and write as we work the Steps. We need to use muscles to move our jaws to speak. We need to *do* the behavioral part of this cognitive-behavioral rewiring job.

How willing are the elected members of this oligarchy to do this work? I think not at all. What I'm hoping is that the sane and healthy folks in America, the twenty percent who are reading this book, are willing to understand this and use their muscles to change. The Internet will allow all of us to be intimately involved in this process. The best ideas and the best people will rise to the top. And I'm hoping that this optimistic group of friendly, 40 million, gathering Americans will be so attractive that the others will be curious enough to check us out! If we can enlist them in this Intervention, I believe that it will be a no-brainer to restore sanity to our government and our nation. We will then be able to be sane stewards for our Earth and for our children.

The next Step, Step Eight will also require us to continue to use our muscles.

13

WOKE UP AND CONSIDERED OTHERS, STEP EIGHT

Step Eight: *"Made a list of all persons we had harmed, and became willing to make amends to them all."*

Up until this point in working the Steps, our focus has been on ourselves. Step Eight, however, asks us to consider the impact of our behavior on others. It is often said that the addict or codependent is a tornado in the lives of others. In Step Eight, we have the opportunity to examine the damage we've done.

I was probably eight months' sober when I got to this Step. My brain was still in the very early stages of recovery. But at least I was no longer filling it, or my body, with chemicals. Steps Four through Seven had invited me to do an inventory on myself, as well as to look at, and let go of, my defects of character.

My sponsor pointed out that my job in Step Eight was simply to make a list of those I had harmed. I was to simply write down some words on paper. I knew what the next Step was, and it scared me -- I knew eventually I'd actually have to make amends to the people on that list. But I also remembered what I had been told over and over. "Do recovery one day at a time and work the Steps one at a time. Do not concern yourself with the future. Trust that if you are present today and doing the work, you will know how to handle some future day. And if you honestly work the Step you are on, you will be able to handle the next Step when you get to it." However, staying relaxed and in the present moment is a hard call for an addict who has spent his life anxiously scanning and scheming for opportunities to get his or her "fix." I had always taken advantage of others. Suddenly being asked to be concerned about others was a new concept!

I had lied to just about everyone close to me. When I was 22, I was living with my mother and working the swing shift in a Pontiac Motors' engine plant in Pontiac Michigan. Part way through my junior year of college, the dean had suggested that a time out from school might inspire me to take college more seriously. In mid-March, Michiganders begin to look forward to the promise of spring. I was bored. I was restless. One evening, I asked my mother to borrow her car so I could drive to visit some friends at college, an hour away. At the school, I met up with my friends and we had a few beers. One of my drinking buddies and I decided on a whim to drive 600 hundred miles to see my girlfriend in Minnesota. On the way back, my friend sideswiped another car while I was making out with my girlfriend in the back seat.

When I got home, I lied and told my mother that the damage to the car "must have happened when it was parked."

I also had cheated just about every employer I had ever worked for. And I was a thief, taking things that were not given to me.

Sears Roebuck was on my list. In high school, I bought a pair of football shoes. I wore them to practice, but the team didn't have enough helmets, and I got beat up pretty bad and was done with football. I took the shoes back to Sears and demanded a refund. I had cleaned them up but it was clear that I had used them, even though I lied and said that I had never worn them. I got the refund. I had also stolen some tools from Sears once. So I put Sears on my 8th Step.

When I worked as a bartender, I stole cash from the club where I worked. When I was a taxi driver in San Francisco, I used the company's Yellow Cab for a lot of personal errands.

There was almost no one close to me that did not belong on the list.

I also began to be aware that I was codependent, although it was years before I was able to fully comprehend that concept and enter recovery for codependency. It is often said that if you scratch an addict you will find a codependent. You will find someone who is addicted to a dysfunctional relationship and who is disrespect-fully trying to "fix" or "change" or "control" another person. I dis-covered that this arrogance and disrespectful approach was just as wrong as stealing from someone; people I had treated this way also needed to go on my amends list. Everyone is entitled to a life, and I have no right to interfere with, or try to change, another person's time on this planet. They are just as entitled to life, liberty, and the pursuit of happiness as I am. Interfering with another person's serenity may be one of the biggest sins we can commit. If I don't like what someone else is doing, I always have the option to simply walk away. If I choose to stay in relationship with them, then it is *my problem*. My serenity is totally up to me.

The more I thought about it the more things went on my 8th Step list.

So, what about our nation? To whom do we need to make amends? If we believe in America, if we vote, if we call ourselves citizens, then we have a responsibility to be aware of how those we elect have behaved, and of those our country has harmed. How we will make amends is the work of the next Step, but in Step Eight we make a list and acknowledge our misdeeds.

The following is a list of just a few of those that we Americans have harmed, and that we, as citizens of America, and through those we elected, are responsible for.

Initially, those who came to American started "clearing the land" of non-Caucasians. In very few cases did we honor the Native Americans' right to own their property. We simply took it. And later we went so far as to kill them, take their children away from them, and, as mentioned earlier, sterilized their women. It is estimated that ten million Native Americans lived here when we arrived, and we have drastically reduced their population. And worse, we continue to relegate them to the status of "different" and marginalize them. Only 80 years ago, our government had a policy that allowed us to enter the homes of Native Americans and take their children. Didn't citizens of another country in Europe, 70 years ago, also enter people's homes and take people away? The Native American population goes on our 8th Step list.

Americans have engaged in the practice of "capturing" Africans as if they were animals and forcing them to comply with our wishes. The capturing and beating and raping of these humans has been a stain on our nation's spirit and continues to haunt us as a wrong that has not been fully recognized. The Africans we made into slaves belong on our list.

The ego-oriented "settlers" who murdered and stole from the original Americans and enslaved Africans also had an entitled view of women. Those who uphold patriarchy, the view of male supremacy, fail to see women as free and independent humans. In many ways, the American founding fathers' (notice, not "founding mothers!") view of women as property still reverberates in our country. Notice that the vast majority of our 536 federally elected officials are men. The same is true of the executives in Big Business and Big Union. Women also belong on our list.

It is simply wrong for the American government to believe that it can control, own, or kill other humans. But we have a rich and documented history of doing exactly that.

Here is a list of some of those America has harmed:

•Native Americans and their land.

•Africans who were sold into slavery.

•Slaves who were abused.

•Women.

•Gay men and women.

•Other minority groups.

•Mother Earth: ecosystems we've destroyed, the rivers and lakes we have polluted, the mountains we have plundered to get coal.

•The buffalo that used to roam the plains.

•The polar bears that are drowning because the icecaps are melting.

•Numerous other animals we have driven to extinction or near-extinction.

We know when we have done something wrong. We feel it in our gut. It colors our spirit and disturbs our serenity. If we want sanity in the world, we need to acknowledge that our behavior impacts others. If you have been paying attention while reading this book, you understand that collectively our behavior has had far-reaching impact on people, animals, plants, the waters, and the sky.

Step Eight asks us to make a list and "become willing" to make amends. What do you feel in your heart when you reflect on the above list of those we as a nation have harmed? Do you notice a sense of shame? Or perhaps guilt? Is there a part of you that "knows" something is just not right?

If we are able to see that America's behavior was wrong, then we need to make a decision. If we, the citizens of America, are going work these 12 Steps and be restored to sanity, then we will need to "become willing to make amends to them all."

To whom do you need to make amends? And are you willing to take out a pen and piece of paper and write down that person's or those persons' names?

Most of us have heard the story about how a butterfly flapping its wings in the Amazon initiates an aerodynamic chain reaction that could result in a typhoon in Asia. Everything affects everything. We are all standing in a galactic force field where forces beyond our awareness influence everything else. Step Eight asks us to look at the bigger picture and list our wrongs. We also need to ask the question, "What have I done to cause myself harm?" If we mistreat ourselves, we impact humanity as well. We may also need to ask, "Am I adding to the world or am I taking from it?" We can refer back to Step Four and remind ourselves of the ways we have failed to live up to our bio-psycho-social-spiritual potential. Remember that millions of people are doing their best to act with integrity and goodness on a daily basis, and we, too, can make that our goal.

Are we willing to stand up and be honest? Are we willing to summon our courage and orient ourselves toward sanity? Are we willing to face those we have wronged?

If we are prepared to take responsibility for our wrongdoing and to make direct amends to those we have harmed, we are ready for the next Step in the recovery of America's greatness.

14

RE-JOINED THE HUMAN RACE, STEP NINE

Step Nine: *"Made direct amends to such people wherever possible, except when to do so would injure them or others."*

To an addict, or a codependent, other people are too often objects to manipulate for personal gain. The addict is driven to get a "fix" through a substance or a behavior; the codependent is driven to get a "fix" by attempting to change another. We have seen how this approach has led to the corruption in our current government.

Up until this point in the Steps, we have been guided by the recovery process and counseled to keep our attention on ourselves, and to stay focused on our own recovery. The life-saving task of recovery requires our full energy and attention. We need to remove as many distractions as possible to give us the best chance of healing. Those in early recovery typically do not have the cognitive or emotional clarity yet to make rational, informed choices about big life events. Our brains' wiring is still being sorted out.

The 12 Steps were read aloud at every 12-Step meeting I attended. By the time I reached Step Nine, I had heard the Steps read many times. I could not help but notice the words, "Made direct amends." "I can't do that," I thought "I don't know how." But over and over I had heard that the task was to do one Step at a time and to trust that, when we got to the next Step, we would be able to handle it.

That turned out to be true for me. I was beginning to become ready to rejoin the human race, as a person with self-awareness and integrity. I was beginning the process of becoming an honorable person. Just beginning! I still had the baggage of decades of selfish, self-centered behavior.

One bright and clear summer Saturday, I walked into the local Sears department store to make amends for what I had stolen from them. I had a check in my pocket made out to them, for fifty dollars. I went to the main office, imagining that I would talk to the manager. I met a clerk who explained that the manager did not work weekends and asked how she could help me. Reluctantly I told her, "I'm a member of a 12-Step program and part of that program is to make amends to those we have harmed. Over the years I have stolen from Sears, and I'm here to make amends, to pay you back." She asked me to have a seat and told me that someone would see me. Shortly, a man arrived and introduced himself as the store detective. Nervously I again explained why I was there and handed him my check. He looked at the check for a long time, obviously thinking about how to respond.

I got scared. Was he going to arrest me? Would I be handcuffed and taken away? Then he looked at my eyes and said, "In the many years of doing this work, I have never had anyone do this. Thank you." Up until that point in my life I had viewed Sears negatively, as a large, faceless, corporate organization. However, on that day, I walked out of Sears with a sense of joy and relief! It was I, not they, who had created the separation and negativity. Sears is just another of God's gifts to those of us who need tools, towels, or tires. I had taken responsibility and closed the abyss that *I had created* between the individuals who own Sears and myself.

Then I drove to Safeway to make amends for stealing some cheese I had taken when I was drunk. I found the manager, who was very busy; I quickly explained my story and handed her ten dollars. She looked at me like I was a wacko, grabbed the money, and sped off.

I was warned that not everyone to whom we made amends would be grateful, or even willing to listen. I was told not to worry about that, because the amends process is not about them. It is about us. We are simply cleaning up "our side of the street." We have no control over how others will receive our amends. Their response is not our concern.

My mother was very happy to hear my amends. I explained about the car and how I was responsible for the damage. I also told her about other things as well. She was delighted that I was sober and in recovery.

What about the unfortunate, black school children I had verbally abused the day I was their teacher? What about the other drivers who shared the road when I drove drunk? What about others I had taken advantage of? My sponsor told me the way to handle these transgressions was to do a "living amends." This means that in my day-to-day actions, I should behave in an honest and honorable way. One way I do this is by seeking out and talking to newcomers at 12-Step meetings and giving them my phone number. I offer to become their sponsor or temporary sponsor, or simply be someone they can call for support. I have worked for nearly 20 years as a Marriage and Family Therapist and drug counselor specializing in family intervention and helping children recover from addiction. And I often donate my time and services to those who do not have the means to pay for help.

How can *we* make amends for the sins of our country? Actually, how can we not make amends for the sins of our nation, since our nation is simply a collection of individuals that includes you and me? If we believe in America, if we call ourselves citizens, then we have a responsibility to make those amends. Why is it that we have days set aside, celebrating the birthdays of presidents, the endings of wars, and the social and economic achievements of American workers, but no days acknowledging the harms that we citizens have done to others?

So what about *me* as a citizen of America? What is my responsibility here? What about my passive support of the insane actions of my government? I believe we have a collective responsibility to make amends for our wrongs. At the close of World War II, several international treaties specified the reparations to be paid by offending countries. Germany paid reparations to Russia and The United States, mostly in the form of machinery and manufacturing plants. Germany paid reparations to Israel and the World Jewish Congress for the Holocaust. The United States apologized to Japan for the American internment of Japanese and paid Japan reparations.

Some countries in post-war or post-trauma circumstances have set up commissions to investigate and disclose past wrongdoing by the government, and sometimes to make restitution to families and survivors of the victims of abuse. In post-apartheid South Africa, under President Nelson Mandela, a Truth and Reconciliation Commission was formed to investigate the human rights violations that occurred between 1960 and 1994. One task of the Commission was to decide how to make symbolic and financial reparations to the families and survivors of the victims. In 2008, the Solomon Islands, following the South African model, formed a commission to address the traumatic experience of the five-year conflict from 1999 to 2004 over Guadalcanal. Journalist Josh Marshall, in a 2005 Talking Points Memo, suggested that America needs a Truth and Reconciliation Commission to examine our involvement in Iraq and to expose the lies, and the lies to cover up the lies, so that we can get the truth on the table, and make amends for these wrongs.

But few governments have matched Germany's production of monuments and museums as atonement for past behavior. In Berlin, both the Holocaust Memorial and the Jewish Museum were built by the German government to express a collective amends for their mistreatment of Jews in World War II. The Germans also built memorials and museums at the site of each of the three main concentration camps.

America has built monuments as amends to its misdeeds in war as well. In the 1990s, the federal government built the National Japanese American Museum, both in apology for the unlawful internment of Japanese in World War II, and as a tribute to the Japanese American soldiers who fought on the side of the United States. Ground was broken in 2009 for a memorial on Bainbridge Island, Washington, to commemorate the almost 300 Japanese Americans who were removed from their homes in 1942. In 2005, after prolonged campaigning by the Avenging Our Ancestors Coalition, funding was granted to erect a memorial to George Washington's slaves, in the Independence Mall in Washington D.C. We need to make these amends, because, if we don't, we fool ourselves about what we have done, we rob ourselves of mental health by unconsciously carrying the shame and guilt of our behaviors, and we hand down the insanity to the next generation.

The addict is self-centered to the extreme and is highly defended. It is a sane person who is humble enough to admit wrongdoing. We are still hearing the echoes of America's wrongs. We have not yet done what is necessary to heal the open emotional wounds we created with slavery, the subjugation of women, the mistreatment of the first Americans, and the destruction done to Mother Nature.

These direct amends need to come from each of us in our own way. We each need to address the original Americans, blacks, and women, and other minorities and say, "I'm sorry. I'm sorry that we have harmed you and your people."

I would like to suggest that influential folks like Rush Limbaugh, Keith Olbermann, John McCain, Harry Reid, the leading media folks, and other public figures say something like this (although it's up to them what they choose to do):

"Folks, I need to tell you something. I have been thinking a lot about a very important topic. I know there are many people watching and listening at this moment. I need to get something off my chest.

"I could say that I was brainwashed or that 'everyone else' is doing it, but that would be copping out. No, I need to take responsibility for this, myself. I need to "man up." The reality is that I am a racist. Seriously. I don't want to return to slavery, and I do want all of us to have life, liberty, and the pursuit of happiness, regardless of skin color. I really do. But the reality is, folks, that our country is racist and I am part of this. I was programmed by America's history of racism and I need to tell you that racism is still alive and well today.

"I've come to understand that my racism is unconscious. It happens in little ways. Like how I turn away from a black person I meet in an elevator. Or deny them an opportunity to be one of my employees. Or, as I have done in the past, not acknowledge the institutional racism that I, and you, are part of.

"I need to make amends to all people of color, to Native Americans, and to women, and to gay people, and to all the others that I have marginalized.

"I need to say this, 'Madam or Sir, I am sorry. I am truly sorry for distancing from you. I am truly sorry for the way I think of you as inferior to me. I am sorry for taking so long to acknowledge this. I am sorry. And, starting today, I will consciously begin the process of rewiring my brain in ways that will acknowledge my racism, or my gender bias, or my homophobia. I will speak up and I will change. I will use my considerable influence to educate others about this abomination and will support a national movement to acknowledge our collective wrongs, through national monuments and re-writing our history books so that children will fully understand our wrongs.

I am so, so sorry.'"

In reality, we *all* need to say this.

Wouldn't that be cool! The next generation of children would grow up believing racism was a part of our past, not our present, and in time, racism would vanish from our lives (just like women not being able to vote is in our past). Let's say a prayer for the influential and the powerful, and the rest of us, to make these amends. I believe that most of us mean well, but sadly, we have not acknowledged our addictions to money, power, drugs, food, and other substances and behaviors, and are not fully sane. And as a result we unconsciously perpetuate very "Un-American" racist and biased practices. We can pray we all get into recovery. But in the meantime, we need to acknowledge that unconscious racism exists.

How can America demonstrate that it clearly understands these wrongs and make amends? One idea would be to amend the Constitution to incorporate the 12-Step model. It may seem like a radical idea, but imagine it. Perhaps we add the 12 Steps to the Constitution as a way of institutionalizing the restoration of sanity to America. Perhaps, now that we are over 200 years old, we add to the Constitution something like: "We acknowledge America has done horrible things. We have been wrong and wish to acknowledge this reality. We Americans have sanctioned genocide, murder, child abduction, homophobia, and gender abuse. We acknowledge these things so that a future America will not make these same mistakes."

We acknowledge past wrongdoing not to diminish America, but to free it to its highest potential. By atoning for past mistakes, we shed the burden of guilt and shame that can keep our nation mired in dishonor and disgrace. The symbolic reparations executed by South Africa's Truth and Reconciliation Commission strengthened that nation; similarly, America's amends can reinvigorate our country.

Perhaps we could hold a "National Amends Day" to commemorate America's wrongs. On this day we would review the horrible wrongdoing of the American government and decide what we could do to make reparations. As part of this effort, we could build a monument on the National Mall. I believe this monument needs to accurately depict the horror of slavery, our genocide of the original Americans, and the dreadful treatment of women.

For blacks, we need to make additional amends for failed reparation attempts of the past. As a part of Reconstruction efforts near the end of the Civil War, General Sherman promised to give freed blacks land from abandoned plantations -- "40 acres and a mule" -- to start a farm. But after Lincoln's assassination, President Johnson revoked the plan, and whites reclaimed ownership of the land. Many blacks went to work for the new white owners, but now worked for wages instead of being slaves. Then, "Jim Crow laws" passed in the 1870s and 1880s made conditions for blacks little better than they had been when slavery was in effect. Racial segregation was mandated, with a supposed "separate but equal" intent, but in reality, facilities for blacks were inferior to those for whites.

We need to make amends to Mother Earth. Oh my God how we have hurt her! Can we ever make reparations sufficient to restore our planet's vitality? It is impossible to remove the poisons we have put into our waterways. It is impossible to remove the mercury that is now in our soils. It is impossible to bring back the animals that are now extinct. We can only *stop doing* more harm and try the best we can to restore what we have destroyed and pray that we are not too late.

We need to make amends: to the Native Americans whose land we plundered; to minorities of all nationalities that we have mistreated; to gays and lesbians whom we have marginalized. The list goes on. Yes, America has done wonderful things but, we, the American people, have committed many wrongs. If we take responsibility for these wrongs and we elect leaders who reflect our better selves, there is bright hope for our country's future.

In Step Nine, we have the opportunity to make direct amends for past wrongs and begin to make living amends, and by changing how we act going forward. We need to do this as individuals and we need to do this as a nation.

In Step Ten, we carry this work into our present life and our future behaviors. We pay attention to our actions and make amends for mistakes as soon as we're aware of them.

In the last section of this book, Part Three, *Into Action*, I describe how we can each take initiative to create personal, national and environmental well-being. In Part Three, I will suggest what each of us can do to continue to make living amends for the wrongs we, as Americans, have committed.

15

STAYING HONEST, STEP TEN

Step Ten: *"Continued to take personal inventory and when we were wrong promptly admitted it."*

Step Nine invited us to make direct amends to those we *had* harmed. What about those people and institutions that we *continue* to harm or will harm in the future? Step Ten addresses this aspect of our recovery.

This "being human" thing is not easy. There is frequent conflict between what you want and what I want, which is natural because we are two different individuals who often have two different agendas. How could it be otherwise? But if we are responsible and sane, we will work it out. We realize that the end goal is serenity and accord, and that we need to be open to a power greater than our egos. At times we will make mistakes, but our underlying love and respect for each other, and our ability to acknowledge our errors, will move us toward resolving our conflicts.

When I was in my addiction I was often angry, and this did not change simply because I stopped drinking and taking drugs. This Step invited me to notice this and make amends when I was wrong. My anger manifested itself in my daily activities. I was usually rude to bank tellers and checkout clerks, if I had to wait in line. On a number of occasions I needed to return to the bank or store and apologize to someone I had treated disrespectfully. My anger often resulted me hanging up on people, and making amends for this behavior meant I had to call a number of people up and apologize for being rude.

The problem, as we have seen, is that most of us are not *always* sane, and that is the reason for this Step. Step Ten reminds us about what we need to do when we sense that we have erred. It reminds us that we need to take responsibility and say, "I'm sorry." And then we need to do the harder part. *We need to rewire our brains so that we don't do that behavior again.*

If we are addicts, we haven't had a lot of functional wiring or sound programming. We've been run by our midbrain's dopamine reward process and haven't spent much time living a contemplative life. If we are addicts, then we will need to do some comprehensive reprogramming to achieve sanity. Perhaps, if we don't blow it, some future Earth will be peopled by the sane. But, for the most part, it isn't us!

Neuroscientists are fascinated by how our brain works. Annually, the Dali Lama and some scientists from M.I.T. and other places, gather to study the brain, and to investigate in particular how meditation affects the brain. We know that meditation can rewire the brain in ways that will create more serenity and peace. We are unlocking many secrets of how we have become the way we are. Remember the 2nd Step? *"Came to believe that a Power greater than ourselves could restore us to sanity."* Notice that it says *"could* restore us to sanity?" I think it is nearly impossible to be completely restored to sanity in a culture with as many flaws as America has. The job is way too complex. Imagine that your job, by yourself, was to rewire the electrical system of the Pentagon, and make it work. I believe that is a fair idea of the challenge we face to rewire our brains and become 100% bio-psycho-social-spiritually sane.

We become saner bit by bit. We need the recovery process to stay on track toward sanity. This is why I continue to go to 12-Step meetings, 30 years after entering recovery. I know of hundreds of people, perhaps thousands, who have drifted away from the program and returned to their addictive behaviors; many of them died early deaths.

What about those who are codependent and the "wrong" they do by trying to "fix" or "change" another person? We see rape as a terrible act of unwanted physical intrusion on another person. Psychological intrusion on another is also damaging. If we are crazy enough to choose to be around addicts, we need to accept the simple fact that we *can't* change them and that our serenity depends on us taking care of ourselves. We will have much more serenity if we do this. There is slogan in Al-Anon: "Dial 911, step over the body, and have a nice day." How others handle their lives is their job. How we handle our lives and maximize our serenity and sanity is *our* job.

Step Ten has us look at the wrongs we commit in current time. We need to be aware and to engage in ongoing assessment and reflection about our behavior. We need to be conscious of our interactions with our partners and friends and colleagues, and with those we encounter as we go about our daily lives. And, we need to be mindful of any harm we do, and promptly admit it.

But there is a larger context. What about each of us as part of the American family? We need to look at what we are doing *today* that is supporting wrongdoing by the politicians we have elected. We need to admit our errors. And then we need to not keep doing the wrong thing, but to make a "living amends" and practice a different behavior than the one we've just admitted was wrong. Inaction when harm is being committed is no longer an option. When we choose to do nothing and to ignore the harm in our midst, we are doing harm. Moliere said, "It is not only for what we do that we are held responsible, but also for what we do not do."

Earlier in the book I described Jon Stewart's interview on *The Daily Show* with Elizabeth Warren, the individual in charge of writing regulations to protect consumers from the addicts on Wall Street. On June 7, 2011, six weeks after Warren appeared on *The Daily Show*, the *New York Times* published an article titled, "Resistance Bogs Down Overhaul of Financial Rules." We all knew *that* was coming! The addicts on Wall Street and their enablers in Congress will continue to rig the system to their advantage and to hell with the citizens, *if we continue to enable this.*

We need to face the fact in real time that we support, enable, and promote this by our passive acceptance of the status quo. Can we admit that we are wrong? Or will we sink back into our TVs, our moneymaking, and our other addictions? I believe that we need to stay awake and alert, and continually review our behavior so we can be aware of our "wrongs," and live freer, happier lives.

One day at a time, we need to admit when we are wrong.

16

FINDING OUR SPIRITUAL SELF, STEP ELEVEN

Step Eleven: *"Sought through prayer and meditation to improve our conscious contact with God* as we understood Him, *praying only for knowledge of His will for us and the power to carry that out."*

This Step asks us to pray only for "the knowledge of God's will." Does that mean I can't pray for rain? For money? To win the war? There is a running joke in 12-Step Programs about this Step. It goes like this. "Prayer works, so be careful what you pray for, because quite possibly God will give it to you. Ignoring this advice, a woman prays for a handsome man who will marry her and have kids with her. Sure enough, the handsome man shows up, they marry and they have kids. But, guess what. He is a womanizer, a drunk, and no good. So be careful about what you pray for." Perhaps we prayed to get rid of Saddam Hussein. We got rid of him, but perhaps we ended up with a much bigger mess. This Step (with its sexism) turns prayer on its head. It asks us to imagine not what we want, but what God wants. What would God want in this situation?

I was about 11 months' sober when I got to this Step, having completed the previous Steps with my sponsor at the rate of about one a month. I'm sure that this Step would not have been possible to "work," much less to understand, had I not completed the prior ten Steps. Remember that the brain of an addict is very much aligned with the small self, the ego -- and not a very healthy ego at that. I understood the world through the lens of my egoic, small, addicted self. As I worked the Steps, my brain's locus of consciousness had slowly been moving back to my rational, prefrontal cortex, and new rewiring was integrating my thinking mind with my emotions, my intuitions, my body, and my spirit. I was beginning the process of building a Self. I was slowly becoming healthier, saner. I had trusted the process and it was beginning to make more sense.

In working Steps One, Two and Three, I had "given up and surrendered." Then, in Steps Four, Five, Six and Seven, I'd been able to take an honest inventory of myself and accept my character defects and shortcomings. In Step Eight, I had acknowledged the harm I had done to others and myself. In Step Nine, I became capable of honestly looking another person in the eye and telling the truth, and in Step Ten, I learned to keep on telling the truth whenever I made a mistake. Now I was facing a quandary. What is "God's will?" How was my small self, my ego, going to grasp this?

By now I was beginning to understand that God, God's will, and spirituality are transcendent experiences, beyond the ego's ability to fully understand. Each of us may have different names for what the 12 Steps call "God" or "Higher Power": Divine Will, God Consciousness, the Greater Good, Mother Nature, The Beyond, The Force, etc. Whatever "it" is, it is beyond our ego's ability to fully grasp it. "It" includes the ego, but is more than the ego. Below is an excerpt from the book *Alcoholics Anonymous*, p. 56.

> *"This man recounts that he tumbled out of bed to his knees. In a few seconds he was overwhelmed by a conviction of the Presence of God. It poured over and through him with the certainty and majesty of a great tide at flood. The barriers he had built through the years were swept away. He stood in the Presence of Infinite Power and Love. He had stepped from bridge to shore. For the first time, he lived in conscious companionship with his Creator."*

Addicts often have drug "highs" that "blow our minds" for a brief period: our first drunk, the first time we took ecstasy, had sex with another, or felt the flood of attention from a cult or religion. However, this "high" is often not a spiritual experience; it is only the flooding of our midbrain with an excess of dopamine! We often mistake this "high" for a spiritual experience and spend the rest of our lives trying to replicate that first, unique experience.

A spiritual experience is different, and hard to describe. It can happen spontaneously. I am regularly blessed with these transcendent moments. I have stopped and watched a bug crawl or a leaf blowing in the wind and marveled at how God, or whatever, created this Universe. These moments are gifts. Mother Nature is awesome. In those brief moments, everything makes sense. I have a pervasive sense of "OK-ness." It is not a "high" feeling, but a feeling of being grounded, content and whole. Even the fact that we may be destroying the Earth and becoming extinct seems, in that moment, to be part of a grander plan for the Universe.

Step Eleven suggests using the tools of prayer and meditation to create these moments. I understand prayer as a practice of asking for guidance. I need to ask, and then listen patiently. "God's will" may not arrive on cue, and when I seek help, I need to wait for answers. Sometimes guidance comes from places we don't expect, such as from the words of a trusted friend. And sometimes it comes from an intuitive thought that arises serendipitously. This book has been like this. I woke up at 3 a.m. six months ago, with an idea that had spontaneously appeared.

As I worked Step Eleven, my sponsor suggested I get on my knees and pray twice a day. At first I balked, but I realized my sponsor's guidance had helped me get this far, so it seemed reasonable to try what he suggested. At first it was awkward, and reminded me of the craziness of my childhood experience with my grandparents. But I began to feel some benefits. When I woke up in the morning, I would get on my knees and say something like, "God, if it is your will, please help me stay sober today." That was it! Later on I would add things like, "help me be more loving" or "help me be of better service to my fellows." But it was always prefaced with, "If it is your will." And at night I would get on my knees and say "Thanks for getting me through the day, sober."

That flea on the horse (my ego) that had been barking out orders was now beginning to relax, and I was beginning to enjoy the majesty of the world unfolding around me. I could give myself a break and trust something beyond my personal desires. I came to understand and experience myself as a complex mix of mysterious parts that I was responsible for but did not always have control over. Yes, I had an ego -- my perception of myself. Yes, I had biological needs that were hardwired from millions of years of evolution. Yes, I had

the ebb and flow of my emotional self, endlessly feeding me information about the world around me as well as within me. Yes, I was
intertwined in the energy of those I am connected to. This was all
true, and yet there was something *beyond* all of this. What was *that*?

How do we handle all of this? I believe the answer is, "not easily."
I believe that life is a challenge and that we each need to find our own
path. We are each responsible for our lives. If we are addicts, we need to
get into recovery. If we are enablers, we also need to get into recovery.
Now, with Step Eleven, I was at a place in my recovery where I could
expand the spiritual aspect of myself. I was now getting to the final facet
of my life that had been damaged because of my addiction. I was now
recovering the spiritual aspect of my bio-psycho-social-spiritual self.

This Step invites us to use meditation to improve our "conscious
contact" with "God." I am blessed to live in a part of the planet
where meditation practices are part of many people's lives. The
practice of meditation has been around for thousands of years. Brain
scientists are beginning to understand what happens in the complex
cells and neuronal networks of the human brain during meditation.
Western medical research is showing that meditation can enhance
health and well-being, lower blood pressure, and reduce anxiety.

Meditation is a discipline of mindfully letting our thoughts and
feelings move through our awareness without judging or reacting to
them. It is not easy -- the mind is an infinite cacophony of conflicting and competing interests that are endlessly being cranked out.
Thinking, feeling, sensing, seeing, hearing, and intuiting are acces-
sible to us in any moment. How do we make sense of all this? How
are we not overwhelmed by it?

Meditation invites us into a practice of *focusing*. It invites us to
move to a place of paying attention to *something* so that we are not overwhelmed by *everything*. The suggested object of focus varies, according
to the particular meditation style. Some traditions suggest a focus on
the breath, others on a phrase that we repeat over and over (a mantra),
and others on an object, such as the flame of a candle.

Quieting the mind through meditation can allow intuitive
thoughts to arise. The stillness of the mind makes space for "conscious contact with God." As with prayer, meditation does not
guarantee immediate insight. However, with practice, meditation
can foster moments of calm and clarity in which we can sense our
Higher Power's "will for us."

In the last part of Step Eleven, it is suggested that we pray not only to know God's will for us, but also for "the power to carry that out." This can be a tall order. Through prayer and meditation we may get clarity or insight or direction about what might be beneficial to think or say or do, but putting this understanding into action can require commitment and fortitude. The wisdom of the Steps, however, has prepared us for this task. Through working Steps Nine and Ten, we have learned to act in honest and honorable ways, to accept our mistakes and to make amends for any wrongdoing. This last part of Step Eleven builds on these practices by helping us discern appropriate and wholesome actions *before* we carry them out. In this way, Step Eleven offers us guidance to behave in positive ways, whether we understand the guidance as coming from God or the Greater Good or Divine Wisdom or our higher Self. It gives us a moral compass so we can discriminate right from wrong and mold our actions to serve for good, rather than to satisfy selfish or smaller motives.

Following, is a prayer from the Big Book of AA:

> *"God, I offer myself to Thee – to build with me and to do with me as Thou wilt. Relieve me of the bondage of self, that I may better do Thy will. Take away my difficulties, that victory over them may bear witness to those I would help of Thy Power, Thy Love, and Thy Way of life. May I do Thy will always!"*

The reality is that a spiritual life for an addict starts with a decision. We are faced with two options. On the one hand we have our small self, our ego, our personality, and our lifetime of hardwired grey matter between our ears. On the other hand, we have the option of opening to and supporting the development of a more integrated Self. Step Eleven invites us to consciously develop this more integrated Self. As part of her ongoing research into spirituality, Colette Fleuridas, Ph.D., professor at St. Mary's College in Orinda, California, has gathered the following list of practices which can support spiritual development: (http://www.spiritresearch.org/)

• Prayer

• Meditation

• Contemplation (spiritual contemplation)

- Worship
- Devotional chanting, singing, toning, playing instruments and/ or using music or sound
- Devotional dance or ritualistic movement (such as mindful walking meditation)
- Body-mind (and/or spiritual) practice (such as hatha yoga, tai chi, or qi gong)
- Physical exercise as a spiritual practice
- Creative arts as spiritual practice
- Spending time alone in nature (with a spiritual or religious intent)
- Spending time with others in nature (with a spiritual or religious intent)
- Service to others (donating time and/or money with a spiritual/ religious intent to those in need)
- Reading spiritual or religious texts
- Listening to audio tapes and/or viewing video tapes with a spiritual or religious content
- Family rituals or spiritual activities (for example, Shabbat or family prayer)
- Community rituals (with a community of faith)
- Personal rituals (done alone)
- The spiritual or religious use of psychoactive substances (such as peyote, Ayahuasca, MDMA, LSD, or psilocybin mushrooms)
- Celebrating religious holidays
- Psychotherapy (transpersonal or depth psychology)
- Bodywork such as massage/Somatic therapy
- Attending church

Individuals who are truly on a spiritual path are interested in and practice many of the activities listed above. Mankind has consciously developed these practices over the centuries, in the quest to further spirituality. Individuals who engage in these practices understand and enjoy the bliss and joy of these experiences. In contrast, I believe that individuals who are using religion or spirituality in service of their egos are typically resistant to surrendering to the wild and wonderful world of spirituality in all its mysterious aspects.

There are many forms of spiritual experiences, but they all share a few common traits. They are beyond our ego. They involve love for self and others. And these experiences allow us to see that everything makes sense, that God's universe is unfolding exactly the way it is supposed to in this moment.

And *in this moment.*

When we are experiencing our spirituality, it is unthinkable to imagine harming another person or harming our planet or lying or cheating or selling drugs to children. When we see people engage in these destructive practices, we can be sure that true spirituality is not present.

How can America work this Step? In reality, prayer and meditation are very personal. But what if the Sane 20% actively meditated and were actively doing the work to find a spiritual basis for their lives? This would begin to move America toward a reliance on common sense and universal values, as opposed to the selfish, self-centered and egocentric behaviors of our corrupt leaders. Can you imagine what it would be like if our leaders were active meditators? I'm sure we would be in better hands if this were true. And what if our leaders declared a National Meditation Day -- a time when we would all have the opportunity to experience slowing down and being still? That would be wonderful.

17

"…IN ALL OUR AFFAIRS," STEP TWELVE

Step Twelve: *"Having had a spiritual awakening as the result of these Steps, we tried to carry this message to alcoholics, and to practice these principles in all our affairs."*

Did Step Twelve really say that? Did it really say, *"Having had a spiritual awakening?"* How can they infer that we would get to Step Twelve and be able to say that we've had a spiritual awakening? I was working on Step Twelve when I celebrated my one-year sobriety birthday. I'd had no drugs or alcohol for a year. I had been to over three hundred and sixty-five 12-Step meetings that year. I had met with my sponsor over a hundred times. I had invested a lot of time in studying and practicing the first 11 Steps.

I was having a lot of experiences that were new, but were they spiritual? It is said that if we enter recovery "we will feel better." What is often left out is that we will feel *everything* better, the good and the bad. Recovery had taken me on a roller coaster, through the unknown and into many new experiences.

Step Twelve was asserting that I was "spiritually awake." I was certainly a lot more clear-headed and aware than I'd been 12 months earlier. I had prayed and meditated, and I had experienced times when I felt guided by intuitive thoughts much wiser than those my marginally healed, thinking brain had been generating. I had moments when it seemed that time slowed down, and I felt peaceful and OK with the world. This being awake to the wonder of the surrounding world was something I had long forgotten. The world softened. I was relaxing into an easy acceptance of others. As I became a trustworthy person myself, I began to trust others as well.

I began to realize that inside me, a light was coming on that had not been on before. I had been a deeply flawed person, but the 12-Step work I had done was, in fact, bringing more and more sanity to my life. As I watched myself telling my story to a newcomer, I began to realize that I had principles that would guide me. I had a network of individuals to lean on to help prevent me from returning to addiction and my ego-centered lifestyle. My midbrain was no longer running the show. And when I was self-centered and made a mistake, I usually was quick to make amends. Looking back, I could see that I would go days without the depression, isolation, and fear that had formally enveloped my life. I realized that I was experiencing a new reality, something that I had never felt or experienced before.

I did continue to have bouts of depression and self-centered behaviors. But I now had tools to better manage these times. When I "relapsed" into egocentric behaviors I would use the tools of recovery. Did I need to make amends to someone? Did I need to make a "program call" and consult with another recovering person? Did I need to reach out to professional help for issues that were bothering me? Would spending some time with a newcomer help put my situation into perspective and remove my suffering? Would reading inspirational literature inspire me? Did I just need to go a meeting, where the fellowship would remind me that I was an accepted member of a loving community?

I was able to see the progression of my consciousness (See diagram). I had been a shutdown, defended, frightened, egocentric man who had just been barely surviving. I had cut myself off from love, spirit, and new information. Slowly I was letting go of many of my addictive behaviors and was allowing the program of recovery to show me a path toward wholeness. I could see that there was much beyond just me. Others mattered, and I opened to them and let them in. I no longer needed to filter information to fit my ego's needs and was able to see that the world was full of amazing and wonderful realities waiting to be discovered. No longer did I block my emotions. I let go and allowed these energies to flow at will. And at times, this wonderful experience would flow over me and cause me to say something like, "Oh my God!" as I was suffused with experiences that I had never had before.

I came to call these moments a spiritual awakening. Yes, I had had similar experiences while taking psychedelic drugs in the 1960s, but they were transitory and always left me with some sort of hangover. What I was now experiencing was just pure delight. Looking back, I could see that I was in the process of developing, or building, what Carl Jung called, a "Self." For longer and longer moments I was aware and allowed the free flow of aliveness within me. My emotions, my feelings, my thoughts, were freely flowing and I was aware of them all happening in the same moment! I could choose to be selfish and egocentric, or not. I was allowing information, undefended connection with others, and something indescribable, to enter my awareness. It is the ability to be undefended and open to all of this at the same moment that I believe describes mental health.

No longer was I driven by my midbrain's need for dopamine -- I was no longer addicted to substances. No longer did I need to defend some crazy belief to justify my actions. No longer were most of my "friends" other addicts.

My life was becoming truly amazing, and I reveled in the newness of it.

But at times, I would regress. I would find myself terribly unhappy and depressed, and I would realize that I had regressed back into my closed-down, defended, egocentric self. I would sometimes find myself just as miserable, even suicidal, as when I was drinking. Actually, my sober years have been a process of moving from the darkness to the light, with regular regressions back to the darkness. In these periods of darkness, my self-centered approach would cut me off from love, connection, and spirituality.

Over time, and with the help of psychotherapy I was able to identify more and more unconscious material that was still impacting me. I had not have had solid, sane, and sober parents to guide me, and so I grew up with some odd views of how to be relationship. Today, three decades later, I still have dark times, but they are much less frequent. And joy and delight, and an awareness of a power greater than myself, have become the norm for me.

I believe that we can all live sane, spiritual, loving, and fun lives. We need to have been lucky enough to have families of origin who modeled this for us, or we need to roll up our sleeves and do what is necessary to "grow up" into high-level wellness.

Clearly the people who make up America have elected officials who do not come close to embodying this level of consciousness. And these leaders reflect the low standards of we, the electorate, who enable our current situation.

Within the first weeks of sobriety the old-timers were advising me to "carry the message" of sobriety to the newcomers. At first it seemed awkward to do this. What did I know compared to the others, many of whom had been sober for many years? They reminded me that the point was not necessarily to help the new guy as much as it was to help me. In fact, reaching out and offering help to the newcomer *as a way for me to stay sober* was a common suggestion.

I had heard repeatedly that "the only way you keep what you have is to give it away." And it was others carrying the message to me that resulted in me getting clean and sober. I would not have known about 12-Step programs without the woman in white who had talked to me about them when I was in a stop-smoking program, or the person on the phone, months after that, when I called a 12-Step Program. I might never have gone to a meeting had some addict not offered to come pick me up and drive me to my first one. I might not have gone back to a meeting the next day, if recovering addicts had not invited me to go out to coffee after that first meeting.

I understood that working with new members was important. What I came to understand was that helping newcomers kept *me* sane and sober. Times were not always good, and I had many really tough periods in my years of recovery. I was told that a very helpful tool for tough times was to work with a newcomer, someone who is just beginning to consider the possibility of looking at his or her addictions. Sometimes, when I was depressed or anxious, I would go to a meeting and talk to the new guys for awhile. *It always helped me.* Ultimately, that is the core of the 12-Step programs, actively helping others *in order for me to stay sane.* My sponsor told me a story about taking newcomers home and letting them sleep on his couch. He said they stole his clothes and burned holes in his couch, "but it was always successful." "You mean they all stayed sober?" I said. "Oh no," he laughingly replied, "But I did!" He carried the message to these folks in order to stay sober *himself.*

The reality is that we can carry the message to other *practicing addicts*, if they are willing to hear it. It is futile to try to carry the message to an addict in denial. The very last thing an addict wants to hear is talk about their addiction, because their "medicine" is what is allowing them to get through the day. As we take initiative through the actions outlined in the last section of this book, we will be carrying the message *to those who are willing to see that we have a problem*, curious about the solution, and then willing to stand up for change and sanity.

It is pointless to try to carry the recovery message to our elected officials, Big Business, Big Union, and the people on the far right and far left. (Remember, we cannot change anyone else, only ourselves.) We can hope that they will awaken to the reality of the harm they are doing. We can hope that they get into recovery themselves. But if we approach them, we can be sure that they will only get more defensive. We can invest our money and energy and votes in people and causes that are aligned with: preserving the earth and helping those in need; eliminating prejudice; providing healthy food for children; reducing our carbon footprint on the planet. But we cannot change the addicts.

The last part of Step Twelve directs us to *"practice these principles in all our affairs."* These principles, these 12 Steps, provide us with a solid foundation for choosing right action. They guide us to be honest, awake and aware, and to seek to do good in *all* our affairs -- from thanking the mailman to buying organic food to minimizing our gas use and reducing our carbon footprint. Mother Teresa said, "Do not wait for leaders; do it alone, person to person."

We need to practice these principles in areas where we can have impact beyond our immediate lives. Asking ourselves: what can we do for the planet; what we can we do for our country; what we can do for people in need? The words of John F. Kennedy are as apropos today as they were fifty years ago: "Ask not what your country can do for you -- ask what you can do for your country." And quoting Mother Teresa again, "If you can't feed a hundred people, then just feed one."

It starts with us. We need to take care of ourselves personally, and extend that care to every other aspect of our lives that touches others and the world we live in. Elizabeth Kubler-Ross said, "As far as service goes, it can take the form of a million things. To do service, you don't have to be a doctor working in the slums for free, or become a social worker. Your position in life and what you do doesn't matter as much as how you do what you do." And John F. Kennedy, "One person can make a difference, and everyone should try."

"Practice these principles in all our affairs" is the suggestion, and that includes our political lives. If we are to make a difference, we adults need to take responsibility for our behaviors. We citizens of America are responsible to do our best to make America the best it can be. We can't shirk this. We don't have a choice. We must care about each other, the world our children will live in, and Mother Nature.

Sadly, the political reality has been depressing, and many of us have opted out. We don't see a reason to vote because both parties seem so corrupt and clueless. The next part of this book explains how each of us can really make a difference. It invites all of us to imagine that we actually are each part of a sane group of people who, if all of us joined together, could actually remove every single elected official and start over. We really could have an America that was restored to sanity. And if we have been restored to sanity, what kind of political reality would we like? If the majority of Americans actually believed in this, we could pull off the American Revolution 2.0.

This year, we are aware of the 10th anniversary of the 9/11 attacks. One of the remarkable stories from that nightmare was the decision of one person on United Flight 93, the plane that crashed in Shanksville, Pennsylvania. One American realized that the hijackers were planning to crash the plane into some important target. That one person spoke up in a way that got another person, and then another, to hear him. And then, together, they stood up and risked everything in an attempt to do the right thing.

You and I are in an equally dire situation. Do we let the oligarchy in power continue to drive America and Earth off a cliff into an insane drunken stupor? Or do we speak up and then stand up? Do we, this 40 million, *get* that we can take control of America?

I say, let's do it!

The next section is about *how* you and I can make that happen.

PART THREE

18

GUIDING PRINCIPLES

What distinguishes human beings from other animals is their larger and more developed cerebral cortex. The human brain is capable of amazing feats, both good and bad. On one hand is the brilliance of Beethoven, Michelangelo, and the folks who got us to the moon. On the other hand is the work of Hitler, the KKK, terrorism, and the acts that have led to environmental neglect. Some of us use our minds to create wonder and joy and harmony; and some of use our minds to create division, pain, and suffering.

This dichotomy is reflected in the behavior of our nearest relatives, the Chimpanzee and the Bonobo. Bonobos are matriarchal and live in peace. Baby Bonobos can completely depend on their elders to protect them and provide them with a safe and sane environment to grow up in. It is as if this tribe has positive guiding principles that inform their actions. The Chimpanzee, on the other hand, is patriarchal and will murder and rape its own kind. Baby Chimpanzees live in a world that is not safe or sane. We see this "Chimpanzee behavior" all around us. Babies born in Israel and Palestine are subjected to endless terror and insanity. The (mostly) men in these nations seem to be driven by ego and have failed to grasp simple and sane principles. The leaders in these countries behave like Chimpanzees. The children in these two countries would be much better off if their parents switched to a new paradigm, one that resembles a Bonobo-like society where the leaders are guided by sane principles.

There are many examples of large social groups that are guided by sane and healthy principles instead of being led by individuals with personal agendas. The recovery community is an example of this.

When we have principles that are sane, principles that we place ahead of our ego's need for control, we have the opportunity to provide safety for our children. I believe providing safety for our children needs to be our bottom line. If our behavior puts children at risk then, I believe, we are behaving like the Chimpanzee. America's mostly patriarchal leaders lack healthy principles. They have put our planet and all of us in dire jeopardy. This is why it is imperative that those who comprise the sane middle of America -- not the extremists on the right and left -- get off their duffs, stand up for sanity, and replace all 536 leaders.

I propose the following general principles to guide Americans and America's new, sane leaders:

- Each of us understands that we are temporary stewards of the Earth. Each of us understands that we must labor to keep the planet unharmed for future generations. Providing for the welfare of the planet is the job of each of us, and every physical act by any one of us is undertaken with the planet's welfare foremost.

- Each of us looks around and becomes aware of the damage that has been done to the planet, and each of us actively works to repair the damage. Each of us will aim to have a small and sustainable footprint on the planet.

- Each of us puts the welfare of children ahead of everything. Every government regulation is based on protecting the welfare of children.

- Each of us does what we can to protect children from negative influences, including drugs, violence, exposure to upsetting images, and being raised by neglectful parents.

- Elected officials agree neither to accept any campaign donation from any business, nor to accept any contribution of over $100 from any individual.

- Each of us honestly strives to understand and respect the underlying values and strengths of both ends of the political spectrum, the left and the right, and to use only positive language in our political statements.

- Each of us seeks to understand how our greed and addictions to alcohol, drugs, spending, hoarding, gambling, electronic screens, sex, food and power keep us from living a full life and prevent us from serving our children and the planet.
- Each of us acknowledges that every human being is prone to addiction. We will honestly examine ourselves and our behavior, and if we recognize that we have any kind of addiction, we will enter recovery, for our own sake and for the sake of those who love us; for America, and for the planet.

We are only recently coming to understand how we humans are prone to addictions that distract us from being able to maintain our principles. As a recovering addict, I know well how this works. Addicts have Chimpanzee-like behaviors. We are self-centered, and will lie, cheat, steal and even murder, rape, and start wars in service of our addictions. Before I began my recovery, I had no principles except the ones that justified my insane addictive behavior.

If our country is going to provide the optimal environment for children to thrive, and is going to contribute to the restoration of the planet, America's addicts need to sober up and get into recovery, or get out of the way. And the enabling codependents need to "sober up" and cross over the line into recovery as well before any fundamental change can occur. As stated elsewhere in this book, I believe that the majority of Americans suffer from addictions or from the effects of living close to an addict. My hope is that these addicts and codependents first recover from their addictions and their codependency. The principles outlined in the 12 Steps have effectively restored millions of addicts to sanity for nearly eight decades. I believe that these principles provide a design for living that can help guide every one of us toward creating a sane and sustainable world.

THE TWELVE STEPS OF ALCOHOLICS ANONYMOUS

1. We admitted we were powerless over alcohol -- that our lives had become unmanageable.
2. Came to believe that a Power greater than ourselves could restore us to sanity.

3. Made a decision to turn our will and our lives over to the care of God, *as we understood Him.*

4. Made a searching and fearless moral inventory of ourselves.

5. Admitted to God, to ourselves, and to another human being the exact nature of our wrongs.

6. Were entirely ready to have God remove all these defects of character.

7. Humbly asked Him to remove our shortcomings.

8. Made a list of all persons we had harmed, and became willing to make amends to them all.

9. Made direct amends to such people wherever possible, except when to do so would injure them or others.

10. Continued to take personal inventory and when we were wrong promptly admitted it.

11. Sought through prayer and meditation to improve our conscious contact with God, *as we understood Him,* praying only for knowledge of His will for us and the power to carry that out.

12. Having had a spiritual awakening as the result of these Steps, we tried to carry this message to alcoholics, and to practice these principles in all our affairs.

(Copyright A.A. World Services, Inc.)

19

REAL REPUBLICANS AND REAL DEMOCRATS

I am very hopeful. I visualize a very different paradigm, a completely different America, as a result of this Intervention. We have seen, in the last section, how an ego-oriented, self-centered addict can change. We have seen how addicts can enter recovery and transform their very nature. These recovering addicts choose to follow a simple path that leads to a transformation. They move from insanity to sanity. We have seen how this process of transformation can be applied to addicts and, by extension, to America. We have seen that when we adhere to sane principles we behave sanely.

And we see that nearly every single elected official, left and right, has sold out America to those who fund their elections. We have seen how money interests, Big Union, and Big Business have purchased their special tax deals and subsidies and protections and lucrative contracts. We have seen how this oligarchy, less than 1% of America, hold the levers of power and dictate the agenda for the rest of us. And how this agenda is bankrupting us, killing our children, and has put our planet at risk. We see how this oligarchy, and the individuals who are part of it, meet the criteria for addiction. We see their *loss of control* over caring about the future. We see their *craving* for "more," at the expense of sanity. We see the *adverse consequences of their behavior* all around us. And, their behavior is *chronic*. Those who comprise the 1% have always seen to it that they got more and kept more than the majority of U.S. citizens.

But I see the best in us, and I wish to disprove Einstein's view that we will destroy ourselves. Primatologist Franz De Waal's brilliant work on primates, I believe, illustrates the core question that humans need to face. Did we humans, and more specifically, did we Americans, evolve from the often-murderous, patriarchal Chimpanzee, or did we evolve from the loving, matriarchal Bonobo? The history of the world has many examples of both forces at work. We have seen angry Americans who are highly defended and seem ready to strike. Children raised in these homes are exposed to objectifying, egocentric talk of "us vs. them" and "the enemy." These adults allow their children to be exposed to violence, killing, and separation. There are also many large communities where children grow up and see adults lovingly interacting, warmly embracing, peacefully celebrating, and adults who protect them from violence and negativity.

Much of America's, and the world's past, has been about power, ego, greed, and "me." This has led to amazing wealth (billionaires), amazing accomplishments (men on the moon), and amazing minds (Einstein, Dali Lama, Steve Jobs). It has also led to a world where billionaires fly in their private, carbon-burning jets, while many of their brothers and sisters starve to death. This approach has led to 1% of Americans setting in motion forces that could drive our country into bankruptcy and the planet into mass extinction.

We have reached a point in our evolution where we are ready for a new political paradigm. What passes for grown-up political parties today is a joke, and anyone who is awake knows it. We can do better. These elected officials have brought us to the edge of financial collapse, runaway spending, high taxes, terrorism, unworkable health-care plans, toxic food, environmental damage, crowded prisons, homelessness, joblessness, and worse. They rig the system so that our only choice is to vote for them over and over again -- or, not vote. In June 2011, one pundit said it might already be too late to run alternative candidates on November 6, 2012 -- this was 17 months before the election!

We have been watching the Arab Spring Uprisings bring down corrupt governments. It is time for our American Fall/Winter/Spring/Summer Uprising. It is time for America to recover the moral high ground. As a country, we need to go to the streets and let our officials in Washington know that we see their game and we are done with it. Even if there *are* honest politicians, they need to sit on the bench for a few innings. Collectively, all 536 of them have failed, and we need to *recall and replace all of them in this coming election cycle.*

We have a great system. America got it right over two hundred years ago. A sane, Democratic government, elected by sane voters, is the ultimate political system. Our institutions are sound. Our Constitution has worked well. The two-party system seems, by and large, to be a good arrangement. We are a proud, strong, and brave country. But we are human and we have our faults. Over the years, we have endorsed some stupid and ignorant practices, including slavery, terrorizing the original Americans, and denying women equal rights. But we changed. We have made progress in some areas, and have seriously messed things up in others. And now it's time for another change. I believe that enough Americans have sufficiently evolved to take this country to the next level.

Numerous recent events have turned the world upside down. Technology has turned on the lights and the microphones, and we all can see that the Emperor has no clothes. He is naked. We see that nearly all of our elected officials in Washington meet the criteria for addiction. They have lost their moral compass. They have become dishonest, immoral, and unethical. We cannot say that they are sane. Many of them went to Washington as good people, but the political system in Washington is corrupt. In order to stay in office, elected officials have had to raise huge amounts of money to buy campaign ads and finance their re-election campaigns. To get money, they have sold out to Big Business, Big Union and the hyper-wealthy. They have given tax breaks and regulation favors to these special-interest groups who have turned around and given the elected officials the money to run their re-election campaigns.

The whole thing is too rotten to try to fix from within the system. Listening to them "debate" makes me want to clean my garage. Our political debates remind me of the conversations at 2 a.m. in any local bar. They are debating while the Titanic is about to go down. We simply need to say "enough" and pick another group of leaders to try to fix this. The local PTA, fire department, or supermarket employees would do better!

Seriously, don't you agree? I may sound outraged, and I am.

I remember a wonderful ad I saw on TV several years ago. In the ad, firemen are running Congress. They are all in their chairs, wearing their fire-fighting gear. An old, gruff, Irish Captain stands at the podium and asks in a loud voice, "Who wants clean water?" The 435 firemen loudly and in unison say, "Aye." The Captain says, "Opposed?" There is silence. He waits a moment and pounds the gavel down. "Passed. What's next?" End of ad.

We all know we have a water problem. We simply need to fix it.

These nitwits in Washington hire tens of thousands of bureau-crats to come up with the same answer that you, I, and a bunch of firemen *already know*! And then they form a bunch of committees to discuss the *merits* of clean water, and then, these elected officials go behind closed doors, ignore the scientists, and do what Big Business tells them to do (keep dumping pollutants in the water to protect "economic growth").

And most of America does not see a problem here!

But 20% of us do see this and are sickened. *We* need to get past our anger, and that means that we need to act. We need to stand up, like aggrieved people around the world have always done. We need to make this Intervention a reality. We need to peacefully go to the streets. We need to peacefully voice our displeasure. That is the first thing we need to do. But the second thing must happen at the same time. We must be ready to stand up and serve our country, like honorable Americans have done throughout our history. We must be ready to run for President, Senator, and Representative. And we need to do the same at our state and local government levels.

And we won't need "them," the moneyed interests, to fund our elections. The media will run the story *for free!* Imagine 40 million people going to the street. That would be news! No strings attached, no favors owed, no campaign donations needed, to get on the eve-ning news!

We need to trust this. We now have Facebook, Twitter, and 24-hour news cycles. We have websites like www.opensecrets.org, that tell us who the Washington officials owe favors to. If we all run for office, we need to trust that the best of us will rise to the top. And we surely could not do any worse than the current crop of lying, cheating, stealing officials who treat us like we are clueless oafs. Sorry, we are Americans, and we know bullshit when we see it and this is clearly bullshit. It's time to tell it like it really is.

I know. Some of you may be thinking, "What about so-and-so? I like him or her." No. I believe we need to have a "restart," and begin with a clean slate. If your favorite person is really good, we will know it. But think about this. Right now, today, government-sanctioned, coal-burning plants are spewing tons of mercury into our environment. Today! Has your favorite politician been *screaming and yelling* and frantically telling everyone who would listen about this murderous practice? I'm sure not hearing him or her.

Some of my Democratic friends, and some of my Republican friends, are upset at me, because I tell them that their favorite candidates are accepting bribes from special lobbies. Both parties actively support the removal of Pennsylvania mountaintops to mine coal that heats the environment and puts mercury and CO_2 in the ecosystem, so that these politicians can get money from the coal miners' union and the mine owners. Some Democrats immorally and unethically accept money from the teachers' union, money that protects bad teachers. The Democrats write regulations favoring Big Law, to get the kickbacks. Democrats put their hand out and take millions of dollars from Big Oil, and overheat the planet. The Republicans do the same, except their funding is skewed toward Big Business. None of this is news. These facts have been in our papers and on the evening news for years.

Only enablers in denial could know the above and think it is "OK." It's not. Seeing the truth and not saying anything in order to protect the addict is enabling. The highly respected U.S. Attorney, Patrick Fitzgerald said the following, "You either speak up and do something about it, or you are part of the problem. That's the only way to look at it." That's why we need to see the truth *and* become ready to stand up and take action. As an Interventionist, I know the entire addictive system must collapse in order to create the space for a new paradigm to emerge. It won't work to keep "some of the old" and try to meld it into something new. ("Half measures availed us nothing." From the book, *Alcoholics Anonymous*.)

No. They all have to go. Keep it simple. This is our country, not theirs. They had their chance and *this* is what they have given us. It is time for the 99% of American citizens not in office to take part in this Intervention.

As part of this new paradigm, let's rethink the nature of our political parties. I've gone to the Republican and Democratic Party websites, trying to find out what they stand for. Take a look yourself. What's there is a bunch of gobbledygook. I know what they stand for. But I don't think *they* know what they stand for! They are like the alcoholic, frantically trying to say just the right words to get you to buy their story, but when you really pay attention, it does not make any sense.

I believe that Republicans stand for personal responsibility and self-reliance. They uphold the integrity and honor of the individual man or woman, who is strong and independent and responsible. The Republican Party endorses the ideals of self-sufficiency and local government. They believe that every able-bodied man and woman must pull their load, no freeloaders. And they uphold the American values of standing up for our country, and even putting their lives on the line to protect these values and our country.

I believe that the Democrats stand for taking care of those in need, the elderly, the disadvantaged, and the children. They sanction using a central government to protect the little guy and to see that business does not hurt the people. They see the good of the larger communities and the role of government in supporting the development of every single individual. They see these larger communities' roles in making sure that everyone has access to health-care, safe working conditions, and education. And they uphold the American values of standing up for our country, and even putting their lives on the line to protect these values and our country.

Which group did you identify with? If you had to pick one right now, which would you choose? Do you lean to the right or the left?

I have to admit that this is a test. I'll let you in on my agenda in a minute.

But which party did you pick? You may think of yourself as an Independent, but I'll bet you did lean toward one of the two parties above. So, if you had to choose, which one would you pick?

OK. Now I'm going to put on my Family Therapist hat and give you a lesson in mental health and what makes good families.

When it comes to relationships, every one of us has two goals. And these goals are in conflict with each other. On one hand, each of us needs to take responsibility for ourselves. If we are adults, no one can or should take care of us. At the same time, each of us must "work things out" with those we are in relationship with: our parents, spouse, children, neighbors, fellow workers, and countrymen. Family therapists call this "the differentiation of self, while in relationship." It turns out that there is no limit to our personal power, personal agency, and autonomy. And there is also no limit to how close, loving, and emotionally available we can be with another person. If we are in an emotionally close relationship, we have to deal with endless conflicts because each person is different. Balancing these conflicting needs is the challenge that every person faces, every day. People in healthy relationships will always find a way to work things out and have fun.

A good example of this happens in families with teenagers. Children need parents who will guide them and keep them safe, and who will set boundaries and say "no" when it is appropriate. Upon entering adolescence, a child naturally begins to become more independent. The teen's drive for independence often conflicts with the parents' need to keep their teen safe. We want teens to stand up for themselves and to desire freedom. And we want loving parents to say "no" when they feel the teen is getting too out-of-bounds. This process naturally leads to conflict. But in a healthy family, the conflicts get worked out and the teen learns about both boundaries and independence.

We want families who will support the individual development of each of their members (the Republican in each of us that leads to self-reliance). And we want families who will support emotionally close and intimate family relationships (the Democrat in each of us striving for cohesion and intimacy with another).

Are you getting it? The core values of both the Republicans and the Democrats are right! Re-read the above paragraphs that describe the two parties. Both of them are right! They just are advocating for different aspects of behaviors found in functional families and functional relationships.

Our current leaders are not functional. Like all addicts, their dysfunction is glaring and obvious. The fact that they are putting each other down, instead of working things out, is a big clue to their dysfunction.

One of the reasons they have strayed so far from healthy values is that the 1% with the money, property, and power have wielded a disproportionate influence over the population. The 1% in power have influenced our democratic governments since we started, even though our founding fathers offered a process that, in theory, gives the power to the people. The problem has been that greed and addictive behaviors have led to corruption and a failure to reach the ideal offered by the founding fathers.

But something has changed. I believe that a combination of America's psychosocial development, the technological revolution, and factors that I don't understand have brought us to a "tipping point." I believe that America is ready for an Intervention on this system, and a new start that will lead us to a much saner democracy.

Of course we all support self-reliance and autonomy, and of course we all want intimacy, connection, and emotional availability. Who could be against any of these things?

Healthy people embody aspects of both parties. We need to support the core goals of both Republicans and the Democrats.

We can no longer support the current politicians who masquerade as "Republicans" and "Democrats." They have forgotten who they were and what they stood for when they got all mixed up with the fat cats, backroom deals, and lobbyists. They have lost their way.

We all need to support Republicans, as the guardians of individual rights and the sentinels who will support and encourage personal development. There are a lot of individuals who understand this and who would be much better Republicans than those who are currently serving. Almost any good teacher or family therapist would be a "good enough" Republican leader. These folks naturally support the personal growth and the self-sufficiency of the individual.

And we really do need to reduce Washington's role in our lives. Our government has become like a giant octopus that sucks money from us. The first President Bush gave a great analogy for the problem with the federal government. The following is the example he used:

Most of us have water heaters that heat our shower water. We go to the shower, turn the faucet, wait a minute; hot water comes out. That's an example of local government. Now imagine that the knobs for the hot water were on a water heater located two floors below, in the basement. We would go to the basement to turn the knob. Climb the stairs and see if the water is the right temperature. If the water were too hot or cold, we'd need to go back to the basement and adjust the faucet, perhaps multiple times. And then when we were done we would need to go back to the basement again to turn off the water.

This, said the senior President Bush, is how the Federal government fails at things that should be done at the local level.

We need to move more of the Federal government's services to the local level. We all could be more Republican, more self-sufficient, and more adult. We need to see that "Big Daddy Washington" is not the answer. Sorry. This means that many of us will need to grow up and become more adult. There should *never* be politicians or a lobby that supports those who play victim (and there are millions of Americans who currently are playing the "game" of "victim." Everyone needs to stand up and pitch in, even if it is only volunteer work planting many millions of trees to suck up carbon dioxide).

And if a business is acting irresponsibly, we will need the Democratic part of us (that says "we are all family") to come in and police the criminal businesses (and there are many thousands of these businesses who pollute, etc.) Some examples of this Democratic side being engaged include: the Clean Water and Clean Air initiatives; or the laws that protect us from lead in paint, or asbestos in insulation. We want a vibrant, free market that allows for innovation and supports business, but we want the common welfare to be protected, also.

We need to support the Democrats as guardians of the general welfare. We need to support that healthy aspect in all of us to protect the family, in this case, the American family. We need to see that our children get adequate education and health-care. Almost any healthy grandmother would make a much better President, Senator, or Representative than the power-hungry, greedy, money addicts we currently have in office.

So we need both of these parties, working together for the best outcome.

But instead of being our humble servants and serving America, our current leaders are driven more by greed than morality. They are obsessively and compulsively lying, cheating, and stealing from us. Right now, they are acting like the out-of-control kids in the book *Lord of the Flies*. It is truly embarrassing to watch, which is why many educated citizens are too frustrated to even get angry. It really is that insane.

Would you invest a few hours a month to restore our country to sanity? Imagine a million people who felt the same way. Imagine if this American Revolution 2.0 "went viral" and *five* million people went to the streets. Imagine *fifty* million people showing up and laughing at the clowns in Washington. And imagine five million people running for office! Yes, *you* for President! Yes, *you* for Senator and Representative. Imagine if everyone showed up and brought sanity back to Washington and local government. Imagine everyone standing up for America!

We can do this. We can take back our country.

Something like this Intervention has already happened many times in the history of the world. The Velvet Revolution occurred when millions went the streets and overthrew the communist government in Czechoslovakia in 1989. The Orange Revolution occurred when people went to the streets in 2004 and forced a corrupt government in Ukraine to re-do a rigged election. Gandhi led millions in non-violent protests that led to India's independence in 1948. Martin Luther King, Jr., inspired by Gandhi's non-violent approach of publicly demonstrating, led America to sweeping changes in our laws, and a public recognition of our institutional racism.

Last October, my wife and I, and 200,000 people, went to the Washington D.C. *Rally to Restore Sanity*. That event was an inspiration, along with what has happened in the Middle East, for the creation of this book. This gathering, organized by comedians Jon Stewart and Stephen Colbert, was dedicated to countering the craziness and insanity that we are all seeing. It also called on us to renew rational conversation at a national level. Two hundred thousand people showed up on the National Mall, with banners and cameras, and peacefully sang, and laughed, and talked, and listened to bands and speeches by Jon Stewart and Stephen Colbert. And, we *had fun*. Americans like to have fun. We are a joyful and loving group of folks.

We need to do it again. And we need to tell our friends to show up. Tell your good friends you want them to run for office. We can do this thing. We have reached the tipping point. It is happening all around the world. The news is coming faster and faster. We are getting linked up, more and more.

We need to have honorable Republicans who understand their task and are ready to serve our country. We need to have honorable Democrats who understand their task and are ready to serve our country. And we need to get off the fence! We all are for healthy families, and we are all for strong, healthy individuals. I suggest, to really and fully comprehend this paradigm, that you switch parties. It *really* doesn't matter!

Seriously, if the core values of both parties were to represent the two different aspects of a healthy person and a healthy family then why would you not support both of them? We need to get rid of our pathogenic beliefs from the old paradigm. We need to toss them aside and allow the possibility of a very different political system, in which both parties disagree and struggle with each other as they press their agenda. But at the end of every day, they embrace each other and laugh, because they see the other party is also right!

Take a moment. If you can't really imagine yourself in the other party, seeing the rationale of both parties, you are not getting the full picture of this paradigm shift. You may still be identified with your party and rationalizing the process to "push your agenda."

Perhaps it would be helpful to imagine re-naming the parties. The Democrats could become the "Family Party," and the Republicans could become the "Personal Responsibility Party," and all serious adults would support both parties' goals. But renaming them may be further down the line. This Intervention will be upsetting enough without trying to also create new political parties. But maybe, after things settle down, in a few election cycles, we could actually re-name our political parties to reflect new political and democratic realities that are based on sound mental health practices.

Each of us must grow up and take responsibility, and wisely support healthy Democrats fulfilling their mandate, and healthy Republicans fulfilling their mandate.

It's time for a change! It is time for an Intervention.

And it is time to start thinking about the wisest among us whom we would love to see as our next elected officials. Seriously. Do this. Dream big. Our next leaders are folks that are not currently on the political stage. We may not even know who they are, and, for sure, we have not imagined them as political leaders.

Until now.

Here are a few examples of potential future leaders that may never have been considered. Recently, there was an American citizen, on the cover of China's edition of *Newsweek*. He was described as China's "most influential foreign figure." He is like a rock star, and people scalp tickets to see him in Japan, South Korea, and China. 15,000 Harvard students have taken his class on "Justice." Can you imagine this brilliant and popular man as the President of the United States? His name is Michael J. Sandel.

Another man has been judged as the "most trusted newsman in America" and is passionately followed by a highly educated group of people who are turned off by the "lame stream" media. They trust his quirky, but deadly accurate, appraisal of the world. His "bullshit detector" is highly attuned, and his sense of humor would be a welcome balm for our troubled times. His name is Jon Stewart, and I would love to see how he would handle stupid politicians. "President Stewart" has a nice ring to it.

Then, there is a female Harvard law professor who worked her way up from a lower middle class Oklahoma family. She tried to stand up for America in the latest financial crisis and was slapped down by the rude power addicts in the Senate. She has a wonderful way of talking that makes sense. Her name is Elizabeth Warren. I would love to see her replace President Obama on the ballot next fall.

These and many thousands of other honorable and smart Americans would be wonderful, inspirational, and honorable leaders. But in this new paradigm, I believe we each need to grow up and take responsibility for our lives, for future children, and for our planet.

I have an amazing life in Northern California. I have a wonderful wife, nice home, great friends, and a rewarding and meaningful job. But I don't think I have a choice to stay the same. I don't think any rational, sentient human who knows the reality of our nation's predicament and the plight of its citizens has the option to stand by any longer and do nothing. It's that bad. We must all act. This is just like World War II, only worse. The problem is more pervasive, and closer to home. Back then everyone needed to step up and pull together. They rationed gas and sugar and butter, and everyone understood why we were doing this. We are on the Titanic, and, like the captain of Titanic, our government's incompetence and corruption, our country's social inequity and neglected children, and the worldwide environmental degradation, is steering us into an iceberg. Our current path is not sustainable.

A lot of wise people agree with me. A recent poll said that over 80% of Americans were unhappy with our government. Interventions happen when we can't stand the insanity anymore and we reach out for help.

I propose that all of us "work" the 12 Steps as part of this Intervention. I believe this comprehensive approach is our best shot. I don't think we have a choice. We have to make a move and we need to do it quickly.

If we do our part, work the Steps, and move toward recovery and sanity, we will no longer simply be pointing out the problem. We will see how we have enabled this, and we will change and be ready to act. We will no longer be standing by and watching helplessly while children go hungry, and go without medical care, and are fed food so toxic that over a third of them will become obese or develop diabetes and die early. We can no longer stand by while children become addicts, because of our failure to take care of them.

The truck driver in Cleveland, the paralegal in Atlanta, the elementary school teacher in Dallas, the insurance salesman in Tucson, the camp director in Wisconsin. You and others can do this thing. We can storm the cockpit of this hijacked country. We can all say, "Let's roll."

Our country is in dire need of radical change. Let's look, one by one, at the areas where we must take sensible measures so our nation can survive. Let's start with our economy.

The following chapters are statements on "what I would do if I were President." I'm modeling what it would look like for *you* to run for President of the United States. I'm doing this to model for *all of us* what I feel we all need to actually do. I believe that each of us must seriously consider standing up for America and serving, in order to manifest this new political paradigm. And I hope this book moves millions to do what I am doing. We all need to rise up and take our country back from the misguided people and the dysfunctional system that have brought us to the precipice. I'm hoping that you all run, or find honorable men and women to run, and replace the 536.

You can count on *my* vote!

20

ENVIRONMENT

This one is painful. Who hasn't had their heart broken at what is happening to Our Mother? Remember Joni Mitchell's song about how they "paved paradise and put up a parking lot?"

For millions of years, the Earth and Mother Nature have unveiled their wonder. Man evolved and learned how to hunt and gather and live sustainably in nature. For a million years, man and nature got along. And then, a moment ago in galactic time, we went crazy. We went insane. We figured out how to set carbon on fire. We went insane, and now we're on track to kill Mother Nature and end all life, if we don't turn this around! And it may already be too late.

The Native Americans lived in peaceful harmony with the earth. Now we've relegated them to a few reservations where they subsist on a fraction of the land they used to protect. If we'd left the Native Americans in charge of our natural resources, would we be in this bad a fix?

It looks like Einstein was right; we are going to destroy ourselves.

It is that serious.

Nothing demonstrates this better than the way money-addicted Big Business, and power-addicted Big Government, and their colluding Big Union, have gone absolutely insane and destroyed large parts of the Earth.

And we are fools for trusting them. *Seriously, we are the fools who put them in charge!*

The ethanol subsidy game is a rigged system enabled by our politicians. The only people who win are the Fat Cats in Big Business, the politicians, and Big Farm -- the large, mainly corn-growing farmers in Midwestern America. Ethanol is touted as an alternative energy to oil, but it takes nearly a gallon of oil to make a gallon of ethanol! So this scheme funds Big Oil. And Big Government colludes with Big Business to brainwash the citizens of Iowa to accept farm subsidies (bribes) to grow corn that's run through Big Chemistry's money machines, to make ethanol that's added to gasoline.

Who wins? The money addicts in Big Business. And the politicians who get bribes to run their endless campaigns. And Big Oil. And Big Farm which gets subsidies. Farmers don't seem to mind ruining their grandchildren's lands and rivers, or are so squeezed economically that they can't see another choice.

Does not sound sane to me. To you?

Who loses? We all do -- in higher taxes to pay for this charade. And, all of us lose as nature is destroyed and pollutants are washed into the rivers and oceans.

The smallish, blue, third planet from the sun, Earth, is heating up. Its inhabitants are running around at a frantic pace, setting all the carbon on fire.

This last year has shown us what the future holds. In July 2011 every single state set record high temperatures! Huge floods, tornadoes, and torrential rain fell. This is occurring because warmer air holds more moisture. And it is warmer because we, you and I, this year, have pumped 31 billion metric tons of carbon into the air; a new record. And we are in a recession. Wait until world economies are humming again.

Earth's rapid warming is setting off alarms on many fronts. The journal *Nature* has recently reported some troubling findings. Scientists at the University of Alaska at Fairbanks are reporting that the ice covering the permafrost is melting. Should this ice melt, it will release vast amounts of methane and catastrophic amounts of carbon dioxide. Jeremy Rifkin, in his latest book, *The Third Industrial Revolution*, says that if this happened, "there is nothing our species could do to prevent a wholesale destruction of our ecosystems and catastrophic extinction of life on the planet."

Obama talked a good game before he was elected. Many of us put our hopes in him to save the environment. But he caved. He sold out. He has become part of the insanity. He sold out his influence to the special interests by giving them what they wanted, so they will give him money to spend on advertising to get re-elected. It is estimated that Obama will spend close to *one billion dollars campaigning, in an attempt to brainwash us into voting for him!*

One billion dollars! What did he have to give up to get that money?

Obama is opening up more land in Wyoming to dig up more coal, to ship east and spread more mercury on America's children and rivers, and pump more carbon into our air. He continues to support the removal of mountaintops in the east, to mine coal in a process that destroys ground water and spews more mercury into our children's food and heats the planet. And he is opening up more drilling in the Gulf of Mexico and Alaska. I had hoped that Obama would be *different*. I now see that I was asleep. I, like most of us, believed in *the System*. I was still in denial of the fact that we are governed by an oligarchy that is run by unethical people.

This Intervention will remove him and all 100 Senators and 435 Representatives from office, and not a minute too soon!

And the Democrats, champions of the little man, champions of big fixes for big problems, stand around with their hands out, knowing that cash will be coming to support this madness! And the Republicans are also standing there with their hands out, waiting for the bribes and their marching orders.

But now the Internet has given us the ability to see that the *whole system* is corrupt and addicted and needs to go away to rehab.

I don't want to run for President, but I don't feel like I have a choice. America is in big trouble and we all need to stand up like we did in World War II. The following are my ideas and proposals. This country is full of honorable women and men who are smarter than I am. And I trust the process. I will do my best, and I trust that they will do their best, and that by combining our collective wisdom through the magic of our wired world, I believe we will choose the best strategies and the best people to create a better America.

Please, think big. Imagine yourself guiding us out of this mess. The Internet is taking us into a new paradigm, and we need a new kind of person to lead us now. We can do this, and we need you.

If I were President, I would ask everyone to read this book, and, if they met the criteria for any addiction, to get into recovery.

And then I would ask everyone concerned about the environment to read Jeremy Rifkin's book, *The Third Industrial Revolution*. This book challenges all of us to think in terms of the paradigm-shifting that is needed for tomorrow.

We all need to go into nature and be still. Some of my most spiritual and enlightened moments have come at such times. I would suggest that everyone go on a vision quest. I believe that we all need to go on a vision quest, every few years. Ten days in the wilderness, with a three-day fast in the middle. We all need to get back to our roots.

If I were President, I would ask Hollywood to take this on. Al Gore's *An Inconvenient Truth* was ahead of its time. That movie was like a newly recovering member of AA, walking into a bar in 1935, and saying, "You can stop drinking." No one would have understood what his or her message was. Before AA was founded in 1935, alcoholics had no hope, no help, and no treatment. They all died or went insane. Today alcoholism is a disease that is simple to treat. When Senator Gore brought his message to Congress, everyone glazed over. No one was ready to hear that message. I would make sure that every person on the planet with a screen to view it had access to his documentary. I would appoint Al Gore as my Secretary of the Environment. And I would see that he received the highest honor America can bestow on its citizens.

I would ask Hollywood to tell the tragic tales of our vanishing wildlife. We all need to know that the Chinese today are shooting elephants so that they can make trinkets! I would propose that we pick a day each year and all go to the streets to spotlight such tragedies. I propose we give China a grade on how it has done to protect the elephants and if they have faltered, that we boycott their goods for a month. The same with Japan. This last year, Japan officially sanctioned the slaughter of over 700 whales! They can do this because there is no consequence for their actions. Boycotts work! If I were President, I would personally meet the ship returning to Japan with the murdered whales. Children around the world have been trying to save the whales. We must listen to our future leaders.

I would ask each of us to restore our backyards to nature. Make room for the bugs and the birds and the butterflies. And get ourselves out of the 90% of the planet that we don't inhabit: the oceans, rivers, lakes, jungles, plains, and air. Once we replace carbon-based energy and have a sustainable energy plan, I would suggest we return our rivers to their natural state, by taking down the dams. We need to see if Our Mother will make it. She has been so terribly molested and attacked that she may overheat and die. We all need to pitch in and pray that she lives. We all need to work to restore her. And we need to see that this is a multi-generational project. It took Mother Earth millions of years to create her masterpiece. It will take many generations to repair what our ego-driven, insane generation has done in just a few decades. There is no way that we can adequately make living amends to Mother Nature. Each of us will die with this on our conscience. Anyone who drives a car or air conditions a home or rides in a jet must wake up to the incredible damage we are leaving for future generations to deal with.

And then I would like all of us to visualize a population that lives in harmony with Earth, a population that has repaired this small blue ball. This future population will have stopped burning carbon, restored the Amazon Rainforest, reclaimed and replanted swathes of destroyed land, and removed the dams. This population will be much smaller. Our descendants will use renewable energy and live in harmony with nature. They will "get out of the way" and wildlife will return. Buffalo will again roam the plains in the millions. Those of us who live in nature will be "off the grid," living like the Native Americans did for thousands of years in the midst of this Eden.

We are all like the two-year-old who has pooped in their pants and is waiting for someone to take care of us.

That's us folks! You and I. We are pooping in our pants!

The sane among us will start this Intervention, get the Powerless Enablers to join us, and we will put some sane folks in Washington.

We need to grasp this. It is only when we come out of denial that we can begin to work on the solution.

Every three months, I would throw a dart at a map of the country and pick a city to visit to find out what it's doing to end its landfills. We need to recycle *everything!* One hundred percent. Mother Earth is not an ashtray! I would take my press corps and my photographers to each city's landfills and walk around and let you see what I am looking at.

We all need to feel ashamed for mutilating our Mother. To be fair, every one of us should go to the landfills and bring home the tens of thousands of pounds of crap we put into them. We should all bring our crap back and put it in our living rooms. It is not OK to treat our precious planet like a garbage can! For us to recover, we need to acknowledge the damage we have done to Mother Earth and her plants and wildlife and oceans and forests. We need to take a fearless and moral inventory of our actions that have harmed our planet, and we need to make amends where we can. And we need to stop the practices that continue to harm Mother Earth.

Let us elect sane and sober Americans who understand this and can help us create a policy to return the planet to its natural temperatures, and our land to "America, the Beautiful." We can be a beacon to the world on sane environmental policies. We can, once again, be admired by the world.

21

ENERGY

Sustainability. We all need to make this word a part of our daily language. Is this or that practice *sustainable?* Can we keep doing this, or that, for the next 200 years without any negative impact on our biosphere? Can we, for instance, continue to increase our oil use? Is this practice sustainable? Can we expect to extract ever more oil from the Earth? Is this practice sustainable? Can we continue to double the Earth's population every 40 years? Our population was two billion in 1920 and it will be fourteen billion in 2100. A seven-fold increase. Is this sustainable? Only a small minority of the world's population uses oil like America. When the world has caught up with us, can we suddenly supply five times as much oil as we do now? Is this sustainable? And, if the population doubles again, and we were using ten times as much oil as we are now using, is that sustainable? How will we get ten times that amount of oil out of the Earth? And what is the impact on the biosphere of burning one hundred times as much oil as we are now?

This is the Titanic, headed straight for that iceberg! But our leaders clearly don't see a problem. Because if they did, we could depend on them to tell us, right? We elected them to lead, and we can trust them, right?

Insanely, politicians today will look us in the eye and tell us that there is not a problem. Why? Because they are lying. Because these greedy bastards are pocketing boatloads of cash! (Or they are illiterate. One presidential candidate actually said that he did not believe in global warming!)

From New Jersey's Governor Christie,

> *"I understand you're angry, and I understand you're frustrated, and I understand you feel deceived and betrayed. And the reason you feel all these things is because you have been deceived and you have been betrayed.* And for twenty years, governors have come into this room and lied to you. *Promised you benefits that they had no way of paying for, making promises they knew they couldn't keep, and just hoping that they wouldn't be the man or women left holding the bag. I understand why you feel angry and betrayed and deceived by those people."*

There is the saying, "Lie to me once, shame on you. Lie to me twice, shame on me." We are all being played for chumps, and we need to grow up and leave the addict. We, the Sane 20% of American voters, now need to take the reins back into our hands, kick everyone out, and start over.

Big Oil, Big Auto, Big Chemistry, Big Farm, Big Union, Big Lawyer, Big Utilities and Big Money have all gone to the back rooms and scratched each other's backs and made deals. And the word "sustainability" is never, ever uttered. It couldn't be, because none of their practices is sustainable.

This has to stop. We need an energy policy that rewards sustainable practices and penalizes Earth-destroying, un-sustainable practices. We need to implement it quickly, and we need to implement it in an orderly way. Again, think of World War II, when we built hundreds of thousands of ships, tanks, planes, jeeps, and trucks *in three years!* And we were done with the war in four! *Those men and women stood up.*

We need to do that now. We need to switch to solar, and wind, and other sustainable energy practices. We needed to have begun that in the 1960s. We put a man on the moon in 1969. We could have ended the practice of burning carbon, but the greedy, money hoarders, and their power-hungry elected enablers, were more interested in feeding their addictions. It must be done, now. We need to think outside the box. We have a solar car that has traveled 12,500 miles -- on sunlight. We have a solar plane that was able to fly continuously for 24 hours, including at night, using solar power alone. We have solar, energy-propelled transportation available right now! Imagine what the future might hold if we had a "Sputnik Moment."

We have the technology to do this. Do we have the will?

Again, Jeremy Rifkin's work with the European Union is worth looking at. His plan, laid out in his book, *The Third Industrial Revolution*, has been evaluated by brilliant thinkers in Europe for a number of years, and aspects of his plan are already being implemented in several European countries. This is doable. The question is: "Do we have time to do what's needed before runaway global heating and population growth and economic problems make this untenable?" Rifkin himself says that this project is a big job, but that he has "not seen a Plan B." Clearly, we need to get moving on a comprehensive plan. Below are the concepts that Rifkin and the European Union have developed and I believe are the best game in town:

1. Move from reliance on fossil fuel to sustainable and renewable energy.

2. Reconfigure buildings to become individual collectors of energy.

3. Install hydrogen and other technologies to store energy in each of these buildings.

4. Connect all of us in America to an intelligent grid where we can all share energy and store energy.

5. Move our transportation fleet to electricity.

When I was an addict, I *knew* something was wrong. For years I just *thought* about doing something about my problem. We *know* we have a global warming problem. We *know* we have a CO_2 problem. We simply need to move from thinking, to action.

Obama sounded like he had a few good ideas at one point, but Washington's rigged addictive system made short order of his renewable energy ideas.

I don't want to run for President, but I don't feel like I have a choice. America is in big trouble and we all need to stand up like we did in World War II. The following are my ideas and proposals. This country is full of honorable women and men who are smarter than I am. And I trust the process. I will do my best, and I trust that they will do their best, and that by combining our collective wisdom through the magic of our wired world, I believe we will choose the best strategies and the best people to create a better America.

Please, think big. Imagine yourself guiding us out of this mess. The Internet is taking us into a new paradigm, and we need a new kind of person to lead us now. We can do this, and we need you.

If I were President, I would ask everyone to read this book and, if they met the criteria for any addiction, to get into recovery.

And then I would ask everyone concerned about energy to read Jeremy Rifkin's book, *The Third Industrial Revolution*. This book challenges all of us to think in terms of the paradigm shifting that is needed for tomorrow.

Then I would ask our most skilled and knowledgeable energy scientists and educators to meet, collaborate, and come up with a plan. The current, elected, officials have not been able to come with a plan. We hired them to do things like implement an energy policy. Would you keep an employee who did not do their job? These addicts have not done their job and must go. I once imagined Obama would do this, but he has caved. He has been driven insane too. He is now in the "Drill, baby, drill" camp. He must go, too.

We need to encourage sustainability and discourage non-sustainability. We need to get real about the true costs of, say, burning coal or oil or natural gas. We must rapidly switch to solar and wind and other sustainable energy sources. We need to turn our furnaces down, or off. We need to turn our air-conditioners down, or off.

I would gather together a new set of thinkers, ones who have been talking about the solution for a long time, such as Jeremy Rifkin. I'd ask them to put together an energy plan in 90 days and present it to Congress. I would expect Congress to give me a bill to sign in another 90 days. It would not be perfect, but it would be a plan, and a serious start.

Currently, we are ripping off the future and ruining our children's planet. How do you explain that to a child? Seriously, go do it. Find a 5- or 10-year old child and tell them what you have done. Look them in the eye and tell them what their future looks like. Really. We are the stewards of their world. We need to let them know how we are doing our job.

As President, I would do my best. I would ask all the adults to gather their children in front of a TV and I would say something like this.

"Good evening, children and others watching me right now.

I'm speaking here as your President. The adults in this country elected me, and my job is to attempt to make the world a better place for you.

What I have to say is hard to say but it needs to be said. It starts out with 'I'm sorry.' We all say, 'I'm sorry' when we make a mistake that hurts someone else. I know you know that. And I'm sure you do the same thing when you make a mistake.

But this is a really big 'I'm sorry.' And it is an apology from all of us adults, including your parents. The apology is to all of you kids.

Maybe 50 years ago, before you were born, we made a big mistake. We really screwed something up bad. We are trying to fix it, but it's pretty bad. We think you are old enough to hear the truth. What we did was we became addicted to burning a really big amount of gas and oil and coal. At first it didn't seem like it was a big deal. But we weren't very smart, and stopped paying attention and before we knew it, it got out of hand and we were burning way more than the Earth can handle without causing problems.

Burning all this carbon has been causing problems. The Earth has been heating up, and this has caused the climate to change, and the polar ice caps and glaciers to melt. These melting ice fields reflect a lot of the sun's heat back into space. Without these reflectors, the Earth is heating up even more, which causes the ice caps to melt even faster.

I'd like to say, 'Don't be afraid.' But I need to be honest with you. This could become a very big problem if we don't fix it. And the reality is that we are not going to be able to fix it completely. We totally screwed this one up, and, speaking for all the adults, I'm so sorry for messing up your planet. You have every right to be really angry with us.

Probably the best we can do now is to slow down this planetary destruction. But it will take many generations to get the Earth back to where it was a hundred years ago. Unfortunately, that burden will fall on you.

I am so sorry to have to report this to you. It is unfair to you. We were really, really negligent, and we are so very, very sorry for doing this to you.

But, Americans can be smart, and resourceful, at times. I'm hoping this is one of those times. I'm hoping that your parents and the rest of the adults in this country will get to work on fixing this problem. It's going to cause all of us to sacrifice some, or even a lot. It will probably mean riding your bike more, and walking more.

And I'm going to need your help, because this will soon become your responsibility. I want you to help your parents do whatever needs to be done. Help them understand how they can save energy. We adults have been so addicted to burning carbon that we aren't even aware when we are doing it.

Hopefully, if we all work together, we can get a handle on this thing.

Again, I'm so, so sorry for what I, and all of us, have done to your world."

Are you ready to say that to the kids in your life? I have. I regularly make these amends to my grandchildren. And we are all going to have to make sacrifices. Nearly all of us will resist this. Why? *Because we are not thinking sanely!* Our egos have become dependent on this lifestyle. Mine has.

We need to get beyond our egos, into our spiritual selves, where we can see the bigger picture; where we can see the wonder of a sustainable planet. Once we are able to do that, I believe we will be grateful and gladly accept the sacrifices we must make, because we finally have sane leadership with a sane plan. We will gladly drive our cars less often. We will need to walk more and ride bikes more and take more buses and Skype and use teleconferencing.

If we grow up in a country that speaks English, we can pretty much predict that we will end up speaking English. If we grow up in a country that is addicted to burning carbon, we can pretty much predict that it will not be easy to give up our "fix," our dependence on burning carbon.

We are in a race. Can we get into recovery and get sane, before the Titanic hits the iceberg? Perhaps we should park our cars, turn off the lights, turn off the furnaces and air conditioners, until we can look our children in the eye and tell them that we are all doing everything we can to stop destroying their world.

22

WATER

Sustainability. This word needs to be on our lips a lot if we want our children to inherit the planet our parents and grandparents gave us. One hundred years ago, we humans had a much smaller footprint on the planet. We have fouled our lands and waters and we need to fix it.

In the mid-1940s, when I was five, six, and seven, I lived in Palatine, Illinois, a suburb of Chicago. Down the street from where we lived was a "swamp." Actually it was probably a little piece of nature man had not touched for hundreds of years. I often went there and marveled at what I saw. Each spring, I watched tadpoles turn into frogs. There were fish swimming and turtles sunning themselves on logs and rocks. The air was filled with the sounds of birds and insects. Butterflies and bees passed overhead. There were dragonflies and water spiders skipping around.

I remember the excitement when a neighbor brought home a huge snapping turtle that had lived for decades in our "swamp." They'd killed it!

Why does man want to kill?

I believe that since the industrial age we "modern men" have lost our way. We have become more and more isolated from nature and failed to show our children its wonder.

When the Caucasians landed in America, the rivers and plains were alive and well. The Native Americans lived in balance with nature. We white people, and our capitalism, over time have run amuck and have seriously wounded Mother Nature.

But I want to prove Einstein wrong. I think we can grow up and act like sane adults, people with common sense. I believe in the best in us. I believe we can to turn this around. If we can go to the moon, we certainly can stop fouling our water here on Earth!

I live in the San Francisco Bay Area. Here, we screwed up the Bay by dumping garbage into it to create more land to fit more houses. Who had this crazy idea? You guessed it. It was the Fat Cats and their buddies in state and local government. They got rich, and we lost the ecology that kept our water clean and the wildlife safe. They looked at the Bay, Mother Nature's complex and amazing and intricate balance of plants and animals, and these greedy bastards saw *money*. They were not sane.

Sane people looked at the Bay and saw a beautiful, flourishing, delicately balanced ecosystem. These sane people saw that every square inch of the Bay served a function in nature. The tidelands and estuaries were the filters that cleaned the Bay waters while providing a sanctuary for millions of birds and other wildlife. The Bay was home to an abundance of fish and sea mammals. It had been this way for millions of years.

How can we repair this? Actually, in 1961, three East Bay women helped mobilize thousands of concerned citizens in a movement to Save the Bay. This "Bonobo kind of thinking" has restored thousands of acres to nature, and thousands more acres are in the process of restoration. Thanks to the work of this grassroots effort, in the past 50 years there has actually been an *increase* in the size and cleanliness of the Bay. This is a heartwarming and precious movement. We are a long way from total repair. A long way, but people of vision are headed in the right direction. Here in the San Francisco area, we need to be stewards of the Bay. When we visit Our Mother, we need to heed the maxim: "Take only pictures and leave only shadows."

I live in Marin County, a beautiful area north of San Francisco. The water that goes down my toilet or sink goes into the Bay. Sadly, my water may contain contaminants that end up in our Bay. Water analysis shows that fish caught in the Bay are contaminated with hundreds of compounds ranging from mercury to cancer-causing endocrine-disruptors, and even penicillin, narcotics, and birth control medications. This is wrong! This is pollution and it must be stopped. Each of us must take responsibility for changing this.

Alex Prud'homme's book, *The Ripple Effect*, says the Hudson River contains cancer-causing PCBs, that there is cow manure in well water throughout the western states, and that most of our waterways contain narcotics and synthetic estrogens, and hundreds of other chemicals. How did this happen? Clearly someone should go to jail. Someone should be held accountable for the immoral, unethical, and insane behavior of the companies that have caused this contamination. Clearly you would think that someone should be imprisoned for ruining our water supply. But the reality is that it is all of us who are doing it. Voters in denial are passively enabling these practices. Apparently we citizens have not been sane enough to see what's happening. We have let the money hoarders and the greedy, power addicts run amuck and pee in our drinking water.

Rivers, creeks, and other wetlands all over America are in trouble. The runoff from industrial livestock feed lots is poisoning downstream waters, as well as the aquifers, the underground bodies of water that supply our well water.

Huge corporations are using Mother Nature as a dumpster! Complex and dangerous chemicals today are poured into our aquifers as a result of fracking. Fracking is a new invention of Big Oil to get *more*. These Chimpanzee-like men set off large explosions in the delicate skin of our planet and then pump chemicals under high pressure to break up the land so they can extract more carbon to sell.

These addicts do not even get the madness of their actions! "Who cares about the ground water? Who cares about heating up the planet? I'm making money!" (And I'm giving money to Congress to make this legal.)

Aquifers are unseen bodies of underground water. The rain that lands on the earth ultimately finds its way into these natural reservoirs. These precious bodies of water have been here for millions of years and provide the well water that many people drink. Can you imagine anything crazier than pumping poison into this ancient, fresh, body of water? The Environmental Protection Agency put out a report in 2004 that said that fracking poses "little or no threat" to the water supply!

(Let's review: 1% are the greedy, money and power Addicts who are destroying the Earth to get even more money and power; 79%

are the anxious and Powerless Enablers, and 20% are also enabling but are sane enough to know something is wrong. This 20% recognize the need to hire an Interventionist and support the intervention process in an attempt to restore sanity.)

So, some part of the 1% (Big Oil) had other members of the same 1% (government scientists) do a study that said there was little or no threat from fracking! They said this, even though the evening news is showing people setting on fire the methane that is coming out of their tap water spigot!

Another part of this 1% (Congress) is authorizing companies that are pumping this fracking fluid into our aquifers to disregard the regulations of the Safe Drinking Water Act in 2005. Congress also authorized Big Oil to keep the ingredients in the fracking fluid secret! (Wonder why.) Some of the chemicals that have been pumped into these ancient fresh water bodies from fracking are carcinogenic; others contain endocrine disruptors, which interfere with the functioning of endocrine glands and hormones. These chemicals also interrupt normal growth and development in babies. Arsenic, copper, vanadium, and many other toxic substances have also been found in the water as a result of fracking. It will be impossible to fix this. Any attempt will only damage it more. For thousands of years to come, if any of us survive, history books will have a chapter about how Americans, in a brief moment of evolutionary time, went insane and did something that had consequences far worse than even what Hitler did. It is easy to see why Einstein could say that he did not think *homo sapiens* was smart enough to figure out how to get along.

Exxon, and Obama, and your Senator, and your Representative are addicted not only to continuing the fracking process, but to increasing it and expanding it! There is no hope of talking to them. There is no chance that a demonstration will deflect this monstrosity. "Raising gas mileage requirements" and "subsidizing electric cars" are matches being lit in a thunderstorm. What all of us are doing is insane. We need to first toss out the 536 elected officials, hire some adults to run the country, and have a serious conversation about how to fix this.

Ultimately, these poisons find their way into our lakes and oceans. This is happening at an accelerating pace, and no sane individual can remain in denial. It's time for an Intervention. It's time to stand up. We really don't have a choice.

> I don't want to run for President, but I don't feel like I have a choice. America is in big trouble and we all need to stand up like we did in World War II. The following are my ideas and proposals. This country is full of honorable women and men who are smarter than I am. And I trust the process. I will do my best, and I trust that they will do their best, and that by combining our collective wisdom through the magic of our wired world, I believe we will choose the best strategies and the best people to create a better America.
>
> Please, think big. Imagine yourself guiding us out of this mess. The Internet is taking us into a new paradigm, and we need a new kind of person to lead us now. We can do this, and we need you.

If I were President, I would ask everyone to read this book and, if they met the criteria for any addiction, to get into recovery.

I would develop a water policy and announce it on TV; it would mandate each and every one of us to help put Nature back together. The answer is simple, but what it requires will not be easy. We can no longer use Nature as our ashtray. If any water is returned to Nature, it must be pure. Pure. Not mostly pure, not almost pure, but pure. Just like it fell from the sky as rain or snow. That needs to be our mandate. It needs to be our goal. Just like we did in World War II, we need to "man up" and make it happen.

I would ask for regulations stipulating that no one can release contaminated water into our water supply. This technology is already available. What happens to the water that is recycled on the Space Station or on nuclear submarines? There are a number of ways to make water less polluted. Here is a list of some of these ways: reverse osmosis, carbon filtration, microfiltration, ultrafiltration, ultraviolet oxidation, electrodialysis, and microporous filtration. But the gold standard is double distillation. This needs to be the goal. We just can't shit and piss in our nest! We are smarter than that!

I would ask you to run for City Council in the city where you live. I would ask you to gather your voters and figure out a way to put *only water that is 100% pure* back into the environment. I want all of us to stop *100%* of the pollution. Not 99.99%. Even water that is 99.99% pure is not sustainable, if we take a long view. *We must always take the long view. We must always think of our children's world.*

We simply have to value our planet. I don't think we realize the tremendous psychological burden each of us carries as we repress the knowledge of the damage we are leaving to future generations. We spend thousands of dollars every year buying stuff -- some of it unnecessary and useless stuff. I don't have a problem with that. I like to buy stuff too. But I know that each of us could give up a little bit of our stuff to restore Nature and live sustainably. *And we would feel good about coming together and making this happen.*

After we've elected new senators and representatives, I would ask every one of them to go home to their local towns and villages and get ideas for stopping *all water pollution* and restoring our creeks, rivers, lakes, and oceans. Americans are smart and industrious, and they can tell us how to make this happen.

Ten minutes from where I live, a local community is restoring a precious waterway. Using taxpayer money, local volunteers are digging out a channel in the wetlands at Muir Beach in Marin County. Until white people arrived, this area was a vital wetland habitat that provided a home for thousands of critters, large and small. Coho Salmon swam up the creeks at Muir Beach to spawn each year as they had for hundreds of thousands of years. In the blink of an eye, white people destroyed this gem.

Today you can see the bulldozers and the dump trucks and the men and women in hard hats, busy undoing what we did. It brings tears to my eyes as I watch them work. I hope I live long enough to see the salmon return. I hope I live long enough to see the Western Pond Turtle come back to the area. I love to pay taxes when I see that my tax dollars are helping undo the damage my people have done.

Each local community will have to come up with its own unique answers. And every three months I want each of our elected officials to go back to our districts and drink the water from our local creeks, river, or lakes. I pledge to do the same thing. I will throw a dart at the map of the United States, and I will go that area and drink the water from the local waterways. I pledge to go to the Detroit River or the Sacramento River or your local river and drink water directly out of it. *And if the water is dirty, I will let you know how I feel after I drink it.* As leaders we need to lead. We need to tell those whom we elect what needs to be done to fix the water. But we need to do something else. We need to educate the citizens in our districts. We need to give them critical feedback about how they have fallen for the Big Lie and how they need to be much more involved in the political system. We can certainly understand why so few get involved. The current American political system is like the crazy alcoholic family down the street. It is painful to watch, and we do our best to ignore it.

Business will squeal, "But this will drive up our costs!"

I would say, "So?"

Come on! We humans are somewhat smart. When nature calls, we don't just crap and piss where we are standing! Only babies do that.

But this is what we are doing! We are crapping and pissing where we are standing!

We have plenty of resources to reclaim our waterways and restore sanity to our water use. We just need to wake up to the out-of-control 1%, our oligarchy, that is using Mother Nature as a toilet. They need to be toilet-trained. Actually, they need to be ousted from office, toilet-trained or not. Stay tuned for the Intervention that will help them to get over this bad habit, or at least get them out of positions of power.

Our current practices are unsustainable. It's unfair to our children that we trash nature. What are we thinking? Yes, profit is part of capitalism, but we also must be moral, ethical, and spiritual. Acting with integrity will bring each of us something much more precious than money. That "something more" will be the serenity you will experience knowing that you were part of the solution and not part of the problem. In the meantime, "Congress, Big Business, Big Union, Fat Cats, get the hell out of the way so that we can clean up your mess!"

We get to start this work when the new leaders we elect take office in January 2013.

23

THE ECONOMY

For years, we have been spending money like a drunken sailor. We need to sober up.

The Iraq war is an example of our leaders' addictive thinking. Who starts a war without good reason? These last guys started two wars and put the expenses on a credit card. The Iraq war cost roughly a trillion dollars. Who paid for it? Our leaders expect their children to pay for it! They are not only greedy, but they are short-sighted.

We have been fools; we have been sweet-talked by the addicts. But we are waking up to a game that is as old as mankind: the rich and the privileged rig the system in their favor; the underdogs have always been underdogs. Things have always been this way. Nature whittles the species through survival of the fittest – the strong and favored thrive, and the weak and less fortunate get the leftovers. Today, 400 Americans have more wealth than 150 million Americans! These members of the oligarchy got that way because they skew the system in their favor.

The Internet has turned this game upside down, and now *the 1% with the power and the money have suddenly lost their advantage.* They are being exposed. We, the Sane 20% of America, have the common sense to see this. The playing field is now level. And we are also realizing that we have a 20-to-1 advantage over the ones who've held the power! This 1%, these elected officials, Big Business, and the hyperwealthy, are waking up to the terrifying reality that the lights are on, and 20% of Americans are standing there, staring at them. They are the stark naked Emperor, and we clearly see their game.

The question is: what will we do with this advantage? Was Einstein right when he said that humans are too dumb to figure it out and that we will destroy ourselves? Or, was he wrong?

Wikileaks, Facebook, Twitter, Tahrir Square, texting, and hand-held computer phones have created a new paradigm. We are in a whole new ball game, but most of us don't actually realize it yet. What the overwhelming majority of Americans know is that what we currently have is bullshit. The old joke of, "If you see their lips moving, they are lying," is no longer funny, and we are actually not sane if we continue to take the bullshit any longer.

We have the numbers. We can fix this thing. You and I. Yes, Federal spending needs to come down, way down. Yes, the Fat Cats, the 1% who have more wealth than over half of the rest of us, need to give up some of their money. If they weren't addicts, they would *want* to give some of it up because they'd understand it is the *right* thing to do for America's children and America's lands. We need more billionaires like Warren Buffet, who understand this. John McCain has so much money he can't keep track of his own property. In the 2008 presidential campaign, reporters asked McCain how many houses he owned; the presidential candidate replied, "I don't know. Maybe six or seven." And he is fighting tooth and nail to make sure none of *his* wealth gets diverted to crumbling schools and breakfast for American children who woke up hungry.

Warren Buffet and Bill Gates have initiated the *Giving Pledge* that encourages the wealthy to give the bulk of their wealth to charity. Many rich Americans are joining this cause: Ted Turner, Michael Bloomberg, Paul Allen, George Lucas, Mark Zuckerberg, and Jon Huntsman are some of the Americans who are showing us what honorable and wealthy Americans can do.

At the Washington D.C. *Rally to Restore Sanity* in October 2010, one sign said, "Paying Taxes Is Patriotic." We all need to pay taxes; it is patriotic and it is right. We each need to pay for our roads and bridges and fire departments. Greece's economy is failing, in part because Greek citizens see their government's corruption, and they, like their leaders, have decided to cheat also -- hence, they are going broke. It is tempting to do the same thing in America, after the latest rip-off by

Wall Street and its Federal government enablers. Every capable adult must contribute. It is not right and it is not patriotic to avoid taxes.

General Electric is a great example of the rigged game that hurts America. A recent article in the *New York Times* nicely lays this out. (http://www.nytimes.com/2011/03/25/business/economy/25tax. html?pagewanted=all). The essence of this article has been one of the themes of this book. G.E. hired former government officials, and former I.R.S. officials, to optimize the company's income by avoiding paying taxes. They bribed Representative Charlie Rangel, chairman of the Ways and Means Committee. Rangel gave G.E. special breaks that allowed the company, in 2010, to pay *no taxes on 4.6 billion dollars in income!* And, right on cue, Mr. Rangel got 11 million dollars in *"donations"* for his home district. Americans were ripped off for a billion dollars in tax revenue that could have been spent benefitting Americans. This backroom deal between Mr. Rangel and G.E. took care of each of *them* just fine. The only problem was that Americans were left out of the loop. This is just one example of how our corrupt system works.

Egypt's Mubarak had billions of dollars one month, and the next month he was in prison. We are not Egypt. Thankfully, we have solid institutions, and we hope those who have ripped us off will repay us because it is the right thing to do. Like all of us, they have been in a fugue, a dreamlike state. We hope that money hoarding, power grabbing, greed, and high-stakes gambling will give way to sanity. My hope is that most of the billionaires will become like Bill Gates and Warren Buffett and do the right thing. We all die naked and alone. *On our death bed we realize that the only thing we get to keep is what we have given away.*

More and more the public is seeing the charade. More and more we see that addiction to money and power drives the actions of these corrupt elected officials and their Fat Cat enablers. I know how this works. I was that addict. I was a liar, cheat, and a thief, and I can still be one, but I know that my serenity depends on being honest and making amends when I catch myself making decisions from my ego. And I know that I must practice selfless giving if I am to keep my serenity.

And, like Scrooge, the Fat Cats could stay in denial and hole up somewhere with their cash. But they will know that *we* know. The Internet will give us news of their continued addictive and selfish ways. We know the financial amends that they owe our country. The billionaire oil barons are in this camp. They dig up oil and destroy the Earth. They cause carbon to be burned, which causes polar bears to drown in the melting glacial waters. It will be very interesting see if and how they, and others like them, make amends for their behavior.

(Today, I opened the latest *New Yorker* and saw a cartoon. A mother polar bear is standing on a tiny piece of ice in the middle of a vast ocean. Her baby looks up at her and says, "Momma? Is Rick Perry real?" I want to weep. The polar bears *today* are drowning because we melted their land from under them.)

This is the world we have been living in. I bought into it, until I had my nightmare. I also had been asleep and confused and unhappy. But the men and women in Egypt woke me up to the possibility of what could happen here. Then it all made sense. This is really much simpler than we imagined. Common sense tells us that this Intervention can and must happen.

An alcoholic family has typically tolerated years of insanity, abuse, rage, financial irresponsibility, and neglected children. Before the Intervention, everyone accepted this madness. They felt they had to, because they didn't think they had a choice. It was all that these sad, sick, people knew. Stephanie Brown, author of *The Alcoholic Family in Recovery*, talks about the "chaos of recovery." The Intervention changes things. The old rules are gone, and the future is unknown. But the Interventionist, and the treatment providers, and the 12-Step programs understand the uncertainty of early recovery. They gently guide everyone in the family along the well-worn and predictable path that leads to sanity. We need to trust this process. It has been successfully helping all who engage in it.

I would hope all the past members of government would get into recovery, "fess up" and make amends. If they did, they would eventually return all the ill-gained money they received while they were serving us. And I'd hope that businesses, unions, lobbyists, and anyone else who has been involved in this corrupt, un-American rip-off would also get into recovery and eventually work Steps Eight and Nine and return that money, our money, to us.

And these elected crooks and their pals could choose not to get into recovery and to hold on to their ill-gained funds, but we would all know, and if they did not make amends, we would treat them like we treat any other practicing addict who ripped us off. We would distance from them and stay away from them because they are dangerous. But we would hope that they would get into recovery and get well.

Either they will "get it" and surrender or they won't.

I like the following definition of "surrender:" "Going over to the winning side."

I believe that it is improper to make money by depleting our natural resources. *Homo sapiens*, as a species, does not own the Earth. It is only the ego-centered, greedy addict that could possibly believe it is OK to trash the Earth in order to hoard more money. The Earth is the heavenly body we get to visit for a very brief time. Earth belongs to the species of plants and animals that inhabit it. There should be no profit from despoiling Earth's natural resources. Any money that has been obtained this way should be used to restore the Earth. These CEO's, these greedy, money addicts, will either understand that they have lost their minds and atone, or they will lie on their deathbeds knowing that their life was a sham. They will die with a bunch of green paper piled up beside them. No one wants that. I believe that this Intervention will help them come out of denial, and that they will go to treatment, become sane, and eventually *return the money* and help us repair the damage.

I would ask the same of Wall Street financiers. They are responsible for their behavior, regardless of the fact that their enablers in Washington intentionally provided them with the loopholes that let them rip us all off. They went to college. They knew that, after the Depression, we had created FDIC insurance, the Glass-Steagel act, and the SEC, to protect us from gambling addicts and greedy folks who put their needs ahead of the needs of their victims. Slowly, they bribed our corrupt officials to take the teeth out of these regulations so that Wall Street could resume their addictive ways.

They were gambling. They are addicts. They are in denial. But I would hope that this Intervention will be successful and they will go to Gamblers Anonymous, get into recovery, and make amends. Hopefully they will repay the billions that they took from us. I believe that hoarding money is a mental disorder. Obsessively and compulsively collecting anything is suspect. The medical doctors who create the *Diagnostic and Statistical Manual of Mental Disorders* are considering including "Hoarding Disorder" in the next edition of the manual. I support this addition.

I hope that our elected officials, Fat Cats, lobbyists, oil barons, special interest lawyers, and everyone else that has in any way been part
of this giant rip-off would also get into recovery, work the Steps, including the Steps about making amends. If your business colluded with
government in ways that gamed the system, harmed people; if you sold
nicotine, toxic food, fuel-inefficient cars, or Credit Default Swaps, I
would hope that you would to do the right thing and make amends,
and return the money to Americans. You will be happier for it.

I believe in capitalism, big time. The opportunity for the individual
to conjure up something new that enriches all of us is a very good thing,
and these individuals should be rewarded. The late Steve Jobs is a perfect example. But the greedy crooks in Washington are blowing this
one. I am a small businessperson, and I need to tell you that I hate the
government's excessive intrusion into my business. I have four part-time
employees, but my taxes are so complex that I need to hire an accoun-
tant! We have a bloated government hindering the free market, and I
believe my approach will go a long way toward fixing this problem.

In recent years, government officials have accepted kickback
money from Big Banks. They have let some businesses "have it both
ways." Big Banks wanted to be capitalists when they could make the
big bucks, but then they turned into sissies and ran to mommy when
they lost their money. No business should be too big to fail. Any business that is too big to fail should cut itself into smaller companies and
be left to sink or swim in the market. This is a must in a free economy.

Our financial state, our economy, is based on trust. The money
addicts and the gamblers, and those with a Hoarding Disorder have
taken us to the brink. Just three years ago, many people lost their
homes and their life savings when the stock market fell and the banks
collapsed. Unemployment is staggering -- more than one out of every
ten able and competent American adults has no job. We, as a nation
of law-abiding citizens, do not want to return to chaos and mayhem.
We need our national economy to get into recovery. Someone in
Uncle Sam's family needs to go to Debtors' Anonymous. Right now,
the median American has a net worth of about 200K and debt of
50K. We each own $50,000 of the national debt. We need to get our
financial house in order. Each of us, including Uncle Sam, needs to
have zero debt and a prudent reserve.

Americans are capable of greatness. Are we ready to take the
next step?

I don't want to run for President, but I don't feel like I have a choice. America is in big trouble and we all need to stand up like we did in World War II. The following are my ideas and proposals. This country is full of honorable women and men who are smarter than I am. And I trust the process. I will do my best, and I trust that they will do their best, and that by combining our collective wisdom through the magic of our wired world, I believe we will choose the best strategies and the best people to create a better America.

Please, think big. Imagine yourself guiding us out of this mess. The Internet is taking us into a new paradigm, and we need a new kind of person to lead us now. We can do this, and we need you.

If I were President, I would ask everyone to read this book, and, if they met the criteria for any addiction, to get into recovery.

And then I would ask everyone concerned about the economy to read Jeremy Rifkin's book, *The Third Industrial Revolution*. This book challenges all of us to think in terms of the paradigm shifting that is needed for tomorrow.

Our economy looks like the work of an addict: multiple credit cards with big balances; borrowing from Peter to pay Paul; piling up debt; creditors knocking on the door; impending bankruptcy; money deals being done out the back door. Always making excuses. Always some story as to where the money went.

Doesn't that sound like what you would hear from an addict?

Sounds like an Intervention is in order.

Let's start with a simple proposition for an economic plan that is used by every sane American, and used in every one of the hundreds of thousands of 12-Step meetings. *We are self-supporting, and we have a prudent reserve.* Period. We don't spend money we don't have, and we save something for a rainy day.

It's a simple principle.

If I were President, I would gather together a group of wise citizens. I'd choose 20 of the newly elected Federal officials. I would task these 20 newly elected people to work for one month to develop a comprehensive economic plan. This plan would have to fix our debt problem, our tax problem, and our spending problem. And this plan would have to be less than 100 pages in length. It would close corporate loopholes and eliminate unwise subsides. And those 100 pages would have to include a new tax code. It would replace the incomprehensible current tax code, which is 17,000 pages long!

Additionally, I would ask each of us, every American, to "step up." We need to adjust all aspects of our money use, probably by no more than 5%. Wouldn't you gladly pay 5% more in taxes or get 5% less in entitlements if it meant that the system was fixed and would ultimately lead to *much lower taxes and a sustainable and secure world?* My guess is that the stock market would soar, and the price of gold would drop, if we actually got our economic engine in gear and stopped mucking up the economic system with complex, contradictory, discriminatory, and anti-market regulations that are designed to make the wealthy even wealthier.

Within 90 days I would then bring this plan to *you*, the new members of the House and Senate, for ratification. And I would expect to sign it in another 90 days. It would not be perfect, but it would be a serious start and would need to be adjusted as we went forward.

And I believe it would only be temporary. We need a bloated government like we need another hole in our heads. Seriously! We have let our politicians create a huge bureaucracy to support their pet projects.

I would invite Jeremy Rifkin to meet with Congress, myself, and all of our respective staff, and help us vision a green economy. He has been advising the European Union on how to go green, create millions of jobs doing it, and possibly save the planet. This has to be the economy of the future. The carbon age is over. What Rifkin and the Europeans have been doing is making this a reality. The plan has been well thought out and makes sense. It is based on 5 pillars:

1. Move from reliance on fossil fuel to sustainable and renewable energy.

2. Reconfigure buildings to become individual collectors of energy.
3. Install hydrogen and other technologies to store energy in each of these buildings.
4. Connect all of us in America to an intelligent grid, like the Internet, where we can all share energy and store energy.
5. Move our transportation fleet to electricity.

I would ask that we all meet once a month and rapidly implement his and others' visions of a sustainable energy policy. Rifkin has been working with the European Union for years, and Europe is far ahead of us. While I applaud their work, I think we can move faster at what they are doing. When Americans put their mind to something, we don't mess around. We ended WWII, put men on the moon, and lead the technological revolution. We just need to get our heads screwed on straight.

This will create hundreds of thousands of business opportunities and millions of jobs. The question is: Can we pull this off before it's too late?

Additionally, I would convene the 400 wealthiest Americans, and I would respectfully ask them what they think they could do for America. I would start with the assumption that they are good people at heart and have simply gotten caught up in the addictive system. I would invite them to see what they could come up with. I'm sure that they love America, and they have simply been enacting the American "success story." They would probably appreciate someone with vision giving their lives more meaning. Perhaps they could put some of their wealth toward paying the unemployed to plant trees, which will reduce our CO_2 emissions.

America's corporations currently are sitting on 2.5 trillion dollars that is doing nothing. Much of that is parked offshore. We need a tax holiday for them to bring it home, and tax incentives, and public recognition for them using their money to save America. Imagine what that money could do.

Gandhi: "We have enough for every man's need, but not enough for every man's greed."

If I were President, I would put three signs on the lawn of the White House, showing the changes in the country's net worth, debt, and savings. I would hope to remove the debt sign as soon as possible. I think our country is on an addiction-induced spending binge. We can, and will, do so much better when we stop letting our egos run our lives and act honorably, and with integrity, to help America recover her financial sobriety.

That is what I would do. I'm sure that you, too, could come up with something that also makes much more sense than what the current leaders are doing.

24

DEFENSE AND FOREIGN POLICY

What would our defense policy look like in this new paradigm, when America got into recovery? What would change? What could change?

Let's start with a look at a name, "Secretary of Defense." We need such a person because people can be mean and angry and dangerous. Some wars make sense. Fighting Germany in the 1940s did. Today's world can be dangerous. But does it need to always be this way? Sometimes having a military gets us in trouble.

Look at the world's reaction to Obama's election. People around the world, like many Americans, pinned their hopes on him. The world is looking for leadership, and we so wanted him to be that leader. I believe that we *homo sapiens* are more like the "Bonobo" than the "Chimpanzee." I believe that our nature is more "make love, not war." Although there are an awful lot of individuals, leaders, and populations that seem to prefer the Chimpanzee, "make war, not love," approach, even if it kills their own children -- something I will never understand.

I believe that our best defense is a great offense. An offense of morality, leadership, and sanity. Something that America has lost. We need to settle down and get our own house in order. I have to admit that I would be tempted to change the name of the Secretary of Defense to the Secretary of Connection. (Just kidding!) My fantasy would be to live in a world where we did not even need to be defensive. Being defensive is *always* appropriate when danger is near.

But what would it be like to live in a world that was safe? That would be my vision. To create a world that did not need armies and guns. Where countries, instead of fighting each other, worked co-operatively to save our planet and celebrate our diversity.

I believe that the primary focus of our species needs to be saving our planet.

> I don't want to run for President, but I don't feel like I have a choice. America is in big trouble and we all need to stand up like we did in World War II. The following are my ideas and proposals. This country is full of honorable women and men who are smarter than I am. And I trust the process. I will do my best, and I trust that they will do their best, and that by combining our collective wisdom through the magic of our wired world, I believe we will choose the best strategies and the best people to create a better America.
>
> Please, think big. Imagine yourself guiding us out of this mess. The Internet is taking us into a new paradigm, and we need a new kind of person to lead us now. We can do this, and we need you.

If I were President, I would ask everyone to read this book, and, if they met the criteria for any addiction, to get into recovery.

On day one of my presidency, I would not change much regarding our foreign policy. The State Department is doing a good job, under the circumstances. I especially like how women leaders have conducted the Libya event. Hillary Clinton, Susan Rice and their teams have quietly, behind the scenes, worked with others to collaborate and integrate the use of military forces from several countries to protect Libya from a cruel dictator.

And the Secretary of Defense and his team have been doing a wonderful job as well, given the current situation. Unfortunately, we have put these fine men and women in our military in harm's way. I would hope to get all nations to come together on the common problems that threaten all of our planet rather than focusing on eradicating terrorists. Our planet is at risk, and that affects every one of us. If we can see that we have a bigger problem, I think that we can focus on that and come together to form an international police force to deal with pockets of "out of control Chimpanzees." As it is now, many countries are acting like drunks with chips on their shoulders, leaving all of us frightened that they may "lose it" at any moment.

All the while the Titanic plows ahead!

However, I have a question that none of us want to face. Do we want our Department of Defense putting down their guns and shutting off our carbon supplies to save the Earth, because we could not get our act together?

I hope it does not come to that. But maybe Einstein was right after all when he said that he questioned whether humans are smart enough to survive as a species.

As President, I would go to the United Nations and give a talk. I would hope that everyone on the planet could see the presentation. It would go like this:

Citizens of Earth: I am here to speak to you, not as the President of the United States, but as a fellow citizen of this small, blue ball called Earth.

I am here to talk about a problem that many of you know about, but many are still unaware of. What I'm talking about is the reality that Earth is in trouble, and that affects all of us and all life around us.

For many decades we have been burning carbon, without paying much attention to the consequences. The reality is that our biosphere is very fragile, and we have been destroying it in many ways. Some of our scientists say that the situation is dire. Others say that we have a problem, but that it is not serious at this point. And there are those who want to believe that there is no problem.

I believe we have a problem, and we need to take seriously what science is telling us. We need to move towards policies that will eliminate the problem.

It is time to Intervene.

We can do this. We can do this, but it will take cooperation among all of us. We need to put our partisan differences aside. We are all citizens of Earth; Earth's air and water have no boundaries.

I call on the leaders of all countries. We must work together. We are the people's servants; it is our job to serve them. We must act in unison and restore sanity to the governments of Earth. We must remember what Mahatma Gandhi said, "Earth has enough for every man's need, but not enough for every man's greed."

And I call on all the people. We need your help. We need you to peacefully stand up and remind all leaders whom they are pledged to serve.

It is time to put down the swords. It is time to see that we are all homo sapiens and to realize that our species is at risk of becoming extinct. All other concerns must be secondary.

I will continue to speak to the other leaders and work to coordinate Earth's rescue efforts. This will be a massive effort, but I believe there is a gift in all of this.

In the past, we have been acting crazily. We have been warring, fighting, raping, and destroying. This crisis, this "hitting a bottom" is forcing us to come together. That is good news.

Working together needs to be our priority.

I ask you, the citizens of Earth, to come together on this. I ask that all of us, every month, stand up and celebrate our humanity. We are all one. At noon on the first Saturday of every month, I ask you to come together for two hours and sing and dance and pray and meditate and love each other. I ask all of us to do this in order to bring awareness to this critical issue.

I and other leaders will join you. Every month we will come to a new time zone and report to you how we are doing in our common effort. I will do this, to make the point that this is a global effort.

This is what I would do, if I were President.

POPULATION PLAN

When I read Paul Ehrlich's 1968 book, *The Population Bomb*, it terrified me. It made sense. We were multiplying like rats, and pooping in our cages. In 1968, I was sinking deeper into addiction, and I checked out for the next twenty years. When my brain came back on line, a few decades later, I listened to the siren song Big Business was singing. In effect, it was saying:

> *"Look, don't worry about the population-growth thing. We got it handled. We have figured out a way to use science to improve on millions of years of God's work. We will rip up huge patches of nature, dam up great rivers, dig up gazillions of barrels of oil and use it to make fertilizer and other chemicals to dump on top of genetically-modified corn and soybeans. We will then run this "food" through big chemical factories and squirt out substances that we will call food. We will add a lot of sugar, fat and salt. Everyone will love it! It will be easy to feed everyone. It's handled, everybody! Chill out and go back to your TV, kick back, grab a beer and some snacks, and relax."*

(Of course, money addicts would say this. They see hunger as a source of money, and don't care a whit about the impact of their behavior.)

Tom Freidman, author of *Hot, Flat and Crowded*, recently wrote: "What were we thinking? How did we not panic when the evidence was so obvious that we'd crossed some growth/climate/natural resource/population red lines all at once?"

He was referring to the spikes in food and energy prices, soaring population growth, tornadoes plowing through cities, unprecedented floods, record heat, displaced people, terrorism, and corrupt governments that are unable to address these problems.

The Earth's human population was two billion in 1920 and it will be fourteen billion in 2100. That's a seven-fold increase. America's population has tripled in the 20th century. From a population of 76 million in 1900, it grew to 281 million in 2000 and is continuing to grow at about 1.3% per year. By 2030, the population of America will be close to 400 million -- almost 30% more than now. If, between 15 and 30 % of American children go to bed hungry now, what do you imagine the situation will be in 2030?

Our population was stable for a million years until we started digging up coal, and then oil, and used these energy sources to produce more food. Today, 364,000 new babies are born every day. We are rapidly consuming more and more "wild" -- wilderness and unharmed land -- and within our children's lives most of it will be gone. The Trans-Amazon Highway is cutting through the center of the Amazon Rainforest and obliterating the last great wilderness.

Today, you and I are part of a system that has brainwashed us to buy all the stuff we buy and to behave the way we do. We need to turn this around. We could do some *positive* brainwashing about the benefits of producing fewer children. Population growth has slowed in Western Europe. And many countries have, or will soon have, negative population growth. The more educated we become, the fewer babies we have. Generally, better-educated people recognize the emotional, financial, and other commitments that raising children entails. I think once everyone comes out of denial and sees the problem, we can move to the solution.

Many schools currently have a "Take a Baby Home" program in place, but it needs to be greatly expanded. Right now some high school students are assigned a "baby" to take care of -- an actual, baby-sized replica of a baby, with a computer chip that mimics a baby's voice sounds. They are tasked with giving up their lives for a weekend to take care of the baby. This "baby" requires constant feeding, holding, bathing, diaper-changing and attending to. Lose focus for a moment and it screams! The computer chip records how well the teen is doing. These teens are amazed at how hard it is to care for a child. And they report that they are *very clear* that they don't want to have a kid any time soon! We would go a long way toward reducing addiction, mental disorders, and burdens on society, if we eliminated unplanned pregnancies.

We would hope that all children are born to sane and mature adults. But sadly, many Americans are born to individuals who are not very mature. We need to address the underlying causes of imma-ture adults having babies. These underlying causes include poverty, addiction, malnutrition, and poor education. When we are able to understand this and see that children are loved, fed, educated, and protected from neglect, abuse, and drugs, we will have made giant strides toward removing the underlying causes of unwanted babies.

I don't want to run for President, but I don't feel like I have a choice. America is in big trouble and we all need to stand up like we did in World War II. The following are my ideas and proposals. This country is full of honorable women and men who are smarter than I am. And I trust the process. I will do my best, and I trust that they will do their best, and that by combining our collective wisdom through the magic of our wired world, I believe we will choose the best strategies and the best people to create a better America.

Please, think big. Imagine yourself guiding us out of this mess. The Internet is taking us into a new paradigm, and we need a new kind of person to lead us now. We can do this, and we need you.

If I were President, I would ask everyone to read this book and, if they met the criteria for any addiction, to get into recovery.

And then I would like all of us to visualize a population that lives in harmony with Earth, a population that has repaired this small blue ball.

I would create a cabinet post, Secretary of the Population, whose mandate would be to raise awareness of the population explosion, worldwide.

I would task this person with the following:

- Expand the "Take a Baby Home" Program to every school-aged child.
- Work with the media to raise awareness of the impact that people have on the planet.
- Work with the United Nations to raise awareness, around the world, of this problem and use our resources to expand the "Take a Baby Home" Program worldwide.
- Make birth-control readily and freely available.
- Expand sex education to prevent unwanted children.
- Encourage the adoption of unplanned children.
- Encourage all nations to provide food, medical care and education to all children.

Education should include:

- Parent education regarding what it entails to raise a baby to age 18: financially, emotionally, educationally, etc.
- What is the effect on the country and the planet's resources of more mouths to feed?
- Consequences of malnutrition.
- Consequences of overcrowding.
- Contraception: if you don't want to become a parent, what are your choices?

My hope is that, given the right information, *homo sapiens* might make it. We have produced democracy, science, and many other brilliant things. Reducing our population significantly should not be that hard. We need to prove Einstein wrong.

That would be my message. And my hope

26

FOOD

I was scared as I imagined publishing parts of this book. I talked to numerous lawyers and writers and friends. The next chapter, in particular, raised some necessary red flags. I assumed that freedom of speech was universal in America, and then I learned that I needed to understand the implications of words like "defamation" and "malicious intent" and "liability."

I learned what you will read in the next pages -- that when Oprah said on her program that she would not eat another hamburger, she was sued. Oprah's words cost her a million dollars in legal fees.

The Big Food industry is huge and does not want certain facts to be made public. As stated in this chapter, they have created laws in 17 states that make it a crime to criticize food. And they will sue, even if they can't win, knowing that it will cost whomever they sue a lot of money to defend themselves. The resulting chilling effect has almost prevented me from writing this chapter.

So, to you Food Industry lawyers, I say this: Please don't sue me. All of the information regarding food in this chapter, and elsewhere in this book, has come from two documentaries: *Food, Inc.*, and *Forks Over Knives*. I have not independently verified the statements in these movies. I am simply reporting what I heard and saw in those films. I do not represent myself as an expert or an authority on food, diets, food production, medicine, or any other aspect of food.

My *personal* experience is clear. The further I get from what Big Food offers, the healthier I feel and the healthier I am. My diet today is almost exclusively plant-based and free of processed foods.

For two hundred thousand years, our ancestors lived in complete harmony with nature. 10,000 years ago some of our forefathers
and mothers learned how to farm and raise animals. For the next
9,900 years we continued to live in harmony with nature. Cancer,
heart disease, diabetes, and strokes were rare or nonexistent. In the
last one hundred years, our "brilliance" and our greed have put
us on a trajectory that is *unsustainable*. We are now like the cartoon
character, Wily Coyote, in *Roadrunner*, who has run off a cliff and has
just realized that he's about to meet a tragic end.

Today in America we have a food policy that is not sane. We
have money-hoarding, greedy CEO's running multi-national Big
Food Businesses. Big Food is bribing government officials to pass
insane, destructive, and goofy laws that will net these companies
even more money. The politicians get kickbacks to pay Big Media
billions of dollars to run *1984*-like propaganda on TV, that the
Powerless Enablers actually believe -- ads that castigate the "other
side," endlessly trying to deflect the voter from seeing the corruption. On top of this, you and I pay billions of dollars in taxes to
finance "Farm Subsidies" that allow Big Food to produce and sell
sugar, fat, and salt-laden products at *below cost*, driving small, organic
farmers out of business.

Why do Americans eat a lot of crap? One reason is that we are
genetically programmed to overeat certain foods as part of our survival mechanism. For two hundred thousand years, our genome had
little contact with sugar, fat, and salt. These items were very rare in
nature. We sought out these nutrients because they were a source of
rich, energy-dense sustenance. When we found them, we would over-
indulge, because they had survival value and we couldn't be sure we
would ever find them again. Because of this genetic hardwiring, the
average person can easily lose control and become addicted to sugar,
fat and salt-containing foods. Given a choice, the genome of *homo
sapiens* will gobble down a fast-food burger and fries (fat, salt, sugar)
instead of fruits, grains, and vegetables, because we are hardwired to
know that we may never find these foods again. Unless we take steps to
stop what's going on in our food culture, this mess will get worse. It is
just as easy to become addicted to these enticing foods as to drugs, and
they are far more prevalent and available than drugs.

We are genetically programmed to become addicted to what
your politician has legislated to make ubiquitous! Our government

gives billions of dollars to multi-national processed-food-creating corporations, and then passes laws that make fat, salt, and sugar very cheap and very available! *Just like a drug dealer who gives away drugs to get you hooked.*

The chemically-altered stuff that Big Food squirts out of their factories is called "food" and has addicted over a hundred million Americans, sickened millions of children, created a national obesity problem, and led to tens of millions of early deaths.

Here are some mind-blowing realities exposed in two recent movies, *Food, Inc.*, and *Forks Over Knives*. Both movies are well sourced and not news to healthy Americans and those who care about and understand the science of food. The Sane 20% of Americans probably already know most this and will not be surprised. However, the majority of America has been duped and is in denial. Big Food, our government, and a lazy Big Media have insanely perpetrated a heinous crime on Americans, and more egregiously, on our children.

- Fact: One in three American babies born after 2000 will get diabetes as a result of eating a diet rich in processed food.

- Fact: Over 30% of Americans have become obese following the diets approved by the "scientists" at the United States Department of Agriculture. (Many of these "scientists" work for, or are consultants to Big Food.)

- Fact: There are laws that make it a felony to criticize this drug-pushing scam. Criticize beef in Colorado, go to prison. There are actual laws in Colorado that say it is illegal to criticize beef. (Most industries are proud of their work. Why would Big Food need special laws, and lawyers standing by, to attack anyone who simply wants to see what is really going on?)

- Fact: Big Food and our "leaders" make it illegal to criticize any of our food! The following is from Wikipedia. "Food libel laws, also known as food disparagement laws and informally as veggie libel laws, are laws passed in 13 U.S. states that make it easier for food producers to sue their critics for libel. These 13 states include Alabama, Arizona, Colorado, Florida, Georgia, Idaho, Louisiana, Mississippi, North Dakota, Ohio, Oklahoma, South Dakota, and Texas. Many of the food-disparagement laws establish a lower standard for civil liability and allow for punitive damages and attorney's fees for plaintiffs alone, regardless of the case's outcome."

- Fact: We spend 2.5 trillion dollars on health-care (five times the defense budget). Treating chronic disease that our drug-dealing leaders are responsible for accounts for 75% of our health-care costs. Our taxes would go way, way, way down if our leaders simply stopped subsidizing Big Food -- simply stopped pushing fat, salt, and sugar.

- Fact: Plant-based diets, as opposed to animal-based diets, *can radically reduce, or even eliminate, obesity, heart disease, strokes, cancer, and diabetes.*

- Fact: The government fails to report the above information because government officials answer to Big Food. They don't want to talk about plant-based diets because it would expose the conspiracy that brings them billions of dollars. Big Food suppresses this information because of their greed. (And *we* gobble up their "food" because we are genetically wired to overeat fat, salt, and sugar. We are suckers for the "drug" they push.)

- Fact: It takes ten times the amount of oil to produce a calorie of animal-based food than it does to produce a calorie of plant food. (And causes more global heating.)

- Fact: The world's cattle, alone, eat enough grain to feed 8.7 billion people, nearly 2 billion more than the population on Earth. With almost 1 billion malnourished people across the globe, redirecting even a portion of the grain used to fatten cattle could feed every hungry mouth on the planet. *(We now have gutless and spineless "leaders" who stand by while babies starve!)*

- Fact: Humans are the only species that drink the breast milk of another animal. Big Food pushes this product on us even though its use by adults can have negative consequences.

- Fact: According to a United Nations report, the livestock industry is a greater contributor to global warming than transportation or industry! (A half-pound burger results in more carbon dioxide being produced than driving a car 10 miles.)

- Fact: 20% of the Amazon Rainforest (an area the size of California) has been cleared and trashed to raise livestock, to support our Big Food and Big Government's pushing a fat, salt, and sugar diet on Americans.

- Fact: For every one-dollar, fast-food burger eaten, we pay close to $25 to treat the medical consequences. For every burger some poor person eats, we all end up paying much higher taxes. Big Food and our "leaders" get their cash up front, and we taxpayers get screwed with higher taxes.

As noted above, in many states you cannot criticize food or the food industry or the food business. Be very careful, because if you do, you may be breaking a law and be sent to prison. It is very, very dangerous to criticize food. The oligarchy has us here. We all need to eat, and trillions of dollars are at stake. And President Obama, and your Senator and Representative have enabled, and are responsible, for this.

In addition to the laws that Big Food got Big Government to pass, thousands of lawyers working for Big Food will initiate frivolous lawsuits against anyone who *criticizes food!* These businesses have a lot to hide and are very defensive, and will aggressively attack us if we even try to see what they are doing.

Oprah, the TV personality, after hearing that people were dying from eating E. coli-poisoned, fast-food burgers, said she would not eat another hamburger. Immediately hordes of attorneys from Big Food came after her. It took thousands of hours and over a *million dollars* in attorneys' fees for Oprah to not go to prison. So, folks, do not criticize Big Food unless you have a spare million lying around to defend yourself, or are willing to risk going to prison.

I'm actually quite frightened that they will come after my family and me and we will be sued and lose everything for pointing out in this book what science already knows. To protect myself from Big Food's lawyers, I am going to hide behind two documentaries that have already done the research, *Food, Inc.* and *Forks Over Knives.* The producers of *Food, Inc.* reported that a portion of the movie's budget was spent on legal fees to defend themselves from Big Food's lawyers. So, Big Food, I simply got all this information from the above-mentioned, two movies. Please don't sue me. (I encourage everyone to check out the sources used by these two movies -- both films are backed by science.)

From *Food, Inc.* comes the story of a middle-class Colorado mom who bought a hamburger for her son at a fast-food restaurant. Days later, her 2-year old son, Kevin, died of E. coli poisoning from the contaminated burger. This fast-food, bad meat disaster had happened many times before, so this mother took steps to get our government to pass a law to protect us. This makes complete sense, except it turns out that our government protects us from the food industry about as well as it protects us from Wall Street or protects children from nicotine, i.e., they don't. Seven years after being introduced in Congress, "Kevin's Law" has yet to be passed.

Kevin's Law is officially known as the Meat and Poultry Pathogen Reduction and Enforcement Act of 2003. It was pretty straightforward. It authorized the Department of Agriculture inspectors to look for dangerous strains of E. coli in meat-processing factories. If they found any, they could shut the factory down until the pathogens were eliminated. After all, this bug was killing Americans. Big Food said that the law would impact "Economic Growth" and force up the price of hamburgers. The reality is that they don't want their costs to increase, and they are prioritizing cost over health. What Big Food also cares about is hiding what it's doing from the public.

Today, 90% of the meat we eat comes from cows that are fed not grass, but genetically modified corn and soybeans in "CAFOs" (Concentrated Animal Feeding Operations.) In these huge setups, hidden away, thousands of cows stand ankle-deep in shit, eating chemically-altered "food." Many of the workers in these plants are illegal immigrants bused from Mexico by Government-enabled Big Business. These poor, shit-covered animals are shipped to top-secret slaughterhouses where more immigrants cut up cow carcasses for distribution to a genome (us) unable to resist overeating the end product (fat, salt, sugar).

(*Food, Inc.* reports that the feed-and-slaughter industry publicly advertises in Mexico to recruit illegal workers, and then buses these illegal aliens to American factories. They are violating the law, and our government officials *know this*. The Republicans support this practice, and the Democrats look the other way. Then, periodically, the government calls in the Immigration and Naturalization Services [INS] to *stage small arrests to make it look like they are doing something to stop this practice.*)

Immoral. Corrupt. They all need to go!

We may think we have a free press, but Big Food's lawyers stand by to silence its critics. The press is our Fourth Estate, and it is frightened to tell the truth about why it can't report this travesty.

Upton Sinclair published *The Jungle* in 1906. He pointed out the shocking conditions in Chicago's meatpacking industry and the corrupt officials who oversaw it. What we have now is much worse. Clearly the mainstream media is afraid to face Big Food and the government-enabled lawsuits.

I wonder what Big Food would not want us to know . . . .

Every year our government gives billions of dollars to Big Food. Big Food is *Big*. I am going to simplify the following. The majority of America's farmers are paid a lot of money to grow *only* corn and soybeans. These farmers are using oil-based, synthetic fertilizer, created by environment-destroying Big Chemical and Big Oil. Producing this fertilizer heats the planet, depletes our carbon, ruins the soil, and creates effluent that poisons our rivers and oceans. Government subsidizes this corn and soybean production so these crops can be grown below cost. Government and Big Food got together and planned this to prevent any competition from small farmers. The American Farmer is *gone!* The Republicans, the standard bearers for capitalism and small business, have been bought off, and in the last 50 years, have helped to *eliminate* small, family-run farms in America. These corn and soybean crops are genetically altered to prevent birds and bugs from surviving anywhere near them, which sterilizes giant swaths of our "fruited plains," killing Mother Earth and causing untold numbers of critters to become extinct. The corn and soybeans are then sent to giant, and nearly top-secret, factories where chemists, using massive amounts of oil, break down these genetically-modified plants into a bunch of chemicals that are then chemically recombined to produce the base materials, that are then recombined again and packaged to look like *food.*

Just read the labels.

The majority of what is available in a supermarket is simply these recombined chemicals, packaged in a way that lures shoppers to buy them, and eat them, causing Americans to become fat and sick. Obesity is skyrocketing. *One third of all people born in the United States after the year 2000 will develop diabetes and could die a horrible and early death.* Please reread that last sentence.

We created this! You and I. We elected these greedy bastards who collude in this immoral and deadly process!

Your Senator, your Representative, your President made the laws and regulations that caused this. If asked, they will spew out some bullshit about how they are not responsible (others guys' fault) or what new agency they will appoint to address the problem. If they are not responsible, who the hell is?

(They all have to go! In 2012. All of them.)

This is insane. These greedy, money-hoarders are costing us billions! But worse than that, they are feeding us "food" that makes us sick and which contributes to bankrupting Medicare. I would much rather pay more to buy food that did not cause cancer, diabetes, strokes or heart disease, or make kids sick and fat. Plus, this would go a long way toward fixing our financial system and saving the planet. *Our taxes and oil consumption would go way down if we stopped this charade.*

Think about it. Just look around. Look at all the obese people. Obese people see a lot of doctors, take a lot of medicines and go to a lot of hospitals. Who pays for this? Medicare, Medi-Cal, Social Security, etc. But there is another, saner approach: recovery from food addiction. I know old people who changed their eating habits and are now healthy and running, swimming, biking in their 70s and 80s. *They have very low, or even no, medical costs!*

In effect, Big Food is saying; "Sorry, we really don't care about the consumer. We don't care about children. We don't care about future economic costs. We have a thing going on here, and we don't want to talk about it." Seriously, they don't want us to see what goes on in their factories.

And we have allowed this. We passively stand by. We all need to wake up and put sane people in charge. If we randomly picked a bunch of farmers who are using sustainable practices and put them in charge of our food, we would save many millions of lives and many billions of dollars! How many Americans died in World War II? Just soldiers alone, over one-hundred-thousand. How many died in Vietnam? Sixty-thousand. How many died in Iraq? Five-thousand and counting. Our current, criminal Food Policy is killing more people every year than the number of Americans who died in all of those wars. Big Food and our bought-off leaders are responsible for millions of very messy, early deaths, every year.

Look what happened when Michelle Obama just mentioned that our kids should eat healthier food. She touched the third rail. *Can't talk about that!* Big Business and its Republican enablers attacked her. Did these elected Republicans, knowing that their own children are being put at a disadvantage by fast food, stand up for science and morality and "what's right," and the future of their children? Addicts are run by their midbrain's need for dopamine. Big Business and government are addicted to power and money. Addicts put their addiction before their children. Of course the elected officials will let their children be disadvantaged to keep the dopamine coming. They are just like the alcoholic who neglects his own children.

Plus, no addict ever "rats out" his dealer. Did the Democrats stand up and support this simple and obvious inquiry about healthy eating? Of course not; they, too, get millions from Big Food. I wept as I watched Michelle Obama, an advocate for children, being attacked by mindless and dangerous addicts. What politicians, Big Business, and the media that support our current sick system did was wrong. They need to make amends to Michelle. Plain and simple.

Rush Limbaugh is right. The *Lame Stream Media* is not sane. Ninety-nine percent of the media did not go ballistic at the insanity of Big Business and Big Government's attack on Michelle's simple but sane views promoting healthy eating for children. Big Media enables the status quo. Julian Assange has a point: Big Media is in bed with Big Business, Big Union, and Big Government.

We are learning that sugar, like tobacco, kills us. Simple carbohydrates containing sugar are beneficial when combined with the thousands of other micronutrients found in *real food, like fruits and vegetables, legumes, nuts and seeds.* But the sugar, and fake sugar, ingested in sodas, candy, cereal, processed bread, canned vegetables, processed meats, and a thousand other products is *not real.* It is manufactured. Ingesting sugar can lead to cancer, obesity, diabetes, heart disease, strokes, developmental delays, and early death. Not only can it lead to those diseases, but it is the reason that one third of children born today are expected to develop diabetes. Processed sugar, in all its varieties, is a bad chemical. But many Americans are addicted to it -- and peddling this chemical makes billions of dollars for Big Business. And millions of dollars get passed on to the leaders, who rig the system.

Now you can see why our government subsidizes sugar!

Robert Lustig, M.D., specialist in pediatric hormone disorders at the University of California, San Francisco, gave a lecture that has gone viral on the Web. Over 1.4 million people have watched it. If you care about saving America, I implore you to watch one of our leading doctors "tell it like it is." The video is called, *Sugar: The Bitter Truth*. The link to the YouTube video is: http://www.youtube.com/watch?v=dBnniua6-oM)

In his presentation, Dr. Lustig talks about high fructose corn syrup, which Big Food erroneously labels "food," and adds to almost every food product found in today's supermarkets. Dr. Lustig calls sugar a "toxin," and a "poison." Five times he calls sugar "evil." He calls high fructose corn syrup "the most demonized additive know to man."

Today, your President, Senator, and Representative are signing off on selling more sugar to children, one third of whom will get diabetes.

"Sustainable farming" is how we have farmed since the beginning of agriculture. Our cows ate grass and fertilized the grass with their poop. Millions of critters, large and small, lived nearby in harmony. When it rained, nature automatically cleaned everything up. *Zero carbon footprint.* This has to be our goal if we are going to keep our planet alive. We must remove the insane leaders who allowed Big Farm to destroy our land. We must restore Mother Earth.

This is the Big Food equation: Money + Government Corruption + Genetic Vulnerability = Addiction That Leads To Massive Killing Of Americans.

Most of us are, or could be, food addicts. I certainly am. I have difficulty passing up my favorite treats, because I am wired by evolution to gobble them up. Hardwired. Millions of us have lost the ability to control our addiction to sugar, fat, and salt. And like all addicts, we are in denial. We get anxious and disturbed when someone mentions anything about the addiction we are denying. In this case, we have the perfect story to confirm Einstein's theory that we lack the capacity to think, and we are going to kill ourselves. Was he right?

Sometimes, when I look around, I think he may be right. We are getting fatter and fatter. Think about it. We adults may choose to kill ourselves. *But our children!* Shame on us! Aren't we also genetically programmed to protect children *with our lives?* How could we allow public schools to feed our children food that compromises their health? How could we allow schools to have vending machines that sell these addictive substances? And how could we take our children to fast-food outlets? And bring home mountains of processed sugar and high fructose corn syrup? We may not have known the science behind overeating, but haven't we noticed our kids getting fatter and sicker and questioned whether what they ate played a role?

Big Business's Addiction to Money + Big Government's Addiction to Power + Human Vulnerably to Overeat Fat, Salt, Sugar + Psychological Defense of Denial = Proving Einstein Correct!

This Intervention will bring sanity back to America and allow us to have the wise leaders that we need to make *real food* a part of our lives.

I don't want to run for President, but I don't feel like I have a choice. America is in big trouble and we all need to stand up like we did in World War II. The following are my ideas and proposals. This country is full of honorable women and men who are smarter than I am. And I trust the process. I will do my best, and I trust that they will do their best, and that by combining our collective wisdom through the magic of our wired world, I believe we will choose the best strategies and the best people to create a better America.

Please, think big. Imagine yourself guiding us out of this mess. The Internet is taking us into a new paradigm, and we need a new kind of person to lead us now. We can do this, and we need you.

If I were President, I would ask everyone to read this book and, if they met the criteria for any addiction, to get into recovery.

I would ask everyone to watch the movies *Food, Inc.* and *Forks Over Knives.*

I would expect to pass Kevin's Law.

I would request that all members of Congress, and the Administration, within 90 days of taking office, and every six months thereafter, visit the CAFO cow, chicken, and pig factories, the food processing plants and the slaughterhouses, and see the effluent (shit) that flows from these concentration camps. I would visit them myself, with the press. We need to turn the lights on!

Next, in a careful unwinding, I would take all the money going to multi-national Big Farm corporations and give it to sustainable and organic farming. For the last 10,000 years, farming has been an honorable occupation. Some of the money we now spend to produce sugar, we can use to hire the unemployed to grow food. Giant agribusiness needs to be replaced by millions of small farms. These farms will thrive, because our post-Intervention leaders will help educate all of us on the basics of raising food. Our government now artificially subsidizes certain food industries. We need to factor in the true costs of real food. We now have dollar burgers and pay three dollars a pound for broccoli. I would move the subsidies to healthy food and away from food that leads to poor health.

I would expose the practice of giving billions of dollars of your money to put cheap heroin on the streets that will addict your kids. Oops, I mean $C_{12}H_{22}O_{11}$, also known as high fructose corn syrup. (Actually, heroin kills 7,000 people a year. High fructose corn syrup has killed, and will kill millions! We get *so* upset at heroin dealers, when the sugar industry is far, far, far more deadly!)

I would propose a rapid, but organized, unwinding of all farm subsidies, as they exist now. I would propose using some of the money saved from discontinuing subsidized farming to educate Americans about sustainable farming. The money saved from ending subsidies would lower our taxes, or go to subsidize the creation of millions of small farms (giving the unemployed still another opportunity for work). I propose that we treat sugar as the addictive chemical that it is. Sugar will be legal, but like other addictive substances, it will be regulated, and it will be taxed, and the revenue from taxes will be used to pay for education and the treatment of food addiction. Just like with addictive substances, parents will keep it away from children. The goal would be to make healthy food available to everyone and to get government out of the process, except when it can contribute to the general good, as in education and treatment of food addiction.

I would ask all students, teachers, government officials, parents, doctors, therapists, and anyone who eats high fructose corn syrup to watch Robert Lustig's YouTube video, *Sugar: The Bitter Truth*. http://www.youtube.com/watch?v=dBnniua6-oM)

I would change the name of the Secretary of Agriculture to the Secretary of Food. I would direct this individual to remove all Big Food employees, or anyone who worked with Big Food, from government positions.

I would ask former President Clinton to tell his story. Remarkable things happen when we move from an animal-based diet to a plant-based diet. Millions know about the magic of recovery from dependence on animal food. Bill Clinton's story is just one of these remarkable transformations. I would consider offering him the job of Secretary of Food.

I would review all government agencies and programs related to agriculture and food. These employees have created, enabled, or ignored this unbelievable nightmare! I would eliminate any grants to science or universities unless they focused on the solution. They have all been complicit in enabling this insane process. I would initiate a national dialogue about sustainable farming, organic farming, and permaculture. The goal would be to provide healthy food to every child *and to collectively celebrate the return of Mother Nature. We do have enough for every person's need, just not for every person's greed . . . for more and more and more.*

27

EDUCATION

All of us are saddened when we think about how our country manages education.

We see the bumper stickers:

"What would it be like to live in a world where schools got 25 million dollars and the Air Force had to hold a bake sale to buy guns?"

Children need to be our first priority. Each of us becomes the person we are because of what happened in the critical, first 18 months of our lives. And the next critical three years. And every year, until we become adults. Every successful mammal prioritizes childcare, even at the risk of being killed to protect his or her young.

Most folks don't understand the stressors placed on today's kids. Children today live in a world where electronic screens seduce them away from nature, and play, and contact with other humans. They grow up in a nation that has destroyed most of their wilderness. They hear that we have screwed up the economy and that we will leave them with the bill. And then they hear that the planet is at risk, and that their clueless parents are "asleep at the wheel" and failing to notice the unfolding tragedy. They text each other, on average, over one hundred times a day. And a recent report says that 70% of them get texts from their hovering, helicopter parents *while they are in class*!

If we care about children, we need to care about their teachers. Sadly, we are misguided here. We need to give teachers better salaries and allocate more funds to school programs. Nationwide, we are cutting back on field trips, sports, marching bands, art, and other activities that many of us older folks so loved when we were in school. And in higher education, California, for instance, used to have one of the best college systems in the land. And it was affordable. Now it is in financial trouble.

We need to get our priorities straight.

> I don't want to run for President, but I don't feel like I have a choice. America is in big trouble and we all need to stand up like we did in World War II. The following are my ideas and proposals. This country is full of honorable women and men who are smarter than I am. And I trust the process. I will do my best, and I trust that they will do their best, and that by combining our collective wisdom through the magic of our wired world, I believe we will choose the best strategies and the best people to create a better America.
> Please, think big. Imagine yourself guiding us out of this mess. The Internet is taking us into a new paradigm, and we need a new kind of person to lead us now. We can do this, and we need you.

If I were President, I would ask everyone to read this book and, if they met the criteria for any addiction, to get into recovery.

And then I would ask all educators to read Jeremy Rifkin's book, *The Third Industrial Revolution.* This book challenges all of us to think in terms of the paradigm shifting that is needed for tomorrow.

I would challenge all of us to take a look at this. We know that there are bureaucracies that suck up money. We know that there are calcified unions that protect uninspired teachers from being challenged to hone their skills and learn new tricks. We have a ton of recent graduates that are unemployed and a lot of retired people who would have a lot to offer as teachers.

We need a "Sputnik Moment" in education to bring about Rifkin's vision of *The Third Industrial Revolution*, which I talk about in other parts of this book. We need to inspire all of us to imagine what we can give to the education system. We need to shake this up. America's education paradigm needs to become more like Steve Job's company, Apple. Apple had no committees. None. People collaborated, brainstormed, and worked towards "what Steve wanted." We need inspired leaders to lead us. If I were President, I would find educators with vision and then give them what they needed to make their visions a reality. Michael J. Sandel, the "rock star" professor from Harvard, is such a leader. He might make a great Secretary of Education.

28

DRUG POLICY

Our drug policy is not working. I know. I treat addiction. And I have known addiction since birth. My father was an addict, and I became an addict. I have been sober for over three decades. I founded and direct an outpatient rehab center that treats teen, young adult, and adult addicts. And, I am a Professional Interventionist. This is my field. I live it every day.

As we have seen, our politicians' greed and addiction to endless kickbacks from Big Business have led to insanity on many fronts. These politicians, like all addicts, have predictably created chaos in the drug field. So it should not come as a surprise that the politicians, Big Business, Big Union and their enablers (that's you and me) have come up with an approach that is insane.

Here are the consequences of their "head-in-the-sand" approach.

Today, children have free access to powerful narcotics and designer drugs that did not exist one generation ago. Today, at your local public school, your child can buy these drugs. Today, nicotine addiction, which kills nearly a half a million people every year, is not being talked about because our politicians get kickbacks from Big Nicotine. Today, 90% of active drug addicts are receiving *no* treatment.

Today, countries like Mexico and Afghanistan are falling apart, as narcotics gangs challenge the state for control. It is estimated that 70% of the money the Taliban gets comes from the sale of heroin to America. We are devastated at the number of Americans killed in Iraq; *during this same period, six times as many deaths have occurred in Mexico, because of our drug policy.*

Today, America is selling guns to Mexico and buying drugs from them. Today, secondhand smoke kills over 50,000 people a year. Today, we are failing to prevent addiction in children. Today, over half of all prisoners in jails and prisons are there because of crimes involving drugs. Today, millions of untreated addicts rob and kill to get drug money. When they're high, they kill and molest our kids. Today, someone is trying to figure out a way to get your child addicted.

This is what you and I have created. You and I are responsible for electing leaders who help create this. This is our "Drug Policy."

How is this working for you? This is what you and I are faced with, today.

This is my field. The insanity makes me crazy. Every day I look at children who have been damaged by the drugs that we allow them access to. *They are our children!* It is the job of adults to protect children! We are failing. We need to grow up, get our act together and protect all children from drug use.

A kilogram of heroin costs $1,000 in Bangkok and $250,000 in New York City. The organized drug dealers have the profit motive and far, far more resources than the drug police. When I worked in San Quentin, it was well known that drugs were readily available there. If we can't keep drugs out of prison, how can we keep them from those who will sell them to our children?

If I were President, I would implement a two-pronged approach to our drug problem. We need to come up with a comprehensive approach that will protect all children from drug use. Nearly every adult addict began his or her addiction as a teenager. And, we need to legalize drugs. We need to legalize drugs in combination with a comprehensive, integrated, national plan that protects *every* child from any substance use.

(To all you adults who are salivating at the thought of legalization of drugs: *First* we have to pass the laws to keep our children free of drugs. *Then* we can talk about legalization. We cannot do one without the other. Children are the vulnerable ones -- children's welfare always comes first.)

What I propose is a radical change in our social norms that would lead to a much saner world. (And *much* lower taxes.) This change will require a society with a broader vision than we currently have, but I believe it is possible to quickly achieve this goal if we put our minds to it.

Let's imagine a world where drugs are legal and taxed. And let's imagine a world where anyone who is affected by addiction receives treatment, because it is approximately 10 times cheaper to provide treatment than to pay for the legal, social, and medical consequences of addiction. Nearly all organized crime would cease, 75% of our prisons could be closed, and we could lay off the Drug Police. This would save billions of dollars and reduce the social upheaval that's resulted in the past from making substance use illegal. And let's imagine a world where every child grows up with their brains and bodies free of addictive substances. The number of adult addicts would diminish drastically, because teens that have not used drugs before age 18 become addicted at a much lower rate than those who use drugs before their brains have matured.

Sounds pretty good, yes?

Some people think that legalization of drugs would lead to more drug use. To these uninformed, let me say the following:

Right now, every drug you could ever want is already readily available!

You must be smoking some weird stuff to think that the legalization of drugs would make them *more* available! Listen carefully, capitalism works. Drug dealers sell drugs to make money. Any drug-seeking person can land on any part of the Earth and, within hours, if not minutes, find and acquire all the drugs they want. Only those who have never visited 'the street' could possibly believe that the legalization of drugs would make drugs more available.

The problem is that currently, drug dealers sell, and give, drugs to children. Which, from a marketing standpoint, makes a lot of sense. They are creating more customers. Perhaps they learned this tragic scam from our elected officials and Big Nicotine, when they were actively peddling their deadly drugs to children. (Or, today, doing very little to prevent it.)

Statistics have shown that teens who do not smoke cigarettes before age 18 have a much, much lower lifetime chance of becoming addicted to nicotine. The reason for this is simple -- by age 18, their brains have developed enough wisdom to understand the dangers of smoking. Sane adults see smoking as a really stupid practice, one that leads to addiction and to death. Up until just a few years ago, the tobacco industry, government officials, and we enablers allowed advertising of tobacco to children for exactly this reason -- children, and younger teens, do not have the judgment to refrain from smoking. By age 18, young adults are beginning to be able to think enough to not fall for slick advertising or peer pressure.

Research has shown the tragic cost to children and society of minors' exposure to drugs.

At what age *should* young adults be allowed to have access to drugs?

Perhaps the question we need to ask is, "when does the brain actually mature and when have we grown up enough to make good decisions?" Neurological research has shown that the brain continues to grow and develop until around age 25. Would 25 be the best age at which to make drug use legal? To keep it simple, I believe we need to start out with 21 being the age for access to all legal drugs and let future leaders make adjustments.

Also, let's imagine the following two interlinked drug laws. The first law would mandate that absolutely no child under age 21 would be permitted use of any recreational drug. The second law would state that there would no longer be any laws restricting the right of adults to ingest any substance, so long as it did not infringe on the rights of another person.

These two laws must to go together.

The only way we can have the freedom of legalized drugs for adults is to effectively protect children from the harm drugs cause. Children have not yet developed the judgment necessary to make adult decisions, like those involved in driving a car or handling firearms. Children who use drugs are at a disadvantage. The younger a child is when introduced to drugs, the higher the probability they will become addicted, and even if they don't become addicted, the higher the chance they will not "make it." These drug-using teens often become the dysfunctional adults who can't take care of themselves and burden our social, legal and health-care systems.

We also need to take another look at adult drug use. Should anyone be able to take drugs, when they are not yet capable of taking care of themselves? One of the quickest ways to get an adult to enter treatment is to say, "either you go into treatment or I will withdraw all financial support -- no food, no housing, no car, no money, no cell phone, no nothing." We taxpayers are giving billions of dollars to addicts, and others who are impaired, because of drugs. This includes people on welfare, food stamps, those collecting workers comp, or those supported by myriad other "safety net" programs. I propose that these individuals will need to be completely drug-free to receive government money. And if they are addicts, they will be offered treatment. We want these people to get off the dole and to pay their share. They can't do that if they are getting high. It may make us crazy to hear about the food-stamp-and-welfare crowd laying around and watching TV while we pay their way. But the bigger tragedy is that we are enabling untreated addiction and sapping the potential of these poor souls.

When I see an adult drug addict, I usually see a developmental crisis. I see an adult who almost always started using drugs in their teen years. I see a family system where the parent and society enabled this teen's drug use. And now I'm looking at someone who *didn't make it.* They did not make it to adulthood and are not capable of being self-sufficient. Without an intervention, and an often-costly treatment process, these individuals will need their mommy and daddy to take care of them forever. Or, we will have to take care of them. They will fill our prisons or become our homeless, who suck up huge amounts of our tax money through various social services.

Nearly all mammals protect their young. And we have a comprehensive set of laws to protect children from harm. We don't allow children to be neglected or abused. Child Protective Services, the police, and the courts will intervene as needed. We don't allow children to work in dangerous conditions. Children cannot drive cars or carry guns until they are old enough to have good judgment. It would be easy to add "no drug use" to the list.

It would be easy. We simply need to wake up and get educated about the facts. And then, make a decision.

It is a parent's job to keep their kids safe. Allowing a child to use illegal drugs is neglect -- plain and simple. It is just plain wrong for us to allow any child to damage their body and stunt their bio-psycho-social-spiritual development. We as a society are just waking up to the horrific risks of the deadly drugs that were not around a generation ago, the reality that addiction is a brain disease, and that effective treatment is available.

Every day for the past 18 years, I have worked with families whose children have become addicted to drugs. Typically these children started smoking pot or drinking in around the 8th or 9th grade. Boom. At that point, many of these children's development slowed down or stopped. It is now two, or four, or ten years later, and these families are finally coming to my office with a huge problem. (10-15% of Americans are or will become addicts, and it almost always starts in the 8th or 9th grade.)

When this happens, I take a deep breath and go to work. What I love is the parent who calls me at the first sign of drug or alcohol use. The *first* sign!

It's simple. The parent sees a potential problem, and they get help. The child understands that his or her parents are serious and there will consequences if they use substances again. These kids will stop. (Unless they are already well into their addiction -- in which case we are lucky to have caught it early and can start addiction treatment when it is the easiest to treat.)

The teen will be angry. We expect the teen to be angry. Healthy teens will push the envelope. Healthy parents set clear boundaries. (If a teen is angry, it's actually a really good sign. They are having their natural grandiosity and narcissism shaped by reality. Parents who fail to "say no" are neglecting their child by failing to teach their children how the world actually works.)

So how do we protect every child from drug use? It's simple. Test them. (Some private schools already drug test all students for nicotine and other drugs.) A saliva sample will show drug use.

But we need to get everyone on board. We, as a nation, need to ask ourselves these questions: "Do we think that protecting children from drugs is a good idea? Do we believe that protecting children from drugs, like we protect them from other kinds of abuse and dangers, is a good idea? Should they be restricted from certain actions and behaviors?" Every doctor, mental health professional, police person, teacher, religion, and nearly all healthy parents will support this.

There will be a lot of resistance from the government and Big Business, who will lose a lot of money. Some adults would resist keeping drugs from children because they would lose their "using buddies." Seriously! Many addicted parents "turn their children on" to drugs (alcohol is a drug) so they have a companion with whom to get high. There will be resistance from the lawyers, because they make money by resisting things. And, there will be a lot of parents who will need to go to parent education classes and visit family therapists, because they don't yet know how to set boundaries and say "No" to their children.

I believe that a sane population will see that parents who allow their child to be damaged by drugs are in the same league as parents who allow their child to be neglected or abused.

Some citizens might invoke civil rights laws or feel that liberties are being violated. I see this as a canard. Children have many rights, but the right to harm themselves is not one of them. Yes, we will need to update our laws to deal with this issue.

I ask you this: can you name one doctor or mental health professional or educator who advocates children having access to drugs (alcohol is a drug)? Not one sane adult wants children to harm themselves. Yes, America would have to change its values to accommodate this. But I believe most parents would embrace a process that keeps their children drug-free until they become adults. (Remember, sending kids to work in factories and mines, and beating them, used to be legal.)

If children were protected from using drugs until age 21, how many on their 21st birthday would choose to smoke cigarettes? Studies show that *very few people* choose to start smoking at age 21. My guess is that cigarette smoking would almost completely cease to exist as the old addicts die off. (Guess who would go ballistic at this idea? Big Nicotine, Big Advertising and Big Government, all of whom will lose the money they get from the tobacco industry's kickbacks. And you *know* what happens to an addict when they have their "fix" taken away from them . . .)

In the world that I propose, everyone would be educated about the brain disease of addiction. Addiction would be recognized as a chronic, medical disease, like diabetes, hypertension or asthma, and treatment would be readily available. Parents and children would be educated about the warning signs of addiction. Parents would seek immediate help for their children at the first sign of any use. And this help would be readily available.

What about those who are mentally ill, or homeless, who cannot make wise choices, and who suffer from a wide variety of psychiatric disorders including addiction? What about them? Right now we spend a fortune on them, and they lie on our streets, suffering terrible lives and cycling endlessly in and out of jails and prisons and hospitals. What about them?

For a small fraction of the money currently being spent on social services, prisons, and lining politicians' pockets, we, as a society, could adopt a compassionate program for mentally ill adults who are unable to care for themselves.

There has to be some sort of treatment that falls between expensive mental facilities and living on the streets. We have come a long way from the lunatic asylums of old, but it is a sad thing how we currently treat our mentally ill.

I wonder a lot about this. Certainly we can do better. There have to be some young idealistic minds out there that can create the next, compassionate thing for this population. What we are doing is not kind.

Here is one idea. Could we give the mentally ill a safe place to receive treatment and get well before rejoining society at large? Perhaps facilities could be created on one of the Channel Islands off California or in Puget Sound or off the coast of Maine. Australia, light.

This may sound odd, and a million critics will find fault with this idea, but to them I say, "OK, what is *your* plan?" We need only look at the current "policy." These poor souls eat out of dumpsters, sleep in doorways, live in our parks, wander the streets, or are put in cages (jails and prisons) and get no help. Is it better to continue to stand by and ignore this tragedy? How long can we ignore these tortured souls among us?

Could we create a society that treats addiction and mental illness humanely and responsibly? We have come a long way as a species, and we can take this next step. It will require leaders with vision. And the impact will be profound. We could eliminate most prisons, reduce taxes, better educate our population, and create healthier families. We could eliminate the specter of untreated addicts and the mentally ill lurking near our children and dying in front of us.

Right now, we are at war with ourselves. Someone said that Osama bin Laden could not have come up with a better plan to disrupt America than our current War on Drugs. It is really a "War on Ourselves."

One part of us wants to eat candy, and another part wants a paternalistic government to protect us from ourselves. I believe that we just need to grow up. We can build a society that is honest about drugs. Addiction will come to be seen for what it actually is, a bio-psycho-social-spiritual disease that can easily respond to effective treatment.

Almost everyone has strong feelings on this topic, and we have a lot to think about before we start down the path toward drug legalization.

We might get some insight from anthropologists who have studied different cultures. Humans have historically used a number of drugs in ways that bring communities together. Indigenous cultures throughout history have been using drugs as sacraments; as ways to enhance spirituality and deepen connection to nature. The Native Americans used Peyote, the South Americans used Ayahuasca, other societies have used psilocybin, marijuana, Ibogin, and, more recently in the west, LSD and MDMA (Ecstasy).

Currently, the federal government is supporting rigorous experiments to confirm what many of us already know. For years, M.A.P.S., the Multidisciplinary Association for Psychedelic Studies, has been quietly promoting legitimate, government-sponsored, scientific research on the positive uses of psychedelics. Researchers are using LSD and psilocybin to treat anxiety in people suffering from terminal diseases. The military is working with medical doctors to use MDMA (Ecstasy) for treating Post Traumatic Stress Disorder (PTSD) in war veterans. And research is now being done on the use of Ibogin to treat addiction.

Many people know a lot about the beneficial use of psychedelics. Research in the 1960s showed tremendous promise for using these drugs to alleviate mental distress and enhance well-being. Bill Wilson, one of the founders of AA, had his lifelong depression helped by using LSD. Some people wonder if his "spiritual awakening" may in fact have been caused by the "Belladonna Treatment" he received in 1935. The government's hysteria in the 1960s and 70s brought legitimate inquiry to a close, although active underground research has continued among professionals around the world.

Slowly, science is proving the value of these substances for legitimate medical and social purposes.

In America, two organizations are authorized by federal law to allow its members to legally use psychedelics as part of their rituals. One is the Native Americans, who can legally use Peyote. The other is the Uniao do Vegetal, an organization founded in Brazil, that can legally use Hoasca, also known as, Ayahuasca. Ayahuasca is a psychedelic that has been used by the indigenous peoples of South America for centuries.

Anthropologists who have visited these Brazilian communities report that Ayahuasca-using communities are socially much healthier and more developed than the people in nearby communities who have adopted the "Western Life" of alcohol and nicotine use.

A case could be made that we might be better off as a society if we were using drugs that led to a loving connection with each other, and with nature. These drugs would include LSD, psilocybin, mushrooms, Peyote, Ayahuasca, and marijuana. And we might be better off not using drugs that make us unconscious, combative, angry, and sick, such as alcohol, narcotics, stimulants, and nicotine.

This makes sense to me, a former hippy, who found love, spirituality, and connection through psychedelics, and ultimately despair, sickness, and insanity when I turned to alcohol.

I don't want to run for President, but I don't feel like I have a choice. America is in big trouble and we all need to stand up like we did in World War II. The following are my ideas and proposals. This country is full of honorable women and men who are smarter than I am. And I trust the process. I will do my best, and I trust that they will do their best, and that by combining our collective wisdom through the magic of our wired world, I believe we will choose the best strategies and the best people to create a better America.

Please, think big. Imagine yourself guiding us out of this mess. The Internet is taking us into a new paradigm, and we need a new kind of person to lead us now. We can do this, and we need you.

If I were President, I would ask everyone to read this book and, if they met the criteria for any addiction, to get into recovery.

I would propose forming a group of wise adults whose task would be to accomplish two goals. The first would be to come up with a comprehensive plan that would lead to the elimination of all recreational drug use for anyone under age 21. The second goal would be to legalize all drugs.

I would, within 90 days, present this plan to Congress for additional study and implementation. I would hope to sign this bill into law in another 90 days. It would not be perfect, but it would be a serious start.

I would create a cabinet post, the Secretary of Substance Use. This person would be responsible for implementing this advisory group's recommendations, which would be along the following lines.

1. We protect children's birthright to healthy brain development, by prohibiting drug use until age 21.

2. We utilize all resources to see that children are drug free. We expand the Child-Abuse Laws to include child drug use. This would include drug testing of all children by doctors, police, parents, schools, and any other facility that children come in contact with.

3. All drugs become legal for adults, aged 21 and over, and are taxed like we currently tax alcohol and tobacco.

4. The money collected from taxing drugs would be used *only* for education, treatment, and research about substance use.

5. We would disseminate the message that allowing any child access to drugs is illegal. Substance Dependence would be recognized as a medical disease, and all individuals suffering from this disease would be treated, for free, using funds from the taxes on these substances.

6. We would all understand that successful addiction treatment, to be effective, *must include the addict's enablers.*

7. We would provide treatment for all inmates who suffer from substance-related disorders. We would free any inmates whose only offense was related to substance use or substance possession.

29

ADDICTION TREATMENT

Homo sapiens has come a long way. We got out of the trees and learned to stand up, make fire, herd animals, and farm. We developed the wheel, and made steam engines, and sent a man to the moon. Today, our technology has transformed just about everything. We have technology that allows most cultures and tribes to communicate and share their wonders. One would think that these accomplishments would put mankind in a really good place.

Except for one very big problem. Our leaders are crazy. They are not sane. They, the 1% running the show, have been captured by their midbrain's need to get more dopamine. They are no longer able to see the big picture. Only the nature of the "fix" to which they are addicted differentiates these "leaders" from the frantic heroin addict, lurking in the shadows. Both types of addicts are unable to see past their next fix.

And, I believe the majority of Americans, to a greater or lesser degree, also meet the criteria for addiction. I fit into this category. Periodically my car somehow takes me to the supermarket, where I purchase a pint of Haagan Dazs and, within minutes, I have consumed the whole thing. The next day, I regret my actions. But I'm getting better. In early recovery, I ate a pint of Haagan Dazs many times a week; now I only do it once every few months. When I was younger, almost every spring, I suddenly found myself purchasing a new motorcycle that I had not planned on buying.

Craving, loss of control, adverse consequences, and practicing the behavior for a long time are the markers of addiction. We all understand that alcoholism is an addiction, and many of us understand the recovery process from addiction. But I believe that most of us have difficulty seeing that many of our common behaviors also meet the criteria for addiction, and that we would benefit from learning how to change and become healthier in these areas.

Take compulsive eating, for example. I live in the San Francisco Bay Area, and our culture is healthier than is the culture of some other parts of the country. As I travel outside of the Bay Area, I am amazed at the number of obese families. Whole families have somehow gone insane and burdened themselves, their children, and the rest of us, with higher medical costs. There are rare, medical exceptions that explain this condition, but the vast majority of these families have succumbed to addictive eating. They know they are fat. They know they would be happier if they were healthier. But they crave their food; they can't control their eating and it is causing adverse consequences; it has been going on for a long time, and it is getting worse. They are addicted.

Here is one way of looking at this. The Drug Dealer came along and said, "Hey, come over here. I've got something you will really like. Here, try it. It's free!" The dealer, of course, is Big Food, and the drug is some amalgam of sugar, fat, and salt. And it might not be free, but it is cheap. It is cheap because our government and our tax dollars made it cheap by giving billions and billions of dollars to Big Farm and Big Food to produce it, below cost. (And of course Big Food then bribes the politicians for that favor.)

Members of these fat families, one in three Americans, are the victims of an addictive system, just like millions of nicotine addicts are the victims of our elected officials colluding with Big Nicotine and pushing their drug on us in order to feed their addiction to money and power. One in three Americans has been exposed to enough chemically-altered, flavor-enhanced, nutrition-depleted food -- and advertisements for this kind of food -- that they have become addicted.

We have seen that there are many kinds of behaviors that can lead to addiction. This book has listed many of them. These range from excessive TV-watching to compulsive eating, and ingesting chemicals, and spending money, and pornography, and computer gaming, and the list goes on.

The bottom line is that the times have changed, and that, for the first time in human history, we have some new problems that need our attention. A hundred years ago, most Americans were simply trying to "get by." They needed to work hard to get food on the table and keep the house warm. While many Americans are still just trying to get by, the times have radically changed. Teens today have easy access to drugs. Fast food and Internet porn are ubiquitous, and many teenagers seem to have merged into electronic screens. We need to acknowledge that addiction is a very big problem; that it affects us all. Taxes would go down significantly if we got a handle on this public health crisis. We would not have to pay the medical costs associated with 45,000,000 nicotine addicts. We would not have to pay the medical costs for the one third of all babies born after the year 2000 who will become diabetic. We could eliminate 70% of the expenses for police and jails and prisons -- which house three times as many addicts as criminals -- if addiction were seriously reduced.

It is estimated that over 40% of families are impacted by addiction, whether the addict is a parent, child, or spouse. What is the cost for this? The mental health of America is simply the sum total of the mental health of its citizens. Does it not seem odd that nearly half of our population is exposed to the insanity of addiction, and that this problem is not being addressed directly?

The reason addiction is not being talked about is clear. The addict is almost always in denial. If we have leaders who are addicted, we would expect that they would not be interested in bringing up the subject. I know I sure didn't want to talk about addiction when I was in my disease.

I like David Linden's book: *The Compass of Pleasure: How Our Brains Make Fatty Foods, Orgasm, Exercise, Marijuana, Generosity, Vodka, Learning, and Gambling Feel So Good.* In an interview aired on National Public Radio, he said, in effect, that he wanted to *enjoy all the pleasures of life, in moderation!* There is nothing wrong with almost any behavior that raises our dopamine level if we can do it in moderation. In fact, I believe that is one of the secrets of a well-lived life. How many different ways can we find to increase our dopamine? Unfortunately, many of us unknowingly have crossed over the line from pleasure to addiction and could benefit from some guidance on this issue.

But first, America needs to come out of denial. We need leaders who are not addicted to lead us in a discussion about addiction and its treatment.

I don't want to run for President, but I don't feel like I have a choice. America is in big trouble and we all need to stand up like we did in World War II. The following are my ideas and proposals. This country is full of honorable women and men who are smarter than I am. And I trust the process. I will do my best, and I trust that they will do their best, and that by combining our collective wisdom through the magic of our wired world, I believe we will choose the best strategies and the best people to create a better America.

Please, think big. Imagine yourself guiding us out of this mess. The Internet is taking us into a new paradigm, and we need a new kind of person to lead us now. We can do this, and we need you.

If I were President, I would ask everyone to read this book and, if they met the criteria for any addiction, to get into recovery.

I would appoint a Secretary of Recovery. This individual's mandate would be to bring awareness to the public that addiction is treatable and recovery is possible.

I would ask him or her to look at the addiction research and at the treatment programs the government has developed. I would have them bring addiction out of the closet and into the light, where we can see the magnitude of the damage that addiction has done to America and to the children who grow up in this world.

I would ask medical schools and mental health training facilities to expand their education on addiction. And I would see that some of the money obtained from taxing the sale of legal drugs went to pay for public service advertising on the disease of addiction.

And I would open up the White House to 12-Step meetings. These meetings would be like the meetings held every day throughout the country. There would be all kinds of meetings: AA, Al-Anon, DA, FA, GA, SLAA, OA, EDA, NA, MA, CA and others. The size of the meeting would be determined by the space available, and attendees would be drawn by lottery from those who wanted to stop their addictive behavior and who asked to go to a meeting.

I would go to these meetings, and also invite the thousands of well-known recovering folks to *come out of the closet* and acknowledge their addictions. You would be surprised at how many well-known folks regularly attend 12-Step meetings.

It is time for everyone to share the joy that recovering addicts feel. Almost without exception, recovering addicts are grateful for their addictions, because addiction brought them into recovery and enabled them to create better lives.

30

VOTING

Right now, the game is rigged. The money, the Fat Cats, the 1% who comprise our oligarchy, have structured our federal election policy so they can stay in power. They use their money and influence to ensure that they control the outcome.

We see the result of this corrupt practice on TV, on the Internet, and in our newspapers. What we see is an elected official, a man or a woman who has been pushed through the sieve of political programmers. These "leaders" have had to sell out so much of themselves to their handlers and those who give them money that the result is a spokesperson parroting the oligarchy script.

Recently, in the Iowa Straw Poll, Rand Paul came within a few hundred votes of winning. As recounted on *The Daily Show*, no major media outlet reported this! Rand Paul does not fit into their mold. And if someone does not fit into the oligarchy's mold, then Big Media has a tendency to ignore him or her.

Go to www.OpenSecrets.com and look. One of the darlings of the left has received 25 million dollars, mostly from unions. And it is well documented that the billionaire oil barons were major contributors to the Republican Tea Party. These powerful, wealthy, and influential forces shape the outcome of our elections in ways that we can no longer tolerate.

It never made sense to allow large entities like businesses and unions to bribe officials as they do now. And I don't think it makes any sense to allow these same special interests to finance TV advertisements for one candidate or another. We humans are programmable. We are all "brainwashable." All of us. I see an ad for this or that product and I want to go buy it. We all do this. That is why we have advertising: to promote business. This is fine. But it is not OK to allow the Fat Cats to use their money for developing slick ads to brainwash the electorate. This smacks too much of something out of *1984*.

We can change this.

They won't change this. They will fight tooth and nail to keep the whole system rigged to their advantage.

But we can. Simply vote only for candidates that don't accept money from businesses.

That was easy.

Another problem: the Electoral College.

Many states are moving to apportion the Electoral College votes as a percentage of the popular vote. Why this has not been done before has never been effectively explained to me. I understand that some committee, two hundred years ago, thought the Electoral College was a good idea, but it no longer makes sense, if it ever did.

We have had a number of presidential elections where the candidate who received the fewest votes won!

It's time to change that.

I don't want to run for President, but I don't feel like I have a choice. America is in big trouble and we all need to stand up like we did in World War II. The following are my ideas and proposals. This country is full of honorable women and men who are smarter than I am. And I trust the process. I will do my best, and I trust that they will do their best, and that by combining our collective wisdom through the magic of our wired world, I believe we will choose the best strategies and the best people to create a better America.

Please, think big. Imagine yourself guiding us out of this mess. The Internet is taking us into a new paradigm, and we need a new kind of person to lead us now. We can do this, and we need you.

If I were President, I would ask everyone to read this book and, if they met the criteria for any addiction, to get into recovery.

Then I would propose two constitutional amendments. The first amendment would abolish the Electoral College and replace it with a popular vote. The second amendment would ban campaign contributions from anyone other than individuals -- no contributions from organizations or unions or businesses or corporations would be legal. Additionally, there would be a financial cap on the amount of money a candidate for national office could receive from any person. I propose $100 as the maximum allowed.

Why does it cost so much to run a campaign? The reality is that information flows freely in our new technological world. We all get to see and hear the candidates on TV and on the Internet for free. The current system is organized around wealthy interests who end up treating us like idiots with their negative and nasty advertisements. Unfortunately, the brainwashing works: it obscures the real issues and makes us not want to vote at all!

One more thing. I would want an historian present at every cabinet meeting. We need to have some historical perspective to ground all of our proceedings. I will also want a teen representative to be present as well. Today's teens will soon be tomorrow's leaders, and we need to speak a language that they will understand; we will periodically need their innocent view on our complex issues. Lastly, I would love to have a woman with an infant in her arms standing at the entryway to our meetings. We need always keep in mind whom we truly serve.

31

GAME TIME

This book has been a challenge. How dare I, a former addict, a flawed man, claim the right to try to pull this off? How could I actually imagine that I could write a book that called for a peaceful revolution in America? Our country is full of really smart people. Obviously I have taken a lot of cues from what has been happening in the last few years.

I've mentioned Mohamed Bouazizi, the honorable fruit vendor in Tunisia who set himself on fire to protest a bad government.

Wael Ghonim was arrested and tortured by the Egyptian secret police. Once free, he told his story on Facebook. Millions read it and went to the streets. I'm proposing we do the same. We can all become Mr. Ghonim and be the modern version of Paul Revere. We can "spread the word" virally, on the Internet. When Osama bin Laden died, I'll bet that 90% of us knew of his death within hours of its happening. Imagine a story like *this* one! And Facebook and Twitter are free.

Asmaa Mahfouz, a 26-year-old Egyptian woman, was upset at her peers for setting themselves on fire to protest the terror- ism of Mubarak's insane government. She went on Facebook and announced that she was willing to put her life at risk and *stand up* for sanity, not kill herself for it. She said, "People, I am going to Tahrir Square." Thousands followed her.

Julian Assange, Wikileaks, and the Internet have let all of us see more clearly what goes on in the back rooms between our elected officials and Big Business. The truth shall set us free.

Today (October 14, 2011) Peggy Noonan, conservative colum-
nist for the *Wall Street Journal*, wrote the following:
"And people have a sense that nothing's going to get better
unless something big is done, some fundamental change is made
in our financial structures. It won't be small-time rejiggering -- a
5% cut in this tax, a 3% reduction in that program -- that will get
us out of this."

The "Tea Party" and the "Occupy Wall Street" movements are
a stirring of our nation's need for "fundamental change." My hope
is that the energy and vitality and frustration of these concerned
Americans can be channeled into this Intervention, and that this
book will become the How-to Manual to make that happen.

Mahatma Gandhi asked people to go to the streets in non-violent protest. His philosophy was grounded in *ahimsa*, non-violence.
His approach helped India gain independence and has inspired
a number of movements around the world that have led to estab-
lishing civil rights and freedom. There was the Velvet Revolution
in Czechoslovakia in 1989 that overthrew the communist government, and the Orange Revolution in 2004, that exposed corruption in government.

It is time for us to stand up for a sane America. I propose that
all concerned Americans go to the streets in peaceful pro- test of the
perilous state we are in. I propose that each of you seri- ously consider running for political office. You can easily do what I am doing.
Write a book. Create a website. My website is www. InterventionO-
nAmerican.com. Create a Facebook page; open a Twitter account;
and run for office.

I propose that we go to the streets peacefully *and have fun*. We
need to *be* the nation that we want to become. We want a world
that will be peaceful, joyful, loving, and fulfilling. And, respectful!
A world in which we never, ever, harm another person or interfere
with another's freedom.

We have examples in our history of people gathering peacefully
to promote a cause.

I remember the free spirited attitude of hippies. When we gathered or marched, we would bring flowers to give to the police! It was
so cool to see everyone with big smiles, including the police, many of

whom were carrying those flowers! We knew how to gather together and have fun. Boy, did we!

There is another group of Americans who, for decades, has been gathering in the thousands and having a wonderful, loving, and fun time. Each year during the week before Labor Day, fifty thousand people congregate at the Burning Man Festival in Black Rock City, Nevada. This in an intentional community that builds a whole city in days, complete with an airport, has a *massive* love-in and art festival, and then, seven days later, takes it all down, leaving behind *not one scrap of litter!* The Federal Government oversees this event, and members of half-a-dozen police jurisdictions wander peacefully among the people. *Nearly everyone, including the police, has fun.*

Then there is the Buddhist community that has, for centuries, quietly and peacefully demonstrated against injustices. You can depend on them to be peaceful. This is another group of individuals that has a wonderful reputation with police departments.

I propose that these three groups, Old Hippies, Burning Man folks, and Buddhists, become our mentors, our guides. These people know how to be peaceful, implement change, and have fun. *Being a jerk just creates more jerks.* There will always be a few people in these gatherings who will have "bad "trips (they are almost always using drugs or alcohol). Back in the 60s, Bill Graham and Dr. David Smith of the Height Ashbury Free Clinic knew how to handle this. They had doctors and nurses wandering among the crowds, attending to those who were having a bad time.

There will be people who will have a problem with this, I know. There are those who are threatened by the idea of change. Many are attached to one party or the other and will feel very upset at the idea of their party's organization being usurped and bypassed. It will be important to welcome everyone into the movement and not engage in any conflict; simply walk away from any vexations.

This *is* the Intervention. (See Chapter 5). We are the "Concerned Others." We get the picture and we are showing up to initiate the process that will lead the addictive system toward sanity. We are respectful and never, ever argue or become contentious. We will be modeling for others what sanity looks like. The goal, in time, is to get the Powerless Enablers to join us. We want them to join us because we make sense *and not because they are wrong!*

Every month, as our numbers grow, more people will join us

because we are inviting, friendly, and our message is attractive. We will simply walk away from the folks who disagree. We will always
cooperate with the police and leave the area cleaner that it was before we arrived.

There are many on the far right and far left who are publically active but could actually harm this movement. I know you mean well, but in the initial stage of this Intervention, we are gathering those who clearly see that *everyone* has been part of the problem, and that fundamental change is necessary. There are sane folks on the right who are frightened about America's insane fiscal policy but are embarrassed at the nutcases and jerks who show up with guns and contentious, angry, and objectionable signs. And there are sane folks on the left who are frightened about America's failure to address the environment and corruption but are embarrassed by the acting out, childish behavior of those who flaunt tattoos, goofy signs, and bare breasts. So to the most outrageous folks in the Tea Party and the Occupy movement I say, "Please stand down." Wait a few months and see how this goes. Give it a chance. Because, at the end of the day, you will need to meet your opposite and come up with a solution. If we are to make it, we will need to huddle together for as long as it takes to come to a sane consensus that they can all support. We must move our energy and focus from talking about the problem to talking about the solution. We need the sane and solid middle of America, the 20% of the voters, 40,000,000 of us, to make a decision to stand up for the planet and the children, and to come together to work toward the solution that *all* the adults on the left and the right can support.

I propose that we gather for peaceful protests at noon on the first Saturday of each month, beginning December 3, 2011. And I propose that we leave the drugs and alcohol at home and remain clean and sober at these gatherings.

Bring flowers, soothing musical instruments, placards and signs, and your own campaign materials. Show up to have fun and be ready to overthrow our government! Also, pick up all the litter you see and take it home with you.

My hope is that this goes viral. I hope each person tells two more people, and so on, and so on. I'm visualizing 40 million of us, each month, gathering and having fun and restoring sanity to America.

I trust us. I trust Americans. We have a rich heritage of doing the right thing. Today what is new and different is the Internet and instant communication. Suddenly anyone can talk to anyone. We have the means to communicate any message, worldwide, in seconds. We are in a different paradigm and we simply need to accept that reality. We can move beyond ego, recover from our addictions, and open to spirit. When we do this, we can see that there is hope.

And we can actually replace all 536 elected officials in 2012.

We will need a lot of organization, but we have millions of the smartest among us. We will to need set up organizations in each state to get the signatures needed to put folks on the ballots. We will need to start identifying the people we want for President and Senators and Representatives. And, we will need to initiate the recall process for all the Senators and Representatives who are not

up for re-election. (Although, if they are honorable they will support this movement, and they will resign.)

I propose that we all become *both* Republicans and Democrats. Let's find the best examples of Democrats who will stand up for the common good and for protecting the vulnerable. And let's find the best examples of Republicans who will stand up for personal responsibility and self-reliance and local government. *And let's make sure that we pick adults who will work with each other because, at the end of the day, we are all wrong if there is one child who is harmed or neglected. And we are all wrong if we are not repairing our planet.*

We don't know if it is too late to save Mother Nature. Actually, it doesn't matter. If we step up, take action, and gather together; if we are peaceful, loving and joyful, we can give it our best shot. And if it is too late, at least we can go to our deaths knowing that we stood up and tried to do the right thing. And that we had fun in the process. God would smile on that.

Are you ready? I say, "Let's roll!"

EPILOGUE

PRINCIPLES OF THE AMERICAN REVOLUTION 2.0

- We will actively work to minimize any negative impact on Mother Nature and to restore Mother Nature everywhere.
- We will strive to diminish carbon burning and to stop burning carbon, as soon as possible.
- We believe that it is wrong to put *any* contaminant into the biosphere.
- We believe in sustainable, organic farming and support the work needed to promote this as the basis for agriculture in our country.
- We understand Mahatma Gandhi's words, "Earth provides enough to satisfy every man's need, but not every man's greed."
- We believe that *every* American is entitled to life, liberty and the pursuit of happiness.
- We believe that every American is entitled to biological, psychological, social, and spiritual wellness, and we will strive to remove all barriers to achieving high-level wellness wherever possible.
- We believe in the potential of every adult to become healthy, except for those who are physically or mentally impaired.

- We will protect all children from negative influences.

- We support all efforts to keep children, age 20 and younger, free from all drugs unless prescribed to them and monitored by their medical doctors.

- We support the legalization and sale of drugs for adults, age 21 and older.

- Taxes collected from the sale of these drugs will be used only for research, education, and treatment of addiction.

- We understand the rationale of both the Republican and Democratic parties and we support both of them and their different, but equally important goals.

- We support elimination of the Electoral College, and the apportionment of election districts to fairly represent the electorate.

- All of our campaigning will be positive. We will respect both parties' honorable tasks.

- Those running for office will not accept any campaign contribution from any business, organization, union, or corporation.

- Those running for office will accept campaign contributions only from individuals and for amounts no larger than $100.

- We will not accept any money from any business, organization, union or corporation while in office.

- We believe that those who have misappropriated funds or enriched themselves as the result of special deals with the government need to make amends and repay the money they have taken.

REFERENCES

Brown, Stephanie and Virginia Lewis, *The Alcoholic Family in Recovery: A Developmental Model*. New York: Guilford Press, 1998.

Alcoholics Anonymous, New York: Works Publishing, Inc., 1939. (Commonly referred to as the Big Book, or the Big Book of AA).

Campbell, T. Colin et al., *The China Study: The Most Comprehensive Study of Nutrition Ever Conducted and The Startling Implications for Diet, Weight Loss, and Long-term Health*. Dallas, Texas: Benbella Books, 2005.

Copernicus, Nicolaus, *On the Revolutions of the Celestial Spheres*. 1543.

De Waal, Frans, *Our Inner Ape: A Leading Primatologist Explains Why We Are Who We Are*. New York: Riverhead Books, 2005.

Ehrlich, Paul, *The Population Bomb*. San Francisco, California: Sierra Club/Ballantine Books, 1968.

Esselstyn, Rip, *The Engine 2 Diet: The Texas Firefighter's 28-Day Save-Your-Life Plan that Lowers Cholesterol and Burns Away the Pounds*. New York: Wellness Central, 2009.

Food, Inc. (Movie), 2009. Directed by Robert Kenner and produced by Robert Kenner and Elise Pearlstein.

Forks Over Knives (Movie), 2011. Directed by Lee Fulkerson and produced by Brian Wendel, John Curry and Allison Boon.

Friedman, Thomas L., *Hot, Flat and Crowded: Why We Need a Green Revolution – and How It Can Renew America*. New York: Farrar, Straus and Giroux, 2008.

Goleman, Daniel, *Emotional Intelligence: Why It Can Matter More Than IQ*. New York: Bantam Books, 1997.

Linden, David, *The Compass of Pleasure: How Our Brains Make Fatty Foods, Orgasm, Exercise, Marijuana, Generosity, Vodka, Learning, and Gambling Feel So Good*. New York: Viking, 2011.

Mate, Gabor, *In the Realm of Hungry Ghosts: Close Encounters with Addiction*. Berkeley, California: North Atlantic Books, 2008.

Mitchell, Stephen, *Can Love Last? The Fate of Romance over Time*. New York: W.W. Norton & Co., Inc., 2003.

Rifkin, Jeremy, *The Third Industrial Revolution*. New York: Palgrave Macmillan, 2011.

Prud'homme, Alex, *The Ripple Effect*. New York: Scribners, 2011.

Tolle, Eckhart, *The Power of Now: A Guide to Spiritual Enlightenment*. Novato, California: New World Library, 1999.

ABOUT THE AUTHOR

L A R R Y   F R I T Z L A N   is a licensed Marriage and Family Therapist, a Certified Addiction Specialist, and a Board Registered Interventionist. Larry has been working in the field of addiction for over twenty years, and is the founder and director of Larry Fritzlan Recovery Services, an intensive outpatient program for families of teens and young adults suffering from addiction. He specializes in doing interventions from a family systems perspective. Larry is also an adjunct professor at the California Institute of Integral Studies in San Francisco. He lives in Mill Valley, California with his wife, Avis Rumney. Visit Larry's website and blog at www.InterventionOnAmerica.com and follow him on Twitter @Fritzlan.